Deadly Waters

David G. Christen

JAY BAHADUR is a Canadian freelance journalist, who has published articles in *The Times, The New York Times, Financial Times* and the *Globe and Mail.* He has worked as a freelance correspondent for CBS News, advised the US State Department on Somali piracy, and has appeared on CNN, the BBC, and the Australian Broadcasting Corporation. Bahadur currently lives in Toronto, where he runs an international news website, Journalist Nation. Follow him on twitter (@PuntlandPirates) and

Deadly Waters

Inside the Hidden World of Somalia's Pirates

JAY BAHADUR

P

PROFILE BOOKS

First published in Great Britain in 2011 by
PROFILE BOOKS LTD
3A Exmouth House
Pine Street
London EC1R 0JH
www.profilebooks.com

First published in Canada in 2011 by
HarperCollins Publishers Ltd

1 3 5 7 9 10 8 6 4 2

Printed and bound in Great Britain by
Clays, Bungay, Suffolk

A CIP catalogue record for this book is available from the British Library.

ISBN 978 1 84668 363 3
eISBN 978 1 84765 436 6

The paper this book is printed on is certified by the © 1996 Forest Stewardship Council A.C. (FSC). It is ancient-forest friendly. The printer holds FSC chain of custody SGS-COC-2061

FSC
Mixed Sources
Product group from well-managed
forests and other controlled sources

Cert no. SGS-COC-2061
www.fsc.org
© 1996 Forest Stewardship Council

*To Ali, without whose infectious love for Africa
this book would not exist*

Contents

Somalia

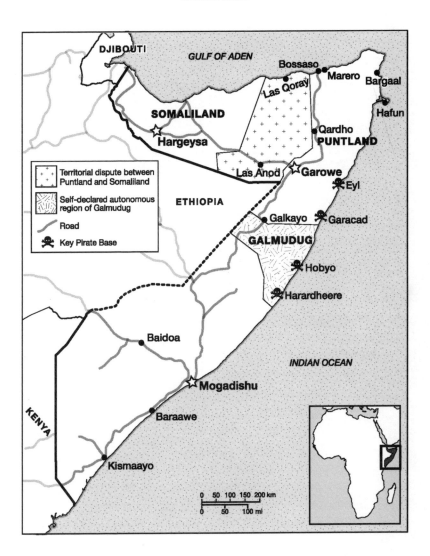

Expansion of Pirate Operations

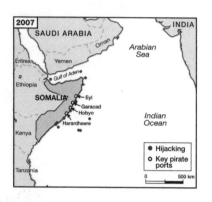
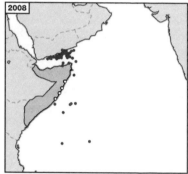
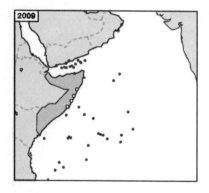
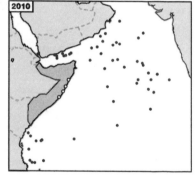

Deadly Waters

Prologue

Where the White Man Runs Away

IT WAS MY FIRST TRIP TO AFRICA.

I arrived in Somalia in the frayed seat of a 1970s Soviet Antonov propeller plane, heading into the internationally unrecognized region of Puntland on a solo quest to meet some present-day pirates. The 737s of Dubai, with their meal services and functioning seatbelts, were a distant memory; the plane I was in was not even allowed to land in Dubai, and the same probably went for the unkempt, ill-tempered Ukrainian pilot.

To the ancient Egyptians, Punt had been a land of munificent treasures and bountiful wealth; in present times, it was a land of people who robbed wealth from the rest of the world. Modern Puntland, a self-governing region in northeastern Somalia, may or may not be the successor to the Punt of ancient times, but I was soon to discover that it contained none of the gold and ebony that dazzled the Egyptians—save perhaps for the colours of the sand and the skin of the nomadic goat and camel herders who had inhabited it for centuries.

The cabin absorbed the heat of the midday African sun like a Dutch oven, thickening the air until it was unbearable to breathe. Sweat poured freely off my skin and soaked into the torn cloth of my seat cover. Male passengers fanned themselves with the Russian-language aircraft safety cards; the women fanned their children. The high whine of the Antonov's propellers changed pitch as it accelerated along the Djibouti runway, building towards a droning crescendo that I had not heard outside of decades-old movies.

The stories I had heard of these planes did nothing to put me at ease: a vodka-soaked technician banging on exposed engine parts with a wrench; a few months prior, a plant-nosed landing at Bossaso airstrip after a front landing strut had refused to extend. Later, in Bossaso, I saw the grounded craft, abandoned where it had crashed, a few lackadaisical guards posted nearby to prevent people from stripping the valuable metal.

This flight was like a forgotten relic of the Cold War, a physical testament to long-defunct Somali-Soviet geopolitical ties that had disintegrated with the countries themselves; its Ukrainian crew, indentured servants condemned forever to ferry passengers along this neglected route.

Over the comm system, the Somali steward offered a prayer in triplicate: *Allahu akbar, Allahu akbar, Allahu akbar,* as the plane gained speed. The whine heightened to a mosquito-like buzz and we left the ground behind, setting an eastward course for Somalia, roughly shadowing the Gulf of Aden coastline.

*　*　*

As I approached my thirty-fifth weary hour of travel, my desire to socialize with fellow passengers had diminished, but on purely self-serving grounds I forced myself to chat eagerly with anyone throwing a curious glance in my direction. I had never met my Somali host, Mohamad Farole, and any friend I made on the plane was a potential roof over my head if my ride didn't show. Remaining alone at the landing strip was not an option; news travels around Somalia as fast as the ubiquitous cellphone towers are able to transmit it, and a lone white man bumming around the airstrip would be public knowledge sooner than I cared to contemplate.

When he learned that I was travelling to Garowe, Puntland's capital city, the bearded man sitting next to me launched into the unfortunate tale of the last foreigner he knew to make a similar voyage: a few months previous, a Korean man claiming to be a Muslim had turned up in the capital, alone and unannounced. Not speaking a word of Somali, he nonetheless succeeded in finding a residence and beginning a life in his unusual choice of adoptive homeland.

He lasted almost two weeks. On his twelfth day in Puntland, a group of rifle-toting gunmen accosted the man in broad daylight as he strolled unarmed through the streets. Rather than let himself be taken hostage, the Korean made a fight of it, managing to struggle free and run. He made it several metres before one of his bemused would-be captors casually shot him in the leg. The shot set off a hue and cry, and in the ensuing clamour the gunmen dispersed and someone helped the man reach a medical clinic. I later learned from another source that he was a fugitive, on the run from the Korean authorities. His thought process, I could only assume, was that Somalia was the last place on earth that his government would look for him. He was probably right.

* * *

Just a few months earlier, I had been a recent university graduate, killing the days writing tedious reports for a market research firm in Chicago, and trying to break into journalism with the occasional cold pitch to an unresponsive editor. I had no interest in journalism school, which I thought of as a waste of two of the best years of my life—years that I should spend in the fray, learning how to do my would-be job in places where no one else would go.

Somalia was a good candidate, jockeying with Iraq and Afghanistan for the title of the most dangerous country in the world. The country had commanded a soft spot in my heart since my PoliSci days, when I had wistfully dreamt of bringing the astounding democratic success of the tiny self-declared Republic of Somaliland (Puntland's western neighbour) to the world's attention.

The headline-grabbing hijacking of the tank transport MV *Faina* in September 2008 presented me with a more realistic opportunity. I sent out some feelers to a few Somali news services, and within ten minutes had received an enthusiastic response from Radio Garowe, the lone news outlet in Puntland's capital city. After a few long emails and a few short phone calls with Radio Garowe's founder, Mohamad Farole, I decided to buy a ticket to Somalia.

It took multiple tickets, as it turned out. Getting to Somalia was an aerophobe's nightmare—a forty-five-hour voyage that took me through Frankfurt, Dubai, Djibouti, Bossaso, and finally Galkayo. In Dubai, I joined the crowd of diaspora Somalis, most making short visits to see their families, pushing cart upon cart overflowing with goods from the outside world. Curious eyes began to glance my way, scanning, no doubt, for signs of mental instability. I was in no position to help them make the diagnosis; by the first leg of my trip, I had already lost the ability to judge objectively whether what I was doing was sane or not. News reports of the numerous journalists kidnapped in Puntland fixated my imagination. I channelled the hours of nervous energy into studying the lone Somali language book I had been able to dig up at the public library; I scribbled answers to exercises into my notebook with an odd sense of urgency, as if cramming for an exam that would take place as soon as I set foot in Somalia.

The last white face disappeared at Djibouti's dilapidated, near-deserted airport, as American F-16s performed eardrum-shattering training manoeuvres overhead. By the time the plane landed in Galkayo, I was the only non-Somali passenger on board.

* * *

The Antonov's first stop was Bossaso, Puntland's northernmost port and most populous city. We wove back and forth over water and land, as Somalia's undulating coastline cut back and forth across the vector of our flight. Out of the scratched porthole, the solid azure of the Gulf of Aden below was broken only by intermittent white cracks marking the location of swells; from the sky, they looked like fissures erupting on the surface of a perfectly smooth blue rock face. As the plane swung back towards the coast, the lines of white increased in number, joined by the occasional fishing trawler cutting its own independent trail across the water.

As we crossed over land, Bossaso came into view. It was the first sign of life Somalia had displayed, a settlement rising out of the vast, lunar wasteland enveloping it. From the air, the city appeared as a clutter of corrugated roof buildings, gathering in a concentrated burst before spilling into the sea. The minarets of occasional mosques poked out of the conglomeration of one- and two-storey structures. A miniature range of denuded mountains, looking like cropped volcanoes, formed a crescent around the city.

The plane banked precipitously and began its descent towards the thin stretch of unclaimed beach lying between city and ocean, in which Bossaso airstrip was nestled. The temperature in the cabin began to rise once more as the Antonov left the higher altitudes. Within a few minutes, the plane had come to a bumping stop on the sand-coated runway.

The thought hit me for the first time: *I am in fucking Somalia.*

Somalia is like a country out of a twisted fairy tale, an ethereal land given substance only by the stories we are told of it. Everything known by the outside world has been constructed from news reports spilling out of the country over the last twenty years: warlords, famine, Black Hawks, jihadis, and now pirates. Along with bananas and livestock, international news is one of the few items that Somalia can still claim to export, and crossing the border from Djibouti into Somalia had brought me from the world of news consumers into the world of news producers.

The stopover was brief; as soon as the Antonov had finished refuelling, the remaining passengers climbed back on board and it took off once more, setting a course for Galkayo, a city straddling Puntland's southern border. The desert below stretched in shades of brown and blond; evaporated riverbeds scarred the pockmarked terrain, carving valleys in their wake. Galkayo is a dangerous place, a crucible where the northern Darod and the southern Hawiye clan families meet, cleaving the city along its east–west axis; the reputed English translation of the city's name, "where the white man runs away," did not put me at ease. Though I had initially assumed that the site marked a decisive victory by Somali independence fighters over British or Italian colonial forces, I later discovered that Galkayo was the location of a much earlier battle between invading Somalis and the non-Muslim indigenous inhabitants.

After another ninety minutes and seven hundred kilometres, Galkayo appeared. We touched down on another dusty landing strip, tires churning to a stop near an expectant crowd. It was the end of the line. I stepped once more down the six shaky steps onto Somali soil, and looked anxiously through the milling throng.

My own name had never sounded as sweet as when I heard it being called from across the landing strip. The voice belonged to Mohamad's cousin Abdirizak, who waved and walked hurriedly towards me. He was short and trim, with a joyous laugh, warm smile, and a receding hairline. Hours of pent-up stress drained out of my body.

Abdi and I proceeded to a customs office, a largely empty building containing a few uniformed officials milling around behind bare wood and glass partitions. One of the bored agents looked me over and demanded twenty dollars for an "airport tax" and another twenty dollars for a visa, which he impressed onto my passport with a stamp that looked to be left over from the days of the collapsed Somali Republic.[1] Asking how long I wished to remain in the country, he scribbled my answer into the allotted field on the still-drying stamp—apparently the twenty-dollar visa was a flat rate.

Abdi led me to a gleaming white-and-chrome Land Cruiser. Perched at either end of the back seat were two UN-trained bodyguards, Said and Abdirashid, who would accompany me like another heartbeat for the next six weeks. They cradled their worn AK-47s between the pant legs of their beige uniforms; crudely sewn on their

sleeves were patches with the letters "SPU"—Special Police Unit—
superimposed on a blue stag's head, the emblem of the Puntland police.

In Somalia, 4x4s are needed to get around even in urban areas;
with the exception of the main thoroughfare, Galkayo's unpaved
streets were worn down to their bare bones, the dirt eaten away by
tire treads to the uneven rock beneath. The surfaces of the buildings, some whitewashed, some matching the dull brown of the road,
were chipped and worn, and occasionally bullet-marked. The more
upscale houses were covered with geometric patterns of vibrant
blues, greens, and yellows, like the colours of a Van Gogh canvas.
Similarly vivid paintings on the facades of shops—bags of flour, cans
of oil, generic bottles of pills—advertised what was sold within. The
Land Cruiser rocked to a stop in front of one of these; the listing
English letters above the entrance read "General Store," and one
of the SPU guards dashed inside and returned with some cream-
filled biscuits and a number of bottles of water. In the mid-afternoon
heat, the streets were largely deserted except for a few children, who
skipped around me cautiously.

The one-lane highway connecting Galkayo to Garowe and Bossaso is the sole road running through Puntland along its north–
south axis, a solitary link stretching across seven hundred kilometres
of desert. Its decrepit state was symbolic of the neglect the region
experienced under former dictator Siad Barre, and from the international community more recently. The three-decade-old Chinese concrete was crumbling and corroded, and craterous potholes turned
the 250-kilometre journey from Galkayo to Garowe into a four- or
five-hour jolting ordeal. It was January 2009, the onset of the first of
Puntland's two dry seasons, the *jiilaal*, and parched shrubs dotted
the barren landscape; the dust clung to my skin until my shirt felt
like fine sandpaper. Piles of bottles, old tires, and the odd stripped
chassis lined both sides of the road; discarded plastic bags, struggling in the clutches of spiny bushes, waved at us spasmodically as
we drove by. Every so often an impassive camel plodded across the
road, slowing us to a near halt.

At irregular intervals, buildings of thatched branches and the occasional panel of corrugated metal clustered into settlements by the side of the highway. The boundaries of these shantytowns were marked by speed bumps built by the inhabitants out of packed dirt and rocks. A few empty gasoline drums blocked the road at the entrance to each village, with two or three listless guards loitering around the makeshift checkpoints.

At one of these pit stops we abruptly turned off the road and pulled into an open-air restaurant, its plastic tables and chairs almost spilling onto the highway. A few words were exchanged, and out came metal plates heaped with sticky rice sopped in goat's milk, flanked by fist-sized chunks of gristly camel meat. My two guards, sharing one of the plates, used their hands to squish the rice into pasty balls, which they proceeded to deposit into their mouths. I decided to use the spoon that had been offered to me, feeling somehow like an elitist in doing so. They looked attentively at me and smiled, waiting for my reaction to tasting camel meat for the first time. I picked at the stringy meat with a knife and my teeth as best I could, smiling back vacuously.

As we ate, a menacing semicircle of youth gradually formed around me, glowering eyes filled with mistrust and suspicion. I tried to lean as casually as possible against the back of my plastic lawn chair, but I was grateful for the SPU.

Four hours down the road, darkness fell. Close to the equator, night arrives startlingly quickly, with dusk relegated to the role of minor broker between night and day. The straight track ahead dissolved into the night beyond the reach of our high beams. No other cars were on the road, and the blackness around us was absolute. We climbed over the last in a series of gentle hills, and the muffled lights of Garowe finally came into view.

Soon we passed a checkpoint where a few yawning soldiers in fatigues hurriedly waved us through, then an abandoned gas station, the UN compound, and many other buildings I was unable to make out. Under the city's muted street lights, Garowe was reduced to a monochromatic grey. Partway through the city we pulled off the main road and struck out onto Garowe's pitch-black streets. Our headlights began to reveal haphazard piles of stone littered around spacious plots of empty land, evidence of Garowe's ongoing building boom. We hit another, miniature, checkpoint, nothing more than a log laid across the path, where a uniformed soldier shouted at us to extinguish our headlights, glanced inside the car, and waved us through.

More soldiers were lounging around the entrance to Mohamad's house. Our driver honked, causing a handful of them to jump to attention and rush to swing open the spiked iron gate. It was past nine o'clock, but multiple Land Cruisers were parked in the driveway and the courtyard was still bustling with activity. Until the last few days, the newly elected president of Puntland had lived here, before moving into the official residence inside the government compound.

I was sleepily ushered through the house and into its only functioning office, where Mohamad sat behind a desk covered by stacks of paper and a laptop. His frame, short and stocky, was the antithesis of the lanky and imperious figure that typified most Somalis. In the pale-green hue cast by the room's only light source, I could not make out the details of his face, not that it made a difference; I had never so much as seen a photograph of the man who was to protect me for the next month and a half. We shook hands and exchanged quick pleasantries.

Soon Abdi and I were back in the dark meandering city corridors, twisting down nameless streets where I saw nothing and remembered nothing, and pulled to a stop in front of a modest-sized residence with a blue gate. We passed through a courtyard and past a set of swinging metal doors into the house. As the SPU set up camp in the courtyard, Abdi showed me down a hall to my room. I tossed down the sports bag carrying my computer, notebooks, and malaria medication next to the bed.

I had scarcely pulled the mosquito netting over the bed before I was asleep.

* * *

I was to spend the next six weeks living in Garowe, a rapidly expanding city at the very heart of the pirates' tribal homeland. My
local partner, Mohamad, was the son of the newly elected president,
Abdirahman Farole, a fact that made me privy to backroom political dealings, stories, gossip, and daily impressions of life that went
beyond the perceptions of reporters flying in to take snapshots of
the gang behind the latest tanker hijacking. During this first trip to
Puntland, I was shocked to encounter no other foreigners until my
final day in the country, when, long-bearded and bedraggled, I briefly met with an Australian television crew hours before flying out of
Bossaso. For an outsider, my access to the region was truly unique.

Contrary to the oft-recycled one-liners found in most news
reports, Somalia is not a country in anarchy. Indeed, to even speak
of Somalia as a uniform entity is a mischaracterization, because in
the wake of the civil war the country has broken down into a number
of autonomous enclaves. Founded in 1998 as a tribal sanctuary for
the hundreds of thousands of Darod clanspeople fleeing massacres
in the south, Puntland State of Somalia comprises approximately
1.3 million people, one-quarter to one-third of Somalia's total land
mass (depending on whom you talk to), and almost half of its coastline. Straddling the shipping bottleneck of the Gulf of Aden and the
Indian Ocean, it was the natural candidate to become the epicentre
of the recent outbreak of Somali piracy.

In writing this book, I had the difficult task of bringing a fresh
perspective to a topic that continues to inundate the pages of news
publications around the world. Pirates make good copy: there is
something about them that animates the romantic imagination. But
reports of daring hijackings in the international section of the news-
paper are the print equivalents of the talking heads on the evening
news; their polarizing effect may attract people to an issue, but they
do not tell the whole story. Descriptions of hijackings are a black-
and-white sketch that I intend to render in colour.

Deadly Waters is about the pirates' lives both inside and outside of attack skiffs: how they spend their money, their houses, the clothes they wear, the cars they drive, the women they consort with, their drug of choice—in short, what makes them human beings, not simply the AK-47-toting thugs who appear in feature articles. Of course, this book is also about what they *do*—the occupation that has made them the scourge of every major seafaring nation. Over the course of my visits to Puntland, from January to March and June to July of 2009—as well as subsequent trips to London, Romania, Nairobi, and Mombasa—I spoke not only to pirates, but also to government officials, former hostages, scholars, soldiers, and jailors. Through this panorama of perspectives, I hope to tell the full story of the most nefarious of modern-day buccaneers—the pirates of Puntland.

1

Boyah

BOYAH IS A PIRATE.

He was one of the "old boys," an original pirate, quietly pursuing his trade in the waters of his coastal hometown of Eyl years before it galvanized the world's imagination as an infamous pirate haven in mid-2008. Abdullahi Abshir, known as Boyah—who claimed to have hijacked more than twenty-five ships—looked down on the recent poseurs, the headline-grabbers who had bathed in the international media spotlight, and it showed; he exuded a self-assured superiority.

It had taken five days to arrange this meeting. Pirates are hard to track down, constantly moving around and changing phone numbers, and are generally not reachable before twelve or one in the afternoon. Days earlier, frustrated and eager to begin interviewing, I had naively suggested approaching some suspected pirates on the streets of Garowe. Habitually munching on narcotic leaves of khat, they are easy enough to spot, their gleaming Toyota four-wheel-drives slicing paths around beaten-up wheelbarrows and pushcarts on Garowe's eroded streets. My Somali hosts laughed derisively, explaining that to do so would invite kidnapping, robbery, or, at the very least, unwanted surveillance. In Somalia, everything is done through connections, be they clan, family, or friend, and these networks are expansive and interminable; you have to *know* one another, and it seems sometimes that everyone does. Warsame,[1] my guide and interpreter, had been on and off the phone for the better part of a week, attempting to coax his personal network into producing Boyah. Eventually it responded, and Boyah presented himself.

I was being taken to a mutually agreed meeting place in the passenger side of an aging white station wagon, cruising out of Garowe on the city's sole paved road. Along this stretch, the concrete had endured remarkably well, with few of the jarring potholes that routinely force cars onto the shoulder from Garowe to Galkayo. Said and Abdirashid perched attentively in the back seat, and in the rear-view mirror was a sleek new Land Cruiser, a shining symbol of the recent money pouring into Garowe. It carried Boyah, Colonel Omar Abdullahi Farole (the cousin of my host Mohamad Farole), and Warsame. Other than our two vehicles, the road was empty, stretching unencumbered through a stony desert dotted with greenish shrubs. The thought that I was being taken to be executed in a deserted field—the unfortunate product of the BBC's Africa news section and too many Las Vegas mob movies—rattled around in my head for a few seconds.

We arrived at our destination, a virtually abandoned roadside farm fifteen kilometres outside of Garowe. Boyah had recently contracted tuberculosis, and Warsame insisted that we meet him in an open space. As we stepped out of our respective vehicles, I caught my first glimpse of Boyah. He looked to be in his early forties, immensely tall and with an air of menace about him; the brief, calculating glance with which he scanned me left the distinct impression that he was capable of chatting amiably or robbing me with the same equanimity. He was wearing a *ma'awis,* a traditional sarong-like robe of a clan elder, and an *imaamad,* a decorative shawl, was slung over his left shoulder. On his feet was a pair of spit-shined ebony leather sandals.

Boyah turned immediately and loped down the dirt path leading towards the farm, Colonel Omar following paces behind him. Threading his way through the mishmash of tomato plants and lemon trees that constituted this eclectic farm, Boyah wove back and forth along the path, like a bird looking for a roosting spot. Finally, he settled on a site in a cool, shady clearing, where an overhead thatching of branches had created an almost cave-like atmosphere. He squatted in the centre of the clearing and began to toy with a *dhiil*—a wooden vat used by nomads to store milk—that someone had left on top of a nearby stack of wood. His mobile phone resting in his right hand, Boyah remained singularly focused on the oblong container in front of him, twirling it on the hardened dirt like a solo game of spin-the-bottle.

Other than the farm's owner and his wife, no one was remotely close by, yet the Special Police Unit officers took up positions at either ends of the clearing with an amusing military officiousness. The meeting place filled with the rest of our party, and I decided it was time to force Boyah to acknowledge my presence. I walked up to him and greeted him with the standard *Salaam álaykum*, and was not surprised when Boyah and those around him responded with startled laughter before quickly offering the formulaic response: *Álaykum salaam*. Somalis were routinely astonished when I demonstrated the slightest knowledge of their culture or language—even a phrase that they shared with the entire Islamic world.

We seated ourselves on some nearby logs and I began the interview. As I forced out my first question through Warsame, I hesitated to use the word "pirate" to describe Boyah. The closest Somali translation of the word is *burcad badeed*, which literally means "ocean robber," a political statement I was anxious to avoid. In much the same way that revolutionaries straddle the semantic fence separating "freedom fighters" from "terrorists," Boyah and his brothers-in-arms did not like to call themselves "pirates" in their native tongue. In an alliterative display of defiance, they referred to themselves as *badaadinta badah*, "saviours of the sea," a term that is most often translated in the English-speaking media as "coast guard." Boyah joked that he was the "chief of the coast guard," a title he invoked with pride. To him, his actions had been in protection of *his* sea, the native waters he had known his whole life; his hijackings, a legitimate form of taxation levied *in absentia* on behalf of a defunct government that he represented in spirit, if not in law.

His story was typical of many coastal dwellers who had turned to piracy since the onset of the civil war almost twenty years ago. In 1994, he still worked as an artisanal lobster diver in Eyl—"one of the best," he said. Looking at his rakish figure, I believed him; it was easy to imagine his lanky form navigating the deepest oceanic crags in the reefs below. Since then, the lobster population off the coast of Eyl has been devastated by foreign fishing fleets—mostly Chinese, Taiwanese, and Korean ships, Boyah said. Using steel-pronged drag fishing nets, these foreign trawlers did not bother with nimble explorations of the reefs: they uprooted them, netting the future livelihood of the nearby coastal people along with the day's catch. Through their rapacious destruction of the reefs, foreign drag-fishers wiped out the lobster breeding grounds. Today, according to Boyah, there are no more lobsters to be found in the waters off Eyl.[2]

So he began to fish a different species, lashing out at those who could out-compete him on the ocean floor, but who were no match for him on its surface. From 1995 to 1997, Boyah and others captured three foreign fishing vessels, keeping the catch and ransoming the crew. By 1997, the foreign fishing fleets had become more challenging prey, entering into protection contracts with local warlords that made armed guards and anti-aircraft guns regular fixtures on the decks of their ships. So, like all successful hunters, Boyah and his men adapted to their changing environment, and began going after commercial shipping vessels. They soon attracted others to their cause.

"There are about five hundred pirates operating around Eyl. I am their chairman," he said, claiming to head up a "Central Committee" composed of the bosses of thirty-five other groups. The position of chairman, however, did not imbue Boyah with the autocratic powers of a traditional gang leader. Rather, Eyl's pirate groups functioned as a kind of loose confederation, in which Boyah was a key organizer, recruiter, financier, and mission commander. But would-be applicants for the position of pirate (Eyl Division) had to come to him, he claimed. The interview was not too gruelling—Boyah's sole criteria for a recruit were that he own a gun and be "a hero, and accept death"—qualities that grace the CVs of many desperate local youth. Turnover in Boyah's core group was low; when I asked if his men ever used their new-found wealth to leave Somalia, he laughed and shook his head.

"The only way they leave is when they die." He smiled and added offhandedly that a member of his band had departed the previous night, dying in his sleep of undisclosed reasons. "You were supposed to meet him," Boyah told me.

What makes for an attractive target? I asked. Boyah's standards were not very exacting. He told me that he and his men did not discriminate, but would go after any ship hapless enough to wander into their sights. And despite their ostensible purpose of protecting Somali national waters, during the heat of the chase they paid no regard to international boundaries, pursuing their target until they caught it or it escaped them. Boyah separated his seafaring prey into the broad dichotomy of commercial and tourist ships. The commercial ships, identifiable by the cranes visible on their decks, were much slower and easier to capture. Boyah had gone after too many of these to remember: "a lot" was his most precise estimate.

He claimed to employ different tactics for different ships, but the basic strategy was crude in its simplicity. In attack groups spread amongst several small and speedy skiffs, Boyah and his men approached their target on all sides, swarming like a water-borne wolf pack. They brandished their weapons in an attempt to frighten the ship's crew into stopping, and even fired into the air. If these scare tactics did not work, and if the target ship was capable of outperforming their outboard motors, the chase ended there. But if they managed to pull even with their target, they tossed hooked rope ladders onto the decks and boarded the ship. Instances of the crew fighting back were rare, and rarely effective, and the whole process, from spotting to capturing, took at most thirty minutes. Boyah guessed that only 20 per cent to 30 per cent of attempted hijackings met with success, for which he blamed speedy prey, technical problems, and foreign naval or domestic intervention.

The captured ship was then steered to a friendly port—in Boyah's case, Eyl—where guards and interpreters were brought from the shore to look after the hostages during the ransom negotiation. Once the ransom was secured—often routed through banks in London and Dubai and parachuted like a special-delivery care package directly onto the deck of the ship—it was split amongst all the concerned parties. Half the money went to the attackers, the men who actually captured the ship. A third went to the operation's investors: those who fronted the money for the ships, fuel, tracking equipment, and weapons. The remaining sixth went to everyone else: the guards ferried from shore to watch over the hostage crew, the suppliers of food and water, the translators (occasionally high school students on their summer break), and even the poor and disabled in the local community, who received some as charity. Such largesse, Boyah told me, had made his merry band into Robin Hood figures amongst the residents of Eyl.

I asked Boyah where his men obtained the training to operate their ships and equipment.

"Their training," he facetiously quipped, "has come from famine." But this epigram, however pithy, did not contain the whole truth. Beginning in 1999, the government of Puntland had launched a series of ill-fated attempts to establish an (official) regional coast guard, efforts that each ended with the dissolution of the contracting company and the dismissal of its employees. The origin of the new generation of Somali pirates—better trained, more efficiently organized, and possessing superior equipment—can be traced in part to these failed coast-guarding experiments; with few other opportunities for their skills, many ex-coast-guard recruits turned to piracy. When pressed, Boyah confirmed that some of his own men had past histories in the Puntland Coast Guard, having joined his group after their salaries went unpaid.

Boyah's testimony revealed another detail of the interwoven

dynamic between pirates, coast guards, and fishermen. Far from being a neutral state actor, the Puntland Coast Guard of the late 1990s and early 2000s worked as a private militia for the protection of commercial trawlers in possession of "fishing licences"—informal documents arbitrarily sold by various government bureaucrats for personal profit. The Puntland Coast Guard thus further alienated local fishermen, and indeed escalated at times into open confrontation with them. Boyah recounted that in 2001 his men seized several fishing vessels "licensed" by then-president Abdullahi Yusuf and protected by his coast guard force. Almost a decade before the fierce acceleration in pirate hijackings hit the Gulf of Aden, the conditions for the coming storm were already recognizable.

* * *

Boyah's moral compass seemed to be divided between sea and shore; he warned me, half-jokingly, not to run into him in a boat, but, despite my earlier misgivings, assured me that he was quite harmless on land. "We're not murderers," he said. "We've never killed anyone, we just attack ships."

He insisted that he knew what he was doing was wrong, and, as evidence of his sincerity, relayed how he had just appeared on the local news radio station, Radio Garowe, to call a temporary ceasefire on all pirate activity. Though I was sceptical that he wielded the authority necessary to enforce his decree amongst the wide range of decentralized groups operating over a coastline stretching almost sixteen hundred kilometres, Boyah stressed that the decision had been made by the Central Committee—and woe to those who defied its orders. "We will deal with them," Boyah promised. "We will work with the government forces to capture them and bring them to jail."

Subsequent events quickly proved that Boyah's radio statement was just so much background radiation. Just days after his announced ceasefire, a pirate gang in the Gulf of Aden committed the first commercial hijacking of 2009, capturing a German liquid petroleum tanker along with her thirteen crew members. The Central Committee has wreaked no vengeance on those responsible.

Boyah himself had not gone on a mission for over two months, for which he had a two-pronged explanation: "I got sick, and became rich." His fortune made, Boyah's call to end hijackings came from a position of luxury that most others did not enjoy. I questioned Boyah on whether his ceasefire had been at least partially motivated by the NATO task force recently deployed to deal with him and his colleagues.

"No," he said, "it has nothing to do with that. It's a moral issue. We started to realize that we were doing the wrong thing, and that we didn't have public support." Their public support, according to Boyah, had taken a plunge last summer when a delegation of local clan and religious leaders visited Eyl and declared to the local population that dealing with pirates was *haram*—religiously forbidden.

The current NATO deliberations regarding possible missile strikes on Eyl did not seem to concern Boyah. "Only civilians live there, it would be illegal for them to attack," he paused, before continuing, "if they do . . . that's okay. We believe in God." Forgetting for the moment his erstwhile promise of a ceasefire, Boyah's tone suddenly turned vehemently passionate. "Force alone cannot stop us," he said, "we don't care about death." Boyah's vocal display of courage was not idle bravado, but the plausible truth of a starkly desperate man. His desperation was not as stark as before he had accumulated his small fortune, but how long his current state of affluence would last was unclear—Boyah announced with pride that he had given his money away to his friends and to the poor, and that he hadn't built a house or a hotel like many of his more frugal colleagues.

As for his plans for the future, Boyah refused to give a straight answer. "That is up to the international community," he said. "It needs to solve the problem of illegal fishing, the root of our troubles. We are waiting for action."

* * *

Throughout our conversation, Boyah had been gazing off into space between my questions, looking bored. Soon he grew restless, mumbling discontentedly as he glanced at the two o'clock sun that "the day is already over." I managed to slip in one final question, asking him for his most exhilarating high seas chase. He immediately brightened up and launched into the story of the *Golden Nori*, a Japanese chemical tanker he had captured in October 2007 about fourteen kilometres off the northern Somali coast.

"Almost immediately after we had boarded the ship the US Navy surrounded it," said Boyah, with the destroyer USS *Porter* the first to respond. Boyah's memory, perhaps augmented with time, recalled seven naval vessels encircling him. Clearly he had told this story before; with obvious pride, Boyah recited by rote the identification numbers marking the sides of four of the vessels: 41, 56, 76, and 78 (the last being the designation of the *Porter*). The swiftness and gravity of this response nearly spooked Boyah's men into fleeing the ship and attempting an escape in their overmatched fishing skiffs. Fortunately for them, the *Golden Nori* was carrying volatile chemicals, including the extremely flammable compound benzene. With mirth lighting up his face, Boyah told me how the American ships were too afraid to fire on the ship for fear of detonating its payload, seemingly undisturbed by the fact that had his assessment been incorrect, he and his men would have been incinerated.

The standoff dragged on through November and into December. "We ran out of food," Boyah said, "and we almost abandoned the ship so we wouldn't start eating the crew." Attack helicopters whirring overhead, Boyah ordered the ship into the harbour at Bossaso, Puntland's most populous city. In case the *Nori's* explosive cargo proved an insufficient deterrent, Boyah added the defensive screen provided by the presence of the city's civilian population.

His perseverance paid off. After lengthy negotiations aboard an American vessel, a pirate delegation finally secured a generous ransom of $1.5 million in exchange for releasing the *Nori* and its captive crew. As part of the deal, the American military guaranteed Boyah and his team safe passage off the hijacked ship. Puntland security forces, waiting on shore to arrest the brigands, could only watch as US Navy helicopters escorted the pirate skiffs to land and allowed the pirates to disembark. I asked Boyah why the Americans had let them escape once they had left the safety of their hostages on board the *Nori*.

"Because that was the agreement," Boyah said. But I already knew the real reason, at least from the US point of view: the Americans would not have known what to do with Boyah and his men if they had captured them. According to international law—to the extent that international law has any meaning in an utterly failed state—the Americans were not even supposed to be in Somali territorial waters. Their hands were tied, and they let the pirates go.

The *Golden Nori* was one of the first major commercial vessels hijacked in the Gulf of Aden, before the international community had truly become cognizant of the problem. During this period, foreign navies tended to give pirates a slap on the wrist: their weapons and boats were impounded or destroyed, and they were released. More recently, states have begun to use the international legal instruments available to them—particularly a UN Security Council resolution permitting foreign entry into Somali waters—much more rigorously. Foreign warships are increasingly interdicting, detaining, and rendering suspected pirates to neighbouring countries to face justice.

Boyah had experienced this approach as well. In April 2008, his gang seized a rare prize, a speedy French luxury yacht on route from the Seychelles to the Mediterranean. Boyah called it the "*Libant*," a clumsy fusion of the ship's French name, *Le Ponant*. After delivering a ransom and freeing the hostages, French attack helicopters tracked the pirates inland to the village of Jariban. On the executive orders of President Nicolas Sarkozy, French commandos launched Operation Thalathine: special forces snipers disabled the pirates' getaway vehicle and captured six of the brigands, subsequently flying them to Paris to face trial. Such a determined, and exceedingly costly, pursuit was a rarity. But the incident illustrated that the international community was starting to take piracy in the Gulf of Aden more seriously—as well as showcasing the touchiness of French pride.

But a military solution alone is incapable of completely eradicating piracy off the Somali coast—nor is one either economically or politically feasible. Boyah's men had been captured or killed with increasing frequency in recent days (his brother was sitting in a Bossaso prison), but it did not matter. Imprisoning them was like trying to use a bailer to drain the ocean: for each pirate captured by the authorities, there were dozens of desperate young men on shore ready to rush in and fill the void.

At its very core, the solution to piracy lies in basic economic principles: the cost-benefit analysis for these men must be shifted to favour more legitimate pursuits. Naval battle fleets can do their part to boost the "cost" side of piracy, but without the alternative "benefit" of meaningful occupations on land, no permanent resolution is possible.

* * *

Boyah had become visibly irritable, and the next pause in my questioning heralded the end of the interview. His bothersome task completed, he rose and started heading back to where the vehicles were parked. As he walked, Warsame casually sidled up to Boyah and slipped him a folded hundred-dollar bill; suddenly the puzzling incongruity between Boyah's irascible manner and his willingness to speak to me was perfectly clear. "These pirates always need money, you know, to buy khat," said Warsame, referring to the stimulant drug religiously consumed by pirates. "Always, they chew khat."

Meanwhile, Boyah had once more leaked out ahead of the rest of us, bounding up the trail alone. Warsame and I gaped as he suddenly took off and effortlessly cleared the metre-wide knee-high bramble patch separating the farm from the shoulder of the highway. With gigantic strides, he ran up the slope to the cars and waited impatiently as we slowly climbed up after him.

It was time for his khat.

2

A Short History of Piracy

SOMALIA WAS NOT ALWAYS THIS WAY. THE COUNTRY OF FAMINE
and bloodshed, the lawless land where Boyah and his accomplices,
like the pirates of yore, have been able to operate virtually unmolested, is the result of one of the most dramatic state collapses in
modern history.

On October 15, 1969, the Somali Republic's second democrati-
cally elected president, Abdirashid Ali Shermarke, was shot and
killed in the northern town of Las Anod by his own bodyguard.
Though he was never proved to have ordered the assassination,
army chief General Mohamed Siad Barre quickly initiated a blood-
less coup that brought him to power for the next two decades.

Siad Barre was not a country person. Holding a profound contempt for the nation's nomadic traditions, he forcibly relocated
whole populations of herders into collective settlements and communal farms. In his relentless drive to urbanize the country, Siad
Barre directed virtually all government investment towards the
capital, Mogadishu, which contained Somalia's only hospitals, universities, and professional opportunities. The city became a magnet
for Somalia's diverse clans, drawing a cross-section of inhabitants
from their traditional tribal homelands. For all his misdeeds, Siad
Barre turned Mogadishu into the jewel of the Horn of Africa, a modern cosmopolis that attracted tourists from all over the world. The

northern desert, conversely, was treated by the regime as a sterile and unproductive backwater.

In the late 1990s, Somalia erupted into civil war. Years of disastrous military campaigns, backward Marxist economic policies, and clan-based discrimination caused an increasingly isolated Siad Barre to fall back on a combination of his Marehan clan network and brutal repression by his security forces. Rebel groups, formed more or less along clan lines, descended on Mogadishu from all sides: the Somali National Movement drawn from the Isaaq clans of Somaliland, the Darod-dominated Somali Salvation Democratic Front (SSDF) operating from present-day Puntland, and the Hawiye United Somali Congress (USC) based in the south.

Siad Barre did not mince words with his adversaries: "When I came to Mogadishu . . . there was one road built by the Italians. If you try to force me to stand down, I will leave Mogadishu as I found it," he threatened. Sadly, he did even worse; when he finally fled Mogadishu in 1991, Siad Barre left the city in chaos.

Following Siad Barre's defeat, Mogadishu was left in the hands of USC warlord Mohamed Farah Aidid, a man best known as the target of the manhunt that culminated in the infamous "Black Hawk Down" incident, in which eighteen US Army Rangers lost their lives. Taking retribution for Siad Barre's persecution of their own clan, Aidid's Hawiye militias hunted down and massacred Darod civilians in the streets. In his book *The Zanzibar Chest*, former Reuters correspondent Aidan Hartley describes in chilling detail the life-and-death importance of clan lineage during the worst days of the war:

> A queue of civilians was huddled at a roadblock before a gang of rebels. As each person was waved through, another came forward and began uttering a litany of names. My guide with the flaming red hair said the people were reciting their clan family trees. The genealogies tumbled back generation after generation to a founding ancestor. It was like a DNA helix, or a fingerprint, or an encyclopedia of peace treaties and blood debts left to fester down the torrid centuries. I was thinking how poetic this idea was,

when bang!, a gunman shot one of the civilians, who fell with blood gush-
ing from his head and was pushed aside onto a heap of corpses.

"Wrong clan," said my flaming-haired friend. "He should have bor-
rowed the ancestors of a friend." [1]

If not quite as inborn as DNA or fingerprints, amongst Somalis the concept of clan operates almost like a mental grammar, an
innate neural structure that defines how one processes and inter-
prets the world. Before Siad Barre's time, it had been customary for
a Somali to greet someone he was meeting for the first time with the
question *Yaa tahay?* "What clan are you?" In his efforts to weaken
the clan system (and thereby buttress loyalty to the state), Siad Barre
outlawed the question, but to little effect; to this day, clan strongly
determines how Somalis assess one another's social position, moti-
vations, and trustworthiness.

Like the Bedouin, Somalis have traditionally been pastoral-
ists, their resource-poor desert environment giving rise to a rigid
and strictly territorial tribal system in which members are fiercely
defended and outsiders ruthlessly attacked. Indeed, the oft-quoted
Bedouin saying "Me against my brother; my brother and I against
my cousin; my brother, my cousin, and I against the world" could
well be adapted to Somalis: "My sub-sub-clan against my sub-clan,
my sub-clan against my clan, my clan against the world." In order to
avoid mutually destructive vendettas, a system of clan law, known as
heer, developed to resolve disputes through traditional rules of blood
compensation, which stipulate the number of camels, goats, and so
on paid to expiate each offence. The murder of a man, for instance,
would demand a restitution of one hundred camels (the equivalent
of about $20,000); a woman, fifty camels.

Despite Siad Barre's attempts to dismantle traditional patterns
of Somali life, clan loyalty remained a more dominant force than
Somali national identity, to the point where it eventually tore the
country apart. In a sense, the whole idea of Somalia was a contra-
diction—an attempt to graft the trappings of a modern state onto a

mode of social organization suited to a centuries-old nomadic life-style. Jobs, business opportunities, military appointments, government posts, and patronage were all awarded through clan networks, reinforcing ethnic divisions and undermining the legitimacy of the central state. Ironically—given its role in sparking Somalia's descent into civil war—the clan system has since ensured a degree of order and social cohesion in many areas, including Puntland and Somaliland, that otherwise might easily have degenerated into their own versions of Rwanda or the Democratic Republic of the Congo. For a country in "anarchy," law and order in some parts of Somalia is remarkably well-preserved.

*   *   *

Many of the Darod lucky enough to escape Mogadishu's urban killing fields fled north to their ancestral clan homeland, which at the time was under the control of the SSDF, headed by the squabbling duo of Colonel Abdullahi Yusuf Ahmed and General Mohamed Abshir. Towns that had been little more than underpopulated crossroads along nomadic migration routes swelled into urban centres. In the years following the outbreak of the civil war, Garowe grew from a population of five thousand to a current estimated thirty to forty thousand.[2]

Though the desert provided a safe haven against the persecution suffered by the Darod in the south, without political unity they remained vulnerable. Leaders of the Harti Confederacy (see Appendix 1), a grouping of the three Darod sub-clans inhabiting Puntland (the Majerteen, Dhulbahante, and Warsangali), looked on with apprehension at the formation of clan polities around them. With the Isaaq-inhabited self-declared Republic of Somaliland to their western flank and the Hawiye poised to extend their control from Mogadishu to much of south-central Somalia, the fear was that without a unified front the Darod would be at a disadvantage in the clan-centred scramble for Somalia's territories.

In May 1998, a conference of Harti clan elders in Garowe proclaimed the creation of Puntland State of Somalia, with Abdullahi Yusuf as its first president.[3] Unlike Somaliland, Puntland did not seek outright independence, but officially maintained its intention to join a future federal Somali state (albeit on its own terms). However, the international community has yet to officially recognize Puntland's status as a semi-autonomous region, and its relations with both the internationally recognized Transitional Federal Government (TFG) and Somaliland have been tense, and at times openly hostile.

For six years following the Garowe conference, Yusuf ruled Puntland as his personal fiefdom. When a 2001 election produced a victory for Yusuf's challenger, Jama Ali Jama, Yusuf did not bother to contest the results; he declared war, defeating Jama over the course of a six-month conflict. It was a rare outbreak of violence in a region that, since its founding, had remained largely insulated from the ongoing instability in southern Somalia.

In 2004, Yusuf headed south to take over the reins of the recently formed Somali TFG, handing over Puntland (after a three-month interim) to former general Mohamud Muse Hersi—a man known by the nickname of Adde Muse, or "White Moses." Hersi remained in power until January 2009, when Abdirahman Farole, an academic who had spent most of the previous twenty years in Melbourne, captured 74 per cent of the vote in an indirect presidential election held by Puntland's "parliament"—a collection of clan elders appointed from the region's seven districts. During and following the election, Farole took a hard-line stance against the buccaneers plying the region's waters, whom he viewed as a black mark on Puntland's international reputation: "The pirates are spoiling our society," he announced to the press following his victory. "We will crush them."[4]

It was a promise he has found difficult to fulfil.

* * *

By the time Farole assumed office in early 2009, sea banditry had become Puntland's only claim to recognition on the international stage. Yet piracy had existed as a Somalia-wide phenomenon since the outbreak of the civil war. As the central government collapsed on land, its ability to control its seas declined commensurately, and a varied assortment of militiamen, fishermen, and dregs of the Somali army all seized advantage. Like darts striking a map, pirate attacks occurred up and down the length of the Somali coast, indifferent to geographical location. These early operations were sporadic, opportunistic, and unsophisticated—little more than groups of gunmen floating in four-metre skiffs a few kilometres away from the shore, waiting for wayward vessels to stray too close. The use of far-ranging "motherships" (fishing dhows or other larger vessels employed as floating bases of operations) was not yet common, and these nascent pirates did not typically venture far beyond the hundred or so miles constituting the traditional sphere of Somali fishermen—well short of international shipping lanes. By consequence, their victims were typically fishing trawlers, whose search for lobster and demersal (bottom-dwelling) fish required them to come close to shore.

The attacks most frequently took the form of "marine muggings," during which the brigands would board the vessel and steal money and everything else of easily transportable value before quickly departing. Like muggings, they sometimes turned violent, as was the case in the very first recorded act of modern piracy in Somalia—an incident that marked the closest the Somali pirates have come to the seventeenth-century stereotype of bloodthirsty buccaneers.

On January 12, 1991, the cargo ship *Naviluck* was boarded by three boatloads of armed pirates off the Puntland coast near the town of Hafun while en route from Mombasa to Jeddah. The pirates took three of the vessel's Filipino crewmen ashore and summarily executed them, before forcing the remaining crew to jump overboard and setting the *Naviluck* ablaze. Only by the grace of a passing trawler were the floundering victims of this "plank walking" saved from the fate of their three comrades.

Not all hijackings were carried out by these sorts of water-borne thugs; some had a veneer of legality. The hodgepodge of rebel groups, militias, and warlords that had inherited chunks of the Somali state (along with the remnants of its navy) began to arrest foreign fishing vessels and extort "fines" for their release. In Puntland, one of the men given this assignment was Abdiwahid Mahamed Hersi, known as Joaar, the owner of a small-scale lobster fishing company who had once employed, as one of his divers, none other than the young Boyah. In 1993, as the civil war continued to rage in the south, Abdullahi Yusuf instructed Joaar to end illegal fishing by foreign fleets off SSDF-controlled territory. In response to this command, Joaar told me, he hired a boat at $200 per day and recruited thirty young men to serve as his marines (I was unable to discover if Boyah was amongst them). According to Joaar's reckoning, he and his men stopped a total of nine Pakistani dhows, bringing them to Bossaso and ransoming three of them back to their home government (there are even rumours, which Joaar denies, that he and his colleagues hijacked a ship out of Mombasa harbour by smuggling a pistol on board in the bottom of a fruit basket). His actions had the desired effect, or so he believed. "Our seas became very clean at that time," Joaar said.

Though he had originally planned to create a full-fledged coast guard, Joaar found himself unable to complete the task. Illegal fishing ships, he said, were under the protection of southern warlords, who took exception to the harassment of their clients. "People were calling my home phone and threatening me," he explained, a fact that helped convince him to shelve his long-term plans.

Acting as he was under orders from the SSDF—the authority in de facto control of the territory at the time—Joaar's exploits are perhaps better described as semi-legitimate privateering rather than outright piracy. In either case, the man some call "the father of piracy" has since put his hijacking past behind him, though he has remained true to his maritime calling: Joaar is currently the director general of the Puntland Ministry of Fisheries, a position he has held since 2004.

* * *

In 1995, two years after the commissioning of Joaar's improvised coast guard, Boyah, Garaad Mohammed (another of Eyl's early pirate leaders), and other Eyl fishermen unleashed their own vigilante brigade upon the seas. At least, 1995 is the starting date Boyah gave me; Stig Jarle Hansen, a Norwegian Puntland specialist who has conducted his own interviews with Boyah, reported him as claiming that "professional piracy" had begun in 1994, but that his group had been engaged in struggles with foreign trawlers as early as 1992. (Momman, one of Boyah's former lieutenants, later told me that the group had begun operations back in 1991.)[5]. The public record lends some credence to Hansen's version of events, showing a sharp rise in both pirate attacks and hijackings in 1994, though the total number of hijackings (four) remained very low.[6]

Boyah and his colleagues were the original models for the oft-invoked media image of the fisherman-pirate locked in a one-sided struggle against the forces of foreign exploitation. They certainly cultivated this impression; if Boyah is to be believed, his operations were directed solely against foreign fishing trawlers, though this claim could easily have been influenced by the desire to justify his actions to the outside world. His tactics were still relatively basic; Boyah repeatedly denied to me that he or his men had ever used motherships, saying they stayed relatively close to shore in their fishing skiffs. Hansen's research attests to this limited range; from 1991 to 1995, almost half of all pirate attacks occurred in Puntland waters, while fewer than one-sixth took place on the high seas.[7]

In 2003, Somali piracy underwent a metamorphosis, thanks to the vision of a complete outsider: Mohamed Abdi Hassan, known as Afweyne ("Big Mouth"), a former civil servant from the distant central coastal town of Harardheere. Drawing on his fellow Habir Gedir clan members (a branch of the Hawiye), Afweyne formed the Somali Marines, an organization that transformed his hometown and its southern neighbour Hobyo—which had hitherto spawned relatively little pirate activity—into the centre of the pirate world.

A capitalist at heart, Afweyne was the first to realize the potential of piracy as a business, and went about raising venture funds for his pirate operations as if he were launching a Wall Street IPO. One repentant potential investor recalled Afweyne's sales pitch: "He asked me to invest USD 2,000, as he was gathering money for his new business venture. He was begging . . . [but] I did not invest and I regret it so much today." [8]

Like any conscientious employer, Afweyne sought to provide the very best training for his employees. Though the old boys of Eyl belonged to the rival Majerteen clan, Afweyne was not one to allow tribalism to get in the way of business, and he personally recruited the most locally renowned pirates—including Boyah and Garaad Mohammed—to work as instructors. The Eyl veterans did not limit their role to that of mere consultants but travelled up and down the coast, organizing and even participating in pirate operations. Even in 2007-2008, after most of the Eyl pirate leaders had returned to Puntland—attracted by the easy hunting offered in the Gulf of Aden—piracy remained the incestuous province of the Majerteen and Habir Gedir clans. Boyah, during our numerous conversations, was not shy about discussing the Eyl-Harardheere connection, readily speaking about "joint operations" between the two groups; one such collaborative effort was the hijacking of the MV *Faina*, the tank-laden Ukrainian transport ship that first splashed Somali piracy across international headlines. Boyah was upfront about Afweyne's business acumen: "Afweyne hand picked his pirate group," he later testified, "carefully designed it to keep costs low, profits high and to maximize efficiency." [9]

In contrast to previous groups, the Somali Marines were extremely well organized, employing a military-style hierarchy with titles such as fleet admiral, admiral, vice admiral, and head of financial operations (Afweyne himself). [10] They exhibited an operational sophistication that matched their corporate professionalism, employing motherships that extended their attack radius hundreds of kilometres from the coast.

Around the same time, other professionally organized groups began to appear. Garaad Mohammed was not content to remain as Afweyne's underling, but formed his own organization, the National Volunteer Coast Guard (NVCG), in the major southern port of Kismaayo.[11] Not only were groups like the NVCG and the Somali Marines more sophisticated in an operational sense, their creative names—which cast them as the defenders of Somali waters against the imperialist incursions of foreign vessels—showed that their PR acumen was keeping pace.

But though their official raison d'être might have been to prevent the theft of Somalia's fish, the Somali Marines showed no shame in attacking those whose intentions were quite the opposite. From 2005 to 2007, the gang targeted World Food Programme (WFP) transports delivering vital food aid to the famine-stricken population of southern Somalia, attacking five vessels and hijacking at least two. Perhaps Afweyne was aware of his potential vulnerability to accusations of hypocrisy; following the seizure of the MV *Semlow* in June 2005, he claimed the vessel's 850-tonne cargo of rice in the name of the people of Harardheere, accusing the international community of neglecting the region.[12] The threat to WFP vessels did not disappear until late 2007, when the French navy began to escort the shipments to port.

As for Afweyne, he has since entered a comfortable semi-retirement, handing over many of the day-to-day operations of the family business to his son Abdulkhadar. Afweyne is perhaps one of the few men to fit the media stereotype of a cash-flush pirate kingpin, having allegedly converted his pirate earnings into a business empire stretching from India to Kenya. He has even enjoyed the dubious distinction of a state reception from eccentric Libyan dictator Muammar Gaddafi, who had revealed a quixotic affection for the Somali pirates during his seventy-five-minute rant at the 2009 UN General Assembly world leaders' summit.

* * *

As a boil festers before it bursts, the 2003–2006 Eyl–Harardheere alliance represented an incubation period for the Somali pirates, a time during which they gradually accumulated capital and experience, continually reinvesting their ransom money in ongoing operations. By the 2008 explosion of piracy in the Gulf of Aden, the pirate business model had already been tried and tested, and sufficient cash was available from previous ransoms to provide gainful employment for the countless volunteers lining up on the beaches of Eyl.

For the poorly educated, locally born youth, the security sector, both public and private, had been the steadiest source of formal sector jobs. It came as a shock, then, when in April 2008 the Puntland government ran out of money to pay its security forces. Many members of the police and army naturally sought alternative employment, and there was hardly a more lucrative career than piracy for a young man possessing nothing but a gun and a desperate disregard for his own life.

Scant other opportunities were available. Puntland's almost non-existent factories provide only a handful of manufacturing jobs, and the already negligible seafood export industry had been suffering on account of both illegal foreign fishing and the decline of lobster stocks. Day labour in Puntland's rapidly expanding cities was one of the only avenues of steady employment open to the estimated 70 per cent of Puntlanders under the age of thirty. While much of the population (65 per cent, according to the Puntland government), remains nomadic, living a traditional pastoral lifestyle outside the formal economy, the increasing numbers of nomads flocking to urban centres in recent years have not found much to occupy their time other than the drug khat.

There *is* legitimate money to be made in Somalia. But the most lucrative business opportunities—livestock export, the transport and telecommunications industries, as well as jobs in government and the civil service—are monopolized by educated Somali expats, who speak English and Arabic and often split their time between Somalia and their adoptive homelands. The result has been a gross socioeconomic gap between those who were able to escape the civil war and those who were forced to remain in Somalia and suffer the brunt of the violence. For the masses of unemployed and resentful local youth, piracy was a quick way to achieve the respect and standard of living that the circumstances of their birth had denied them.

* * *

Before the presence of the massive naval flotillas that now jam Somali coastal waters, the risks were fewer, but the payouts were also relatively paltry. One of the Somali Marines' most noteworthy prizes in the early days was the MV *Feisty Gas*, a Hong Kong–flagged liquid petroleum tanker captured in April 2005. In exchange for her release, the Marines received a mere $315,000, likely about one-tenth the sum they might have received five years down the line. Since then, ransom amounts have crept steadily higher, with each new precedent exerting an upward pressure on future payments. At the time of writing, the highest recorded ransom had reached a staggering $9.5 million, paid in November 2010 to free the oil super-tanker *Samho Dream*.

Later generations of pirates owed their extravagant multimillion-dollar ransoms to the negotiating abilities of the pioneers. Indeed, the triumvirate of Afweyne, Boyah, and Garaad Mohammed could be compared to the hard-nosed leaders of a newly formed labour union—though in their struggle for higher wages they admittedly employed stronger-arm tactics than typically seen in collective bargaining. The lucrative ransoms for which they fought predictably attracted a new influx of independent groups to the industry—what I refer to as the "third wave" of piracy in Puntland. Many of these pirates were opportunists without histories in fishing, often disaffected inland youth. Yet their recent entry into the field did not stop them from telling any apologist reporter who would listen that persecution by foreign fishing fleets had driven them to their desperate course.

* * *

Harardheere's piracy dominance temporarily came to an end in 2006, when the Islamic Courts Union—an Islamist political movement—seized control of the south of the country and cracked down on pirate operations, claiming that the practice violated Islamic law. This paved the way for piracy to relocate to the next logical locale: back to Puntland, the gateway to the Gulf of Aden. From 2007 to 2008, Eyl was the undisputed capital of the Somali pirate empire, until the establishment of the heavily patrolled maritime safety corridor in the Gulf of Aden allowed Harardheere to reclaim the title in late 2009.

International recognition of the problem was sluggish. Though mariners in Somali waters had for years been keeping their eyes nervously glued to their radar displays, the triple intrigue of arms, oil, and Americans was needed for the Somali pirates to make international news headlines. The galvanizing event was the September 2008 seizure of the Ukrainian transport ship *Faina,* which combined the mystique of high-seas buccaneers and international weapons trafficking: in contravention of a UN embargo, the *Faina* was carrying Soviet-era tanks destined for southern Sudan, likely with the full knowledge of the Kenyan government. Two months later came the daring hijacking of the MV *Sirius Star,* a Saudi supertanker carrying $100 million in crude oil; seized a shocking eight hundred and fifty kilometres southeast of Somalia, the incident marked the furthest the Somali pirates had ventured out to sea at the time. Finally, in April 2009, pirates attacked the *Maersk Alabama,* the first American cargo vessel to be hijacked in two centuries. A tense three-day standoff with an American warship, worthy of a Hollywood script, ended with three Navy SEAL sniper bullets to the hijackers' heads and the lone survivor brought back to face US justice in a New York courtroom. The *Alabama* incident catapulted Somali sea piracy to the attention of the American public, and convinced editors around the world that the pirates were worthy of their front pages.

This trinity of hijackings that seized the imagination of the average news consumer were the brainchildren of the founding fathers of Somali piracy: the *Faina* was a joint operation between Boyah's and Garaad Mohammed's gangs and the Somali Marines, the *Sirius Star* hijacking was carried out by Afweyne's group alone, and the *Alabama* attack was publicly claimed by Garaad.[13]

The Somali pirates had come of age.

* * *

The basic characteristics that made Puntland an ideal spawning ground for pirates had existed since its founding in 1998. Why, then, did it take ten years for piracy to develop into the present epidemic? Four main causes explain the rise of piracy in Puntland: geopolitics, environmental factors, economic adversity, and breakdown of governance (two other principal factors, illegal fishing and toxic dumping, and the Puntland Coast Guard, will be discussed in Chapter 4).

In geopolitical terms, two factors lent Puntland a comparative advantage in the piracy "industry": its location and its relative (but tenuous) stability. The benefit of its geography is readily apparent: situated right at the intersection of the Indian Ocean and the Gulf of Aden, Puntland straddles one of the busiest shipping lanes in the world. More than 20,000 commercial vessels, or about 10 per cent of global shipping, transit through the Gulf of Aden each year.

Second, Puntland's isolation from the ongoing civil war in the south as well as its semi-functioning government ensured that pirate organizers would be left in relative peace to plan and carry out their operations. Piracy is not so much organized crime as it is a business, characterized by extremely efficient capital flows, low start-up costs, and few entry barriers. Pirates, almost as much as businessmen, require a certain level of order and predictability for their enterprises to prosper (and to avoid getting ripped off by actual organized crime networks). Roger Middleton, a Horn of Africa expert with the London-based think tank Chatham House, summed it up eloquently for me: "Puntland was the perfect area for pirates to operate because it's just stable enough, but also ungoverned enough. You don't have the chronic instability you have further south . . . There's too great a chance of getting caught in the crossfire and too many competing interests to pay off."

The link between political stability and the frequency of pirate attacks has some convincing empirical support; when Puntland descended into violence, piracy was the first business to suffer. In 1992, for instance, the year when Abdullahi Yusuf was locked in a fierce conflict to prevent the Islamist organization al-Ittihad al-Islami from establishing a Puntland foothold, piracy completely disappeared from the region. In 1994–1995, after Yusuf had triumphed and relative peace was restored, the frequency of pirate attacks began to creep up once more.[14]

The theory holds for Harardheere and Hobyo as well, which are located in another autonomous region—Galmudug—insulated from the chaotic south. Galmudug, with an administration far weaker than even Puntland's, was perhaps an even more ideal business environment for pirate entrepreneurs—a fact that the astute Afweyne was able to capitalize on.

Somaliland, in contrast, possesses a Gulf of Aden coastline comparable to Puntland's, yet the few pirates originating from the region have been swiftly arrested and incarcerated by the local authorities. The difference is due to Somaliland's greater political stability, a product of its robust history of democracy and inter-clan consensus. Its central government can exert control over its territory in a way that Puntland's leaders, who must navigate a much more fractured clan landscape, cannot. In the south, in short, the pirates had to fear other criminals; in Somaliland, the danger came from a more traditional source: the police.

Environmental circumstances also contributed to the rise of piracy. The population of Puntland is largely nomadic, and depends heavily on the seasonal rains to sustain their livestock herds. From 2002 to 2004, Puntland suffered its worst drought in thirty years. Herds were decimated, and much of the nomadic population flocked to urban centres in search of food. With an estimated 600,000 across Somalia directly affected by the dry spell, the governments of both Puntland and Somaliland declared a humanitarian emergency. Although there is no conclusive evidence, it is possible that this drought drove those traditionally dependent on livestock to rely on fishing as a source of sustenance, with the result that the standard encroachment by foreign fleets on Somali fisheries may have been viewed as especially egregious.

Just as Puntland was on the verge of recovery from this crippling drought, Mother Nature supplied her own solution to the water shortage. On December 26, 2004, one of the most powerful tsunamis in recorded history struck near the Indonesian island of Sumatra, sending waves as high as thirty metres surging across the Indian Ocean. The coastal areas of Puntland—though more than 4,800 kilometres from the tsunami's epicentre—did not escape. Over three hundred people were killed and the livelihoods of forty-four thousand affected.[15] The tsunami devastated the region's fishing economy, destroying an estimated six hundred boats and damaging 75 per cent of the fishing gear beyond repair.[16]

One of the tsunami's indirect contributions to the piracy outbreak was the (literal) exposure of toxic dumping in Somali waters. Residents of Eyl and nearby coastal towns related how the tsunami's waves had broken open and scattered ashore previously submerged toxic waste canisters, causing an increase in the incidence of radiation sicknesses amongst the local population. Though a brief UN fact-finding mission to the area found no evidence to corroborate these claims, the perception that foreign nations have used Somalia as a toxic dumping ground has served as both a rallying cry and a post hoc justification for the pirate movement.

The four-year delay between the drought and tsunami and the outbreak of piracy makes it difficult to finger them as immediate causes. But these environmental factors undoubtedly exacerbated the general level of poverty and suffering in Puntland, increasing the pool of candidates for pirate recruiters.[17]

Puntland's declining economy also provided an additional incentive to turn to turn to piracy. From 2006 to 2008, the region experienced unbridled hyperinflation that drastically reduced the standard of living of the average citizen. Puntland still uses the shilling, the currency of the defunct Somali Republic, though only the highest denominations of five hundred and one thousand shillings remain in use (the latter bill is worth approximately three cents). While US dollars are used for larger transactions, shillings remain the staple choice for everyday purchases, and are typically exchanged in bundles of 100,000.

From a high of 14,000 shillings per US dollar in 2006, by August 2008 the exchange rate had fallen to a record low of 35,000 per dollar.[18] In Garowe, Bossaso, Qardho, and Galkayo, protesters filled the streets to express their anger over the rising price of goods, blocking roads and pelting government buildings with stones. General Hersi's administration responded with a desperate attempt to fix an exchange rate of 18,000 shillings per dollar, a measure that even a totalitarian state would have found difficult to enforce.

Counterfeiting was a problem I noticed almost immediately upon my arrival in Puntland. For a currency that had not been minted in almost two decades, it was astounding how many crisp thousand-shilling notes proclaimed "Mogadishu 1991" in unfaded orange ink. Indeed, nineteen out of twenty local bills looked as if they had been printed by a cheap photocopier. It was not until early 2009, when local sheikhs launched a campaign to dissuade the organizers of counterfeiting operations, that hyperinflation began to come under control; by March, the exchange rate had stabilized at 29,000 shillings per dollar.[19]

Puntland's economic woes were mirrored by the decline of its political institutions. As hyperinflation escalated, the salary of a regular soldier in the Darawish (the Puntland army) dropped almost threefold in real terms, from more than seventy dollars in 2006 to less than thirty dollars in 2008.[20] President Hersi continued to pay his forces in printed money until, in April 2008, he stopped paying them altogether. As mentioned above, many soldiers and policemen abandoned their positions and turned to piracy; a local crime wave ensued, and May saw the first increase in pirate attacks, a trend that took off following the end of the monsoon season in August.[21]

Prior to the discontinuation of its pay, the Darawish had already been depleted in raw numbers. When Puntland strongman Abdullahi Yusuf had accepted the post of president of Somalia's Transitional Federal Government (TFG) in 2004, he took about a thousand Puntland soldiers (out of an estimated five thousand) south to Mogadishu to serve as his personal militia, funded out of government revenue.[22] With this weakening of the security forces, the Puntland government's ability to project its power throughout its territory declined. "Puntland's capacity to investigate piracy onshore, always weak, had totally collapsed," writes Stig Hansen.[23]

Following Puntland's military decline, its always-tense relationship with its western neighbour, Somaliland, worsened precipitously; in October 2007, Somaliland forces invaded Puntland and captured the town of Las Anod, capital of the disputed Sool region. Though this invasion was not in itself a direct contributor to the piracy outbreak, it was indicative of the Puntland government's loss of control. Rival clans to the Osman Mahamoud-dominated administration, such as the Isse Mahamoud, began to assert their independence from the central government, and Isse Mahamoud–inhabited areas like Eyl became lawless enclaves ideal for pirate operations.

* * *

The history of Somali piracy has been, one might say, a tale of two cities: Eyl and Harardheere. Like the Paris and London Dickens wrote of, the towns were hotbeds of revolutionary sentiment, seething against oppression and injustice. In Eyl, a band of angry young twentysomethings headed by Boyah and Garaad Mohammed formed the simmering nucleus that developed into the modern Somali piracy movement. "Boyah was a pioneer," one local journalist told me. "He showed the others the real potential of piracy."

Puntland's semi-lawless status made the region an ideal training ground and business environment for the early pirates; relatively peaceful, it was free of the organized criminal gangs, Islamist groups, and covetous warlords that plagued the turbulent south. From 2005 to early 2009, as the central government disintegrated under increasing economic and political pressures, pirate groups gained the freedom to operate with complete openness and virtual impunity.

Yet much of the early history of Somali piracy is still clouded in obscurity. With few outside observers present on the ground, little reliable information about the country is available to academics and journalists, and many past (and present) pirate attacks go unreported by shipowners. This dearth of credible information has created an opening for conjecture and speculation, with the result that, as with the buccaneers of yesteryear, a number of present-day myths about the Somali pirates have already sprung up.

3

Pirate Lore

EDWARD TEACH (OR BLACKBEARD, AS HE IS MORE COMMONLY known) was reported to have tied sulphur fuses into his beard, which he would set alight before going into battle in order to give himself the appearance of the devil. It is said he liked to drink a burning mixture of gunpowder and rum, and that, after he was killed and decapitated by the Royal Navy, his skull was fashioned into a silver chalice. Another legend holds that the Barbary corsair Barbarossa ("Red Beard"), Blackbeard's North African predecessor, tortured the inhabitants of a small Greek island in order to discover the location of a town concealed by a precipitous gorge. As the bloodthirsty pirates descended upon the town, mothers threw their children over the edge of the cliff in order to save them from being sold into slavery.

Passed down through the centuries, such tales are probably as apocryphal as the stories of buried treasure, peg legs, and Jolly Roger flags, yet they have become part of our collective image of the swashbuckling buccaneer. Somalia's modern sea bandits may lack some of this colour, but, aided by the news media's inexorable search for a good yarn, they are already on their way to amassing their own canon of folklore.

MYTH #1: SOMALI WATERS ARE TEEMING WITH PIRATES.

In recent years, information technology has made twenty-four-hour-a-day news coverage a reality, with the unintended result of making the world seem much riskier than it is. Given the international media focus on every daring hijacking off the Somali coast, sailing through "Pirate Alley"—the shipping lane from the Indian Ocean through the Gulf of Aden—may appear as dangerous as a seventeenth-century trip across the Spanish Main in a gold-laden galleon. But before you abandon your plans for a career in the merchant marine, ask yourself, What are the actual chances of being hijacked by Somali pirates? When you switch off the six o'clock news and examine the numbers, they turn out not to be very high. In 2008, about twenty-four thousand commercial transits through the Gulf of Aden led to only forty-two successful hijackings, according to the International Maritime Bureau, a global body devoted to combating maritime crime.[1] In short, the average sailor faced *less than a 1 in 550 chance* (0.17 per cent) of being taken hostage on a given voyage—not all that much worse than the effectively 0 per cent chance on any other sea route in the world.

Of course, for some this figure will be significantly higher; to the poor sailor on a supertanker with a maximum speed of eight knots and a low freeboard, the Gulf of Aden might start to look uncomfortably similar to the Spanish Main.

MYTH #2: THE PIRATES ARE IN THE POCKETS OF SOMALI ISLAMISTS.

By all measures, Somalia should have been one of the most economically successful African nations: it has the continent's longest coastline, is strategically situated on the Suez Canal shipping lane, and has a long-standing history of trade and entrepreneurship. Sadly, events have taken the country along a different trajectory, and for the last two decades the international community has been trying a variety of strategies to piece it back together. Initially, the United Nations embraced the "building block" approach, which focused on supporting and engaging with the relatively stable mini-states within Somalia, such as Puntland and Somaliland. The logic was that if these regions became bastions of peace and security, their stability would spread to the more turbulent areas surrounding them. Once a number of such "blocks" were in place, reassembling a federal government would be a relatively easy task.

This all changed in 2000, when the Somali National Peace Conference held in Djibouti produced the Transitional National Government (TNG), an ultimately ineffectual attempt to restore central government to the country from the top down. After the TNG went bankrupt and collapsed, it was replaced in 2004 by the current Transitional Federal Government (TFG). Choosing to view these national reconciliation attempts as legitimate expressions of the will of the Somali people (despite the fact that Somaliland—representing a quarter of the nation's territory—continued to seek outright independence), the international community threw its backing behind the TFG.

International support for the central government became further entrenched in 2006, when Ethiopian troops disastrously invaded Somalia in order to overthrow the Islamic Courts Union (ICU), an Islamist political movement that had wrested control of Mogadishu and much of the south from the TFG and competing warlord factions. The Ethiopian intervention drove ICU's moderate leadership into exile and sparked a radicalization of the organization, as the ICU's extremist military wing, Al-Shabaab, splintered from the group and launched a brutal insurgency against the Ethiopian occupiers. The US government had already been wary of the ICU's Islamist ideology and its potential links to Al Qaeda, and had backed the Ethiopian invasion with air and logistical support; the emergence of Shabaab turned the TFG into a key ally in the war on terror. No longer was the TFG merely the latest phase of a strategically irrelevant country's struggle with anarchy, but the last bulwark against an Islamist takeover of the Horn of Africa. This perception was reinforced in March 2010, when Al-Shabaab officially declared its affiliation with Al Qaeda, and in July, when

Shabaab carried out its first suicide attack outside of Somalia, setting off bombs in two bars in Kampala, Uganda, packed with World
Cup revellers.

Following the overthrow of the ICU, the TFG underwent another
transformation. Under pressure from the international community,
it merged with the Alliance for the Re-liberation of Somalia (ARS),
an "opposition party" hastily formed by the self-proclaimed moderate ICU cadres who had fled into exile in Eritrea and Djibouti.
The repentant Islamists were accommodated with 275 new seats
in the Somali parliament, doubling it to an absurdly bloated 550
members. The leader of the ARS (and former ICU chief), Sheikh
Sharif Ahmed, was elected president of the new body. Since 2009,
members of Sheikh Sharif's government have been huddling in their
Mogadishu barracks, their daily docket of business more concerned
with surviving the continual onslaught of Shabaab militants than
administering the country.

Drawn by YouTube videos, foreign jihadis have come flocking to
Somalia from around the world, including Pakistan, Afghanistan,
Canada, Britain, and the United States (Omar Hammami, known as
Abu Mansoor "Al-Amriki," one of Shabaab's more notorious online
recruiters, is a US citizen born in small-town Alabama). With its
suppression of women, glorification of martyrdom, and visions of a
global caliphate, Shabaab embraces the kind of Islam the war on terror thrives on. In the areas under its control, the group has banned
sports, music, and even bras; those who transgress the group's strict
Salafi interpretation of sharia law face amputation and medieval
executions (girls as young as thirteen have been stoned to death for
the "crime" of adultery).[2] Shabaab's radicalism was new to Somalis,
who had traditionally practiced a moderate, Sufi-influenced variety of Islam. Up until a generation ago, it was common for women
to uncover their heads; these days, the Arab style of dress, with its
accompanying headscarf, is virtually ubiquitous.

In a world dominated by the discourse of the war on terror, various policy analysts, journalists, and politicians pushing particular

agendas inevitably began to speculate about pirate cash ending up in the hands of terrorists. One of the early claims came from the London-based publication *Jane's Terrorism and Security Monitor,* which reported that Shabaab had provided the pirates with funds, bases, and "specialist weapons" in exchange for a share of the ransoms as well as pirate training in "naval tactics."[3] The image of turbaned Islamists instructing pirates in sharpshooting in return for sailing lessons would be laughable if it did not have such serious implications for the safety of hostages; a Shabaab-piracy connection would effectively prevent the paying of ransoms, since in most Western countries it is illegal under any circumstances to transfer funds to a designated terrorist organization.

History, at least, seems to be against those who would claim an Islamist-pirate conspiracy. In 2006, the Islamic Courts Union began pushing north, reaching Harardheere in August. Dubbing piracy un-Islamic, or *haram,* ICU militias shut down operations in Harardheere, forcing many pirates into Puntland (as mentioned in Chapter 2, the ICU clamp-down in Harardheere partly accounted for the rise of Eyl as Somalia's piracy capital). Despite the potential loss of revenue, evincing such an attitude—at least publicly—was necessary for the ICU to maintain the legitimacy of its fundamentalist ideology. It was able to afford its pious airs; the group reportedly receives substantial funding from affluent supporters in Saudi Arabia and the other Gulf states.

During my months in Puntland, I questioned every pirate I met about Islamist ties, and received the same vehement denials from every one. Nonetheless, some indications of a relationship between Al-Shabaab and the pirates had emerged by late 2009, or so said my source in the Somali diplomatic community. On October 2, the Spanish tuna boat *Alakrana* was seized by one of Afweyne's attack groups and brought to Harardheere (the thirty-six hostages were released seven weeks later for a reported ransom of $4.5 million). Before arriving in Harardheere, however, the pirates stopped at the Shabaab-controlled port of Baraawe, where two hijackers headed for shore in a small skiff. They had hardly left the ship before a Spanish navy helicopter intercepted and arrested them.

"They were supposed to meet the Shabaab leaders in Baraawe and bring them to Harardheere," my source explained. "As it turned out, the leaders had to make the trip by road." The incident, he argued, was "ultimate evidence" of a connection between Shabaab and the Harardheere pirates, a relationship that he said had been brokered by Afweyne himself. "Shabaab could be receiving anywhere from 5 per cent to 60 per cent of the ransom," my source said. "And according to my information, it's much more than a gentleman's agreement for money. Al-Shabaab itself seems to be training for acts of piracy—becoming, in effect, 'sea Mujahedeen.'"

Nevertheless, there was still no evidence, fourteen months later, that any Islamist group had launched a "piracy division." But this may change; in a repeat of the 2006 ICU clamp-down, Hizbul Islam—the then second most influential Islamist group in Somalia, after Shabaab—invaded Harardheere in May 2010, chasing many of the resident pirates north to the town of Hobyo. Like the ICU, both Hizbul Islam and Shabaab have publicly declared piracy to be *haram,* but the lure of large sums of money may have spawned a reinterpretation of the scriptures; there are reports that the remaining Harardheere pirates have begun to split their ransoms with both Islamist groups.[4] In the cynical words of my diplomat source, "Nothing is *haram* if it supports the insurgency."

In Hobyo, conversely, the pirates have decided to fight 'em rather than join 'em. Mohamed Garfjani, a Hobyo pirate strongman believed to have hijacked a half-dozen ships, has built up an organized militia consisting of several hundred men, eighty heavy machine guns, and six technicals (flatbed trucks mounted with light anti-aircraft guns).[5] In an effort to stave off the Islamist expansion, Garfjani has placed his muscle in the service of local officials of Galmudug, the semi-autonomous region in which Harardheere and Hobyo are located (the Galmudug administration, it must be said, has never exercised effective control over the towns).

Links between pirates and terrorists undoubtedly exist, but they are isolated and incidental—opportunistic individuals with Islamist ties who happen to dabble in piracy investments on the side. Shabaab, as an organization, does not yet have conclusive systematic links to the pirates, and the pirates have good reason to keep it that way. As one Somalia analyst put it to me: "If I'm a pirate and I'm giving money to Al-Shabaab, I can be pretty sure that some American is going to find out and drop a bomb on my head. It's simply a very, very bad business decision."

MYTH #3: SOMALI PIRACY IS RUN BY AN INTERNATIONAL CRIMINAL CARTEL.

Many theories have sprung up to explain the astounding success of the Somali pirates in snatching vessels from right under the guns of Western naval armadas, almost all of which seem to rest on the assumption that the Somalis could not possibly be doing it on their own. Security firms, media outlets, and law enforcement agencies have all alleged the existence of a vast and sophisticated international crime network providing funding, equipment, and intelligence to their local Somali minions—conjuring the image of a sinister Bond film villain pushing buttons on a giant maritime navigation display.

One of the strongest and most outlandish claims came in October 2009, when Interpol announced that Somali piracy was controlled by "transnational crime syndicates." "It is organized crime," Jean-Michel Louboutin, executive director of police services at Interpol, bluntly told the Agence France-Presse (when I attempted to contact Mr. Louboutin to clarify his statement, a public relations rep informed me, without elaborating, that he had been misquoted).[6]

I asked Toby Stephens, a London-based crisis response lawyer, about these claims. The principal function of Stephens's firm is to "convince" a hijacked ship's various insurers to put up the ransom money, and his job had taken him almost as far as the negotiating room during the ransom bargaining process. "We've been involved with various security services in tracing the pirates' phone calls, as well as their assets," said Stephens. "There have been definite instances of calls coming to telephones in London. The criminal network certainly extends beyond Somalia, but my perception is that it is not nearly as organized as people think," he continued. "I think the pirates are a disorganized bunch, but they do have contacts—friends, family, whoever it may be—in places around the globe. And they draw on those, but it's not a mafia-style organized crime network."

On the ground, there is little to back up the tales of international conspiracy. Pirates operate in relatively small, decentralized groups of twenty to fifty—essentially, relatives and friends who come together for the purpose of a mission, then disperse once the task is complete and the ransom has been divided up. The loyalty of the average pirate is to the money, not the Don.

Nor is there any evidence of the rivalries and turf wars one would expect in an organized crime environment. While isolated cases of gang infighting have resulted in deaths, no pirate organization maintains a standing "hit squad," and inter-group conflict has been virtually non-existent. There seem to be plenty of cargo ships to go around.

Pirate money certainly passes back and forth across international borders, but this movement is not necessarily extralegal. The Somali diaspora is one of the most interconnected and interdependent in the world, and the international exchange of funds should be viewed as family finances, rather than the monetary trail of a transnational criminal cartel.

MYTH #4: PIRATE GROUPS EMPLOY HIGHLY SOPHISTICATED INTELLIGENCE NETWORKS

Accompanying the claims of transnational pirate crime networks have been numerous media reports suggesting that pirate organizations are being fed vital shipping data enabling them to pick and choose targets from the tens of thousands of vessels charting the Indian Ocean and Gulf of Aden each year. In May 2009, for instance, Spanish media cited a European military intelligence report claiming that pirates were targeting specific ships identified by a team of "well-placed advisers" in London. "These consultants," the report read, "are in constant satellite telephone contact with pirate commanders on land, who can then pass details of the layout of the vessel, its crew, route and cargo to their colleagues at sea." The article went on to insinuate that the passing of such information, if true, represented a major intelligence failure on the part of the UK government: "It was unclear why leaks of such sensitive details appear to be coming from Britain."[7]

In reality, these so-called sensitive details are practically public knowledge, available to anyone with an Internet connection and access to an online maritime tracking service, such as Lloyd's Marine Intelligence Unit. By paying a subscription fee, users—such as these hypothetical "consultants"—are able to continually monitor the course and position of virtually any commercial shipping vessel in the world, as well as its cargo, crew manifest, and other details of interest to pirates (such as freeboard and maximum speed). But it is not clear that such information would be particularly useful; even with access to a maritime tracking service, intercepting a vessel on the open sea is not nearly as easy as it may seem. For security reasons, the vessels' exact coordinates are delayed by at least five or six hours, and plotting an intercept course using the commercially available GPS device a pirate attack group is likely to possess is an extremely formidable task. Even missing a pre-selected target by as little as half an hour would put a vessel moving at ten knots out of visual range, exposing its now-aimless pursuers to an increased risk of being picked up by international naval patrols, or even dehydration, starvation, and death. In myopically chasing a single target, moreover, the pirates would probably have to pass over a host of other perfectly suitable ships.

Roger Middleton voiced his own reasons for rejecting the existence of a sophisticated pirate intelligence network: "Why on earth would you need intelligence to hijack a ship in the Gulf of Aden? Spend half an hour googling and you can find where the shipping lanes are and therefore where the best targets are likely to be. You go north, and maybe left a little bit, and then you just wait." Middleton conceded that the vast Indian Ocean presented them with a greater navigational challenge, but argued that their basic strategy had remained unchanged. "If there were a certain ship sailing through the Indian Ocean and you wanted to catch it, then of course you'd need intelligence. But that's not the nature of this crime . . . it's not an intelligence-led crime—it's opportunistic. It's like walking down the street looking through windows: you see one that has a single glazing, so you smash the window, go in, and steal the TV."

The major hijackings hitting the news are bound to create the impression that pirate gangs purposefully go after only the juiciest of targets. But of the over two hundred vessels to have been successfully hijacked, only five—four oil supertankers and the tank transport MV *Faina*—could be considered "ideal targets." For the average pirate—ragged, ill-equipped, and often without enough food and fuel to get him home—any ship that floats is a welcome oasis in the desert.

MYTH #5: PIRATE DOLLARS ARE FUELLING A PROPERTY BOOM IN NAIROBI

The Nairobi suburb of Eastleigh, unofficially known as "Little Mogadishu," is a slice of Somalia transported into Kenya; the roads are unpaved and perpetually clogged with noisy traffic, and khat leaves litter the ground between colourful rows of open-air kiosks. As he dropped me off at the outskirts of the sprawling neighbourhood, my Kenyan taxi driver earnestly cautioned me to stay alert. "Somalis don't argue with you," he warned. "They just stab you."

House prices in Nairobi have risen two- and threefold over the last five years, and angry local residents have naturally turned to Somalis—already viewed with suspicion by native Kenyans—as convenient scapegoats. Since the piracy outbreak two years ago, the scapegoating has included allegations that pirate dollars are in large part responsible for the rising costs.[8] A few days earlier, a University of Nairobi medical student I had met on the streets downtown echoed the concerns felt by many Nairobi residents. "Somalis are buying all the land from the Kenyans," he exclaimed. "How? Where do they get all the money?"

Strolling down the streets of Eastleigh in December 2009, I could not deny that the neighbourhood was in the midst of a building boom. Alongside the broad thoroughfares carving up the suburb, layers of scaffolding snaked around the shells of six-storey buildings under construction. I stopped and began to question passers-by, and soon a small mob had gathered around me. I asked the crowd for their thoughts on a recent broadcast by the Kenyan Television Network, which had sent a team to Eastleigh with the express purpose of looking for pirates. "All they found were Toyota Surfs and *mirra* [the Kenyan term for khat]," one man shouted out. "That's not enough evidence!"

Irrespective of whether pirates are hiding out in Eastleigh, a rough calculation is sufficient to dismiss the notion that piracy has had anything to do with the skyrocketing demand for Nairobi land. At the time, pirate ransoms had not totalled more than $125 million; given how much pirate booty is blown on cars and khat, it would be a miracle if as much as a tenth had made its way from Somalia into the Nairobi property market. And $12.5 million in over two years could not noticeably affect average property prices in even the smallest slum of a global city like Nairobi.

Though admittedly not as glamorous an explanation, the Nairobi property boom has been a result of the Kenyan government's investor-friendly policies over the last half-decade—not the laundered proceeds of pirate kingpins.

*   *   *

Looking beyond the mythology that has coloured the reality of piracy both past and present, there are some striking similarities. Despite their notorious reputations, the pirates of old, like Somali pirates today, usually left their hostages alive (after all, they needed to provide an incentive for crews to surrender without a fight). Like the Somalis, they were spendthrift; Captain Kidd was the only pirate known to have buried treasure, and he did not do so very often (pirates didn't—and still don't—plan for the future). Even in their organizational cultures, the two groups are remarkably similar; like the Somalis, pirate crews on seventeenth-century vessels more resembled associations of shareholders than servants indentured to a despotic captain.

Among the Somali pirates, of course, not all shareholders were equal.

4

Of Pirates, Coast Guards, and Fishermen

THE DAY AFTER MY FARM MEETING WITH BOYAH, I WAS SITTING AT the dining-room table of my guest house in Garowe, sipping a cup of Shah (sweet tea) and waiting for Abdirizak, my host and interpreter, to bring me a pirate. Before long, I heard Abdi's station wagon pulling through the fortified iron gate and into the courtyard, and he soon appeared with a sullen youth in tow. Consistent with the Somali nickname culture, Abdi introduced him as Ombaali, meaning "the burdened camel"; I learned only later that his real name was Abdulkhadar.

After interviewing a man considered by many to be the father of piracy in Puntland, I was speaking with one of its unknown sons. Over the course of three hijacking operations, Ombaali had served as one of Boyah's foot soldiers; he was a "holder," a low-ranking member of the group brought on board to guard the crew once the vessel had been captured and taken to harbour. Or so he claimed; when I later asked Boyah about Ombaali, he waved his hand dismissively and denied ever employing him.

Ombaali, though only in his mid-twenties, had crooked and rotten teeth, perpetually bared in a leering grin, and his eyes were bloodshot. His hunched frame, petite and almost childlike, barely filled out the standard combat fatigues of a Somali militiaman. A former truck driver, Ombaali had grown up in a poor inland village,

Hasballe, that lies in the corridor running from Garowe to Eyl, inhabited by the Isse Mahamoud sub-clan of Boyah and the gang's other Eyl-born leaders.

Ombaali seemed able to remember scant details of his pirating career. He claimed that the three ships on which he had served were hijacked sometime in 2008, though his most precise guess was that they were taken during "the early months of the year." The only other facts he was able to recall were the nationalities of two of the ships—Japanese and Yemeni—and, not surprisingly, the exact ransom amounts.

"We got $1.8 million for the Japanese tanker," he said, of a vessel carrying a cargo of crude oil. "And $1.6 million for the other one." The owners of the smaller Yemeni ship, on the other hand, did not deem the vessel or her crew to be worth ransoming, and in the end the gang simply let it go. Checking up on his story afterwards, I discovered only one vessel captured in 2008 that matched Ombaali's description: the MT *Stolt Valor*, a Japanese-owned chemical tanker hijacked in the Gulf of Aden while transporting oil products. Although the ransom paid to release the ship—reported to be between $1 million and $2.5 million—fits Ombaali's account, the *Stolt Valor* was seized on September 15, hardly "the early months of the year."

Ombaali paused to take a pinch of sugar from the bowl in the middle of the table, casually depositing it into his mouth. I hurriedly offered him some tea for the second time, but he shook his head, seeming surprised at my solicitude.

There were fifty individuals in his gang, he said, of whom fifteen were "attackers"—those who carried out the hijacking—and the remaining thirty-five were holders, such as himself. Ombaali differed slightly from Boyah in his account of how ransoms had been divided, telling me that 50 per cent was split amongst the attackers, 30 per cent went to the investors, and the remaining 20 per cent to the holders; unlike Boyah, Ombaali had no recollection of any money going to charity. Given that an attacker earned almost six times as much as a holder, I asked Ombaali why he had been content to settle for a blue-collar position.

"There is a management board, run by Boyah and others, that selects the attackers," he explained, presumably a reference to Boyah's Central Committee. "If I had stayed with the group, eventually I would have become an attacker."

Eight of the group's attackers, said Ombaali, had previous histories with the Somali-Canadian Coast Guard (SomCan), a private security firm that provided coast guard services to the Puntland government from 2002 to 2005, and again in 2008. "They were the most experienced at attacking and capturing," said Ombaali. They were probably also the most expert at marine navigation, including the operation of global positioning systems and other equipment. "GPS was very important," Ombaali confirmed. "We would never launch an operation without one."

The group had an interpreter, a Mogadishan named Yusuf, who had the dual responsibility of communicating with the crew as well as handling the ransom negotiation with the shipping company. Before working with Ombaali's group, Yusuf had been involved with a much more nefarious hijacking—though the case is perhaps better described as a kidnapping at sea. On June 23, 2008, pirates belonging to the northern Warsangali clan seized the German sailing yacht *Rockall* in the Gulf of Aden and brought it to the fishing town of Las Qoray, whereupon the middle-aged couple on board were taken ashore and force-marched into the mountains of Sanaag region. After being held for fifty-two days, during which they were allegedly abused and brutally beaten by the pirates, the Germans were released for a reported ransom of $1 million.[1] Yusuf's references from his previous employers must have been laudatory, because Ombaali's gang quickly sought his services. "We knew him from that operation, so we gave him a call," said Ombaali.

Interpreters, I would later learn, are in such high demand that they essentially functioned as independent contractors, hiring themselves out to various pirate groups and moving from job to

job. Many translators are simply English-speaking members of the
Somali diaspora out to make a few quick dollars in their homeland—
where English is rarely spoken by the local inhabitants—while others establish themselves as *dilals*, professional negotiators who take
pride in exacting the best possible price from shipowners.

From his two operations, said Ombaali, he had received a total of
$50,000.[2] Unlike some of his more spendthrift colleagues—who had
blown their earnings on cars and khat—Ombaali had invested in his
future, using a portion of his profits to construct a house. "The rest I
invested in a pirate operation," he said. "But I got unlucky. They were
at sea for a long time, but they didn't find any ships."

Whatever Boyah's actual level of control over the day-to-day
operations of the gang, Ombaali's testimony made it clear that
the position of investor was open to anyone who had the money.
Like many pirate operations, Boyah's extended group apparently
employed a shareholder structure, with Boyah and the other members of the "management board" responsible for gathering funding
from local investors and organizing the crew.[3]

With his dreams of early retirement dashed, Ombaali was forced
back to work, albeit in the public sector; with his sub-clan, the Isse
Mahamoud, now in power, he had had little difficulty in finding a job
with the Puntland armed forces. If Ombaali was to be believed, this
opportunity might have prevented his foray into the pirate world.
"The reason that I became a pirate was that the government was not
functioning," he said. "With the new government, I have expecta-
tions that things will change. If they do, I will stay a soldier. If not,
I'll go back to the pirates."

Ombaali was evidently still struggling with this dilemma when I
returned to Puntland five months later. By that time, he was working
as a driver and bodyguard for Omar, one of my interpreters. When
Omar fired him for incompetence, Ombaali repeatedly threatened
to return to piracy unless he was reinstated. Following the failure of
this strategy, Ombaali somehow got hold of my phone number, and
would call me up to three times a day for no apparent reason.

Throughout the interview, Ombaali had sat squirming in his chair, his manner suggesting more the subject of a police interrogation than a friendly exchange. By the forty-minute mark I had clearly nearly exhausted his limited supply of patience, and he began to grumble about being late for an appointment. I squeezed in one final question: With hours of idle time and few diversions, how did he and his fellow guards get along with their hostages?

"We gave them the best treatment," he said. "We never stole anything from them, even their cellphones."

"But what if you had not received any ransom money?" I asked.

Ombaali leaned back in his chair and calmly replied, "Then we would have killed them all."

* * *

The decision to kill, thankfully, was not in Ombaali's hands, but in those of his fishermen bosses—the long-serving generals of the Central Committee, most of whom, years earlier, had begun the struggle against foreign incursions into their fishing waters. Since the foreign destruction of Somali fisheries is commonly cited as the impetus for piracy, it may be surprising to discover that fishing has never played much of a role in Somalia, either as a means of sustenance or as a sector in the formal economy.[4] In fact, prior to the 1970s virtually no Somalis engaged in fishing as a livelihood, and it was traditionally viewed as a somewhat ignoble occupation.

Like any good Marxist dictator, Mohamed Siad Barre sought to re-engineer his country's society and patterns of life. Aiming to reduce the population's overreliance on livestock, Siad Barre attempted to alter cultural attitudes about the value of fish, even going so far as to broadcast daily educational jingles over the radio exhorting nomads to "eat fish and make profit from it."[5] Natural disaster afforded him a more direct means of getting his message across; following severe droughts in 1974 and 1986, Siad Barre forcibly resettled tens of thousands of nomads into coastal towns, which soon developed into fishing communities.

In 1999, in response to persistent complaints from these communities about foreign fishing, Puntland president Abdullahi
Yusuf brought in the British private security firm Hart Security
to supply coast guard services to the nascent state. Yusuf did not
contract Hart directly, but instead used an umbrella organization
of local businessmen, the rapidly formed Puntland International
Development Corporation. One of these intermediaries was Kha-
lif Isse Mudan, a hotel proprietor and major shareholder in Golis
Telecom, Puntland's largest mobile phone company. In February
2009, I met with Mudan in the office of the hotel he owned on the
outskirts of Bossaso.

Working as partners, said Mudan, the Puntland government provided the coast guard's single ship and weaponry, with Hart Security
responsible for the selection and training of its marine force. For the
task of patrolling the sixteen-hundred-kilometre coastline of Puntland, Hart was given one twenty-metre trawler and a multi-clan
force of seventy local men, armed with two aging ZU-23 Soviet anti-
aircraft guns—weaponry on a par with that which the more prudent
foreign fishing trawlers had begun to carry.

Hart Security's principal duty was to prevent illegal, unregulated, and unreported fishing in Puntland waters, and its operations
were funded by selling official government fishing licences, issued
through the Puntland Ministry of Fisheries, Ports, and Marine
Transport. The licensing revenues were collected by Hart and split
almost evenly with the government, the latter taking a 51 per cent
share. "They were like joint venture investors," explained Mudan. For
a fragile natural resource like the fisheries, a for-profit approach to
licensing had obvious implications; the success of Hart's operation
was defined not by the tranquillity of the waters it patrolled, but by
the profits it generated, which in turn depended on the number of
licences issued. The Ministry of Fisheries lent only a thin veneer of
lawfulness to the process, as it had no policy in place to regulate the
issuing of licences—nor any reliable marine research on which to
base such a policy.

Despite Hart's support for foreign fishing companies, Mudan insisted that neither the firm nor its clients had entered into confrontations with local fishermen. "It was a very smooth operation," he assured me. Only five or six licences had been sold to short-range trawlers, and these had strict restrictions that prevented them from coming in contact with locals. "The trawlers weren't allowed to use very small-mesh nets," said Mudan, "or to come within less than ten miles of the shore."

According to Mudan, Hart focused its patrols in the waters from Hafun to Hobyo, a stretch of about six hundred kilometres in which most illegal fishing occurred. But even this reduced range consisted of a length of coastline greater than that running from Boston to New York, which Hart patrolled with one lone ship. In order to facilitate this immense job, the company set up observation posts in towns along the coast, from which it received daily reports via high-frequency radio, informing its forces of any suspicious ships fishing in the vicinity.

Hart's effectiveness was severely limited by the sheer territory its sole ship was tasked with patrolling. However, the company managed to arrest a number of foreign fishing vessels, most notably the Spanish fishing ship *Alabacora Quatro*, whose owner Hart successfully sued in a UK court, winning an undisclosed settlement.

Hart's patrols rarely brought its ship into contact with any pirates; the company's only significant encounter occurred in 2000, when the cargo vessel *Mad Express* was hijacked after experiencing technical problems near Bargaal. According to Hart chief Lord Richard Westbury, a former SAS officer, the pirates' level of sophistication was far below what they have demonstrated in recent years. "Basically, the pirates jumped off the ship. One injured his ankle," Westbury related in a January 2009 interview. "They certainly had no skills to operate in the way they are currently operating."[6]

* * *

Hart's operations in Puntland continued until 2002, when the company was unwillingly squeezed out of the business by the sudden arrival of the Somali-Canadian Coast Guard (SomCan), a private security firm headed by a former Toronto taxi driver named Abdiweli Ali Taar. The circumstances under which SomCan ousted Hart were decidedly suspicious. After the Puntland presidential election of 2001, which resulted in the victory of challenger Jama Ali Jama, the incumbent Abdullahi Yusuf attempted to oust Jama in a military coup. During the ensuing civil conflict from 2001 to 2002, the Ali Taar family—who belonged to the same Omar Mahamoud sub-clan as Yusuf—supported the former warlord in his fight against Jama. When Yusuf prevailed, the Ali Taars began operations in Puntland's waters. The brief civil war had also played itself out within the ranks of Hart's multi-clan coast guard force, which split into opposing factions; when fighting broke out near Hart's bases of operation, the firm packed up and set sail for the United Kingdom.[7]

A few days after speaking with Mudan, I met with two of SomCan's top executives, Said Orey and Abdirahman Ali Taar (elder brother of Abdiweli), on the patio of the same hotel. Joining us was Captain Abdirashid Abdirahim Ishmael, the commander of SomCan's marine forces.

Said Orey was quick to provide me with his no doubt partial explanation for Hart's hurried exit from Somalia. "Hart Security failed in its task," he claimed. "They weren't interested in the job. Hart failed to bring in sufficient equipment to properly protect the coast, and so people wanted a local company to do the job."

Though run by Somalis, the company did not represent much of a break from the past, being yet another private venture. SomCan seamlessly continued Hart's coast guard fishing licence business model, on an even greater scale. During its glory days, from 2002 to 2005, SomCan boasted an armada of six patrol boats and a force of four hundred marines, and claimed to have identified and arrested a total of thirty illegal fishing vessels. During this period, the company was heavily involved in selling fishing permits, with a quarterly licence fetching about $50,000. These revenues were supposed to be channelled through the Ministry of Fisheries, but the company was alleged to have often bypassed the ministry and sold fishing licences directly to foreign concessions.

"Some licences were coming from the ministry," Mudan had told me a few days earlier, "and some were issued by SomCan itself. I saw one of them, in Dubai. And it was not issued by the ministry; it was signed by Abdiweli Ali Taar."

Puntland specialist Stig Jarle Hansen, who has conducted extensive research into the use of private security in the region, agreed. "As I understand it, Abdiweli Ali Taar was authorized to sell licences," he told me. "They were sold through networks, but SomCan was in the end responsible."

Unlike Hart, SomCan required foreign fishing companies to obtain a Somali agent to represent them. Once the companies— mostly Korean, Thai, or Japanese concerns—had established ties with a Somali businessman, local government militiamen would be placed on their ships to provide protection, particularly from hostile local fishermen. In many cases, the fishing companies also hired additional security through their Somali agents. "SomCan was keeping the security of their own licensed ships, instead of keeping the security of the sea," explained Abdiwahid Mahamed Hersi "Joaar," the long-serving director general of the Puntland Ministry of Fisheries.

SomCan's tripartite role as law enforcer, trade commissioner, and independent contractor enabled the company to establish what could be described as a maritime protection racket. From 2002 to 2005, the coast guard served directly as an agent for the Thai concession Sirichai Fisheries, guaranteeing the company's security in Somali waters and protecting it from local fishermen-cum-pirates, even to the point of posting its own armed guards on the decks of Sirichai's ships. Sirichai's relationship with SomCan was literally skin tight; according to Noel Choong, director of the International Maritime Bureau's Piracy Reporting Centre, Sirichai went so far as to provide uniforms for the coast guard troops.[8]

If there was any conflict of interest in a government coast guard protecting a private client, it was lost on Orey. "Yes, we were the agent for Sirichai," he said. "It was always the best company at following the rules and regulations."

SomCan's penchant for defending a select group of foreign fishing ships ran directly counter to the coast guard's raison d'être and brought it into conflict with local fishermen. For this reason, said Orey, the Ministry of Fisheries kept a close eye on the activities of licensed ships. "There were always inspectors from the Ministry of Fisheries on-board ship, whose duty it was to check if they were using legal equipment, and to protect local fishing boats from them," he said. "Sometimes these ships would overrun small fishing boats, and the inspector's job was to stop them, to keep them away from the locals."

Despite these measures, confrontations were common. According to Hansen, SomCan actively defended both foreign and domestic "licensed" fishing vessels from local fishermen. "Local fishermen were often unable to obtain the proper permits," he said, "and were forcibly prevented from fishing by the coast guard." Exacerbating the problem was the fact that SomCan-licensed ships would routinely come within close range of the shore. "They were coming two miles from the shore. Several times they destroyed nets," Mudan had told me. "Foreign fishing ships came very close to the shore and local fishermen started firing on them. SomCan responded."

SomCan's first coast-guarding stint came to an inglorious end in March 2005, when its employees hijacked a fishing trawler operated by Sirichai Fisheries, the company's own client. In another incident that blurred the distinction between coast guards and pirates, three SomCan guards on board the fishing trawler *Sirichainava 12* seized control of the vessel, demanding an $800,000 ransom for its release. Their actions provoked a quick and decisive response; within hours, a joint British and American strike team freed the ship and took the renegades into custody. The US Navy subsequently transported them to Oman, after which they were brought to Thailand and sentenced to ten years' imprisonment for piracy. (The hijackers served only a few years of their prison term; in 2007, President Hersi arranged their release under unknown circumstances.)

What had prompted their ill-advised gamble was not completely clear. One report suggested that the hijacking was provoked by the non-payment of the guards' monthly $200 salary. Orey insisted that the men had been paid in full, but had simply gotten greedy.

In either case, the hijacking was an utter disaster for SomCan, costing the company its job with the Puntland government—at least temporarily.

* * *

SomCan received a second chance three years later. Two years after the company's dismissal, in 2007, the Saudi private security firm Al-Habiibi briefly assumed coast guard duties in Puntland, but was fired in February 2008 for refusing an order to liberate the hijacked Russian tugboat *Svitzer Korsakov*. Then-president General Mohamud Muse Hersi turned back to SomCan, which was more willing than Al-Habiibi to serve as pirate hunters.

From between the pages of his daily planner, Orey produced a folded copy of SomCan's current employment contract, signed with Hersi's government in July 2008. As had been the case with Hart, all licensing and fine revenues were to be split 51 per cent–49 per cent, with the Puntland government responsible for supplying the coast guard's ships, weapons, and equipment.

In recent days, the pirates had been presenting a challenge not seen during SomCan's previous coast-guarding tour, but Orey was confident that his company was ready. "It is over the last eight months that we have done our best work," he said. In October 2008, for example, SomCan had mounted a successful operation to liberate the hijacked MV *Wail*, a Panamanian-registered bulk carrier containing a consignment of cement owned by a local Somali businessman. Captain Ishmael, who led the rescue operation, described how the SomCan flagship, flanked by its two speedboats, had surrounded the pirates and dispatched a negotiator to discuss the situation. As the speedboat carrying SomCan's envoy approached the hijacked transport, the pirates opened fire, killing the craft's operator. In the ensuing firefight, SomCan marines captured ten of the hijackers, sustaining one injury and minor damage to their ship.

SomCan's other encounters with pirates had been less bloody, and even more successful. Orey cited three naval assaults against hijacked fishing ships held near Hafun, which in each case resulted in the bandits abandoning the vessel and melting before SomCan's onslaught. The objects of these rescues were all local Somali or Yemeni vessels, which, according to Orey, the pirates had intended to use as long-range motherships.

Despite these successes, Orey was quick to acknowledge that SomCan had a long way to go. Although the company possessed three cast-off patrol boats obtained from the Japanese coast guard—as well as two speedboats—the cost of fuel usually limited it to deploying only a third of its "fleet." [9] The company operated no coastal radar tracking stations and did not employ satellite surveillance; the only intelligence it received was conveyed by radio or telephone. SomCan was, in effect, a "Dial-a-Coast-Guard," whose counter-piracy activities were limited to after-the-fact responses: either commando-style raids on captive vessels, or, if given timely tip-offs, anticipatory assaults on land.

Even setting aside the difficulties in response time, the SomCan patrol ship's armament rendered it run-of-the-mill competition for many of the illegal fishing vessels it was routinely tasked with observing and intercepting. A few weeks earlier, Orey had been personally supervising a routine patrol from Bossaso to Hafun. As the SomCan ship was returning to port, it came across four foreign fishing vessels in close proximity to one another, each armed with an anti-aircraft gun, which Orey sardonically described as "almost the exact same kind as ours. They saw the anti-aircraft guns on our deck," he said, "and that was enough. They opened fire." Outmatched, the SomCan crew had few options. "Of course we fled," said Orey, "there was no way we were ready to fight them." Fortunately, no one was injured or killed in the engagement.[10] But the incident illustrated that SomCan was in need of a more lethal deterrent than the "Coast Guard" lettering on its ships before it would be able to administer justice in Somalia's anarchic waters.

* * *

After the dissolutions of Hart and SomCan in 2002 and 2005, respectively, their employees melted like a tide into the coastline. As Ombaali's testimony suggests, some of them discovered that their nautical training had practical applications at the opposite end of the employment spectrum from law enforcement. In an October 2008 report by the British think tank Chatham House, Captain Colin Darch, skipper of the hijacked Russian tugboat *Svitzer Korsakov,* related that several of the vessel's captors had previously belonged to the Puntland Coast Guard. "One pirate called Ahmed told us he had been in the coast guard," he said, "and only Ahmed and one or two others who had also been coast guards understood our engines."[11]

The involvement of ex-Puntland Coast Guard marines in piracy is hardly surprising. The skills and experience possessed by former coast guards—trained to a European standard in sharpshooting, maritime navigation, and boarding and seizure operations—made them perfect employees for the new businesses springing up around the Gulf of Aden. The Somali pirates who burst onto the scene in 2007 and 2008 were organized to a level attested by the immediacy of their success, and by the millions of dollars that were literally airlifted their way. Long-range motherships and advanced navigation systems like GPS and radar made it possible for them to carry out deep-water operations. These technologies—as well as larger investments in fuel and weapons—extended the pirates' attack radius hundreds of kilometres from the coast. During the extended hunting trips into the wilderness of international waters that characterized this new wave of pirates, a former coast guard's knowledge of GPS systems, radar, and the more complex engines on board the mother-ships would be an invaluable asset.

* * *

The peaceful election of Abdirahman Farole—a PhD candidate from Melbourne's La Trobe University—in January 2009 was regarded as something of a landmark in Puntland politics; he was only the second civilian Somali leader, along with Somaliland founder Mo-hamed Egal, since the assassination of Somali Republic president Abdirashid Ali Shermarke in 1969. During his political campaign, Farole promised to get tough on piracy, a stance he has reiterated in media interviews since his election. Hoping to tease out the specif-ics of his plan, I spoke with him at the presidential compound in the centre of Garowe.

Farole, meaning "fused toes," was a nickname that the president had inherited from his great-grandfather. In his mid-sixties, Farole was diminutive, but the intensity of his almost-feline eyes com-manded an authority that his body did not; they seemed to swallow anyone meeting his gaze. The president was an erudite man, fluent in English, Arabic, and Italian, and his first sentence to me inaugur-ated a half-hour lecture on the history of Somalia's current tribula-tions; finally, I managed to steer the conversation towards the topic of the Puntland Coast Guard.

"We are nowhere near being able to establish a functioning coast guard," Farole began bluntly. "This force must be professionally trained and equipped with speedboats, telecommunications, and GPS technology, heavy weapons, and a continual supply of fuel," he said, at a cost that the Puntland government was unable to shoulder. With his administration struggling to keep up with monthly army wages of $30, financing the monthly coast guard salary of $300 (a necessary wage, said the president, for a highly skilled job requiring long periods spent absent from families) for a hundreds-strong force would be impossible without international financial assistance.

"Money will also be needed to reward marines who successfully capture pirate vessels," said Farole, adding that additional funds would be required to satisfy traditional Somali clan law, or *heer,* which requires compensation to be paid to the families of soldiers killed in action. Hearing the president speak, it was clear that he anticipated much blood being spilt—for him, a resolute and dogged fight against piracy would be a war, with casualties unavoidable. "Unless you truly get the will and commitment of the people behind you," said Farole, "you cannot win any war."

Winning a war also requires a command of logistics, an area in which the president admitted Puntland was notably deficient. The region possesses close to half of Somalia's thirty-three-hundred-kilometre coastline, yet communications, radar, and satellite centres in the Indian Ocean and the Gulf of Aden—which would provide intelligence and coordination to the coast guard—are yet to be established. Additionally, mechanisms are still required to integrate the Puntland Coast Guard with the institutions of NATO, the European Union, the International Maritime Bureau, and individual foreign navies.

The president had little faith in the ability of a private security firm to overcome these formidable challenges. When I asked about SomCan's future role as coast guard, his response was guardedly noncommittal—but not optimistic. "I don't believe they will be effective for this difficult task," he said. "Because they didn't do anything in the past." For the moment, at least, the president was not looking to hand over SomCan's job to anyone else once the company's present contract expired.

"We are not prepared to create a coast guard without international help," Farole said, adding that the fight against the pirates would be in the hands of Puntland's regular ground troops, deployed from their Bossaso garrison. For Farole, however, international concerns over piracy were of secondary importance to those closer to

home. "Measures need to go beyond preventing piracy against commercial ships," he said. "Piracy is [the international community's]
problem—well, it's ours too—but what is *specifically* our problem
is illegal fishing." Until illegal fishing was curtailed, the president
was adamant that the ministry's days as a licence printing press were
over: "We are not planning to issue any fishing licences before we
have full control of our seas."

The Puntland government's dream of gaining sovereignty over
its seas remains distant. Puntland currently relies almost entirely on
foreign warships to provide ersatz coast guard services in the Gulf
of Aden and the Indian Ocean (only the day before I spoke with the
president, the French navy had handed over nine Somali captives to
Puntland officials—a far more tempered response than the overzealous Operation Thalathine). But operating an international armada
at a cost of tens of millions per month is not sustainable; eventually,
a locally owned coast guard, one free of Hart's and SomCan's unsavoury legacy of profiteering, will be required to safeguard Somalia's
dangerous waters.

* * *

On June 30, 2009, SomCan's contract with the Puntland government expired, and—not surprisingly—was not renewed. During
the last few months of its tenure, SomCan—perhaps still hoping to
prove its worth to the new administration—continued to hunt illegal fishing ships with furious resolve. On March 12, the company's
boat headed out of Bossaso harbour on patrol, and on March 31
it caught up with two ships fishing illegally near Hafun. After escorting them back to Bossaso and impounding them, the SomCan
owners were greeted with an irate reaction from the Ministry of
Fisheries, which produced copies of two licences that it had recently
issued to the vessels (which were subsequently released). Apparently, just a few months after Farole had assured me of his government's intention to scrap the corrupt fishing licensing schemes of

past Puntland administrations, the arbitrary issuing of licences had seamlessly resumed.

These developments were not welcomed by Said Orey, a fact he made clear on the porch of my Garowe residence shortly before the expiration of SomCan's contract. "We are entitled to collect 49 per cent of the proceeds of all fishing licences sold by the Puntland government, but the fishing ministry won't even tell us it's selling them," he said, looking disgusted. "It's clear that people from the Ministry of Fisheries are working with illegal fishing interests."

A few days later, over lunch at the house of a mutual friend, I asked Director General Joaar about the ministry's renewed interest in the licence-printing business. "Yes, we started selling licences again—with the permission of the president—for forty-five-day periods," he admitted. "But only six have been sold so far."

When I brought up SomCan's contractual right to almost half the revenue from the licences, Joaar waved his hand dismissively.

"Said Orey is himself a pirate," he declared. "Our office still hasn't received a copy of that contract. It was a deal that was completely under the table."

SomCan and the Ministry of Fisheries butted heads for a second time towards the end of May, after the company attacked and arrested three more foreign fishing vessels in the vicinity of Bargaal. These vessels, according to Orey, were entirely different from the two arrested in the March incident, but Joaar insisted that two of the three were the exact same ships SomCan had erroneously captured two months earlier. "This time, I told them: 'If you think you can capture those ships, go ahead and try—because they have security on board,'" said Joaar. This security had been provided by the Puntland government after the vessel's previous run-in with SomCan, as Joaar freely admitted. "If we give them licences," he explained, "we are responsible for what happens to them."

The SomCan patrol ship had nonetheless confronted the vessels, and, after they refused to surrender, opened fire. Responding to the fishing vessels' distress calls, the Spanish warship *Numancia*, the flagship of the European Union fleet, arrived and attempted to mediate the situation. After receiving confirmation from unidentified onshore ministry officials—relayed through the *Numancia*—that the ships were legally licensed, SomCan disengaged and left the scene. Following the episode, Orey told me, he received a personal rebuke from the office of the president.

At best, these incidents revealed a buffoonish lack of coordination between the Puntland government and its supposed official coast guard; at worst, an endemic state of venality and double-dealing within the Puntland Ministry of Fisheries that had been granted President Farole's blessing. In any case, the ministry's—and Joaar's—antipathy towards SomCan seemed somewhat self-defeating: without a coast guard backing it up, one wonders why any foreign fishing vessel would ever bother to buy a Puntland licence. But the potential loss of revenue did not seem to dampen Joaar's sense of triumph over his adversaries.

"SomCan is finished," he said, wiping his hands together. "No more."

* * *

SomCan's demise, however, did not bring an end to the Puntland government's dalliances with private security contractors. In November 2010, Puntland entered into a deal with Saracen International, a South African private security firm with no clear address, to "train and mentor" a "Puntland Marine Force." [12] Even by the standards of the murky Hart and SomCan deals, Puntland's agreement with Saracen had all the transparency of a muddy lake. The firm—whose Ugandan subsidiary has been fingered by the UN Security Council for training rebel paramilitary forces in the Congo—is headed by Lafras Lutingh, a former officer in the Civil Cooperation Bureau, a notorious apartheid-era internal security force. [13] Several months after the announcement of the Puntland deal, Saracen was revealed to be covertly backed by Erik Prince, founder of Blackwater (now

Xe Services), the much-maligned military contractor implicated in the 2007 deaths of fourteen Iraqi civilians. Saracen is currently in the process of training a one-thousand-strong anti-piracy militia in Puntland, equipped with 120 pickup trucks, four armoured vehicles, and six patrol aircraft.[14] The funding for this ambitious program, Somali officials initially announced, would come from an unnamed Middle Eastern country (later revealed to be the United Arab Emirates) with a vested commercial interest in keeping the Gulf of Aden shipping lane pirate-free.

The Puntland government, it seems, is yet to learn the lesson of the last decade. Far from being an impartial government actor, the coast guard operated as a business enterprise, generating its own revenues through the sordid sale of fishing permits to private clients. Instead of preventing violent confrontations between the locals and foreign fishing fleets, the coast guard took sides, posting armed guards on the decks of a select group of foreign vessels. In doing so, it accentuated the grievances that were driving the local fishermen to commit feats of piracy.

After doing its bit to accelerate the rise of piracy in Puntland, in 2005 the SomCan Coast Guard itself took a turn at hijacking. When the company subsequently dispersed, many of its former employees, trained to *combat* piracy, themselves joined the burgeoning ranks of pirates sweeping into the Gulf of Aden. In early 2009, SomCan completed the circuit, actively recruiting so-called "reformed pirates" into its ranks.

First in line was one of Eyl's most notorious sons, the infamous Garaad Mohammed.

5

Garaad

IN THE EVER-SHIFTING WORLD OF PIRATES, COAST GUARDS, AND
fishermen, the movement amongst the three professions has never
been in only one direction. As some coast guards have transitioned
to piracy, so have some pirates made the shift into coast-guarding. Of
this latter trend, there is no better example than Garaad Mohammed.

Like many pirate pioneers, Garaad grew up as a fisherman in Eyl,
joining his comrades in the struggle against illegal fishing. Beginning in 2003, Garaad, along with Boyah and the other Eyl veterans, travelled south to Harardheere to provide training to Afweyne's
Somali Marines. Garaad's bloodline made him an ideal inter-clan
go-between; his father belonged to the Isse Mahamoud of Eyl, but
his mother was born Habir Gedir, the same sub-clan as Afweyne and
the other Harardheere pirates.

Shortly after he began joint operations with the Marines, Garaad
founded his own group, the National Volunteer Coast Guard (NVCG),
an organization based in the southern city of Kismaayo that specialized in targeting small boats and fishing vessels. But even after the
formation of the NVCG, Garaad's affiliation with Afweyne and the
Harardheere gangs did not end, and he continued to finance gangs
operating out of central and northern Somalia.

On April 8, 2009, four of Garaad's henchmen, operating from
the commandeered Taiwanese fishing vessel *Win Far 161*, attacked

the MV *Maersk Alabama* several hundred kilometres off the central Somali coast as she was steaming towards Mombasa. In what was the first piracy of a US-registered vessel in two centuries, the hijackers boarded the vessel and took Captain Richard Phillips and two other American citizens hostage on the bridge. As the leader of the attackers attempted to locate the rest of the crew, he was ambushed in the darkened engine room by the *Alabama*'s chief engineer, Mike Perry, who, though armed only with a knife, managed to overpower him. After the leader was released in a bungled attempt to exchange him for Captain Phillips, all four hijackers fled in the *Alabama*'s cramped lifeboat, taking Phillips along with them.

The destroyer USS *Bainbridge* was the first US warship to arrive at the scene, as if guided by the spirit of her namesake, Commodore William Bainbridge, a nineteenth-century naval officer who had played a pivotal role in the war against the Barbary pirates of northern Africa. A tense hostage standoff with the lifeboat ensued. Over the next three days, the increasingly jittery pirates—whom Phillips nicknamed "The Leader," "Musso," "Tall Guy," and "Young Guy"—subjected him to sadistic psychological torture, the details of which Phillips related in a book about the incident, *A Captain's Duty:*

> "When we kill you, we're going to put you in an unclean place," the Leader said. "That's where I'm taking you now."
>
> "What does that mean?"
>
> They explained that they knew about this shallow reef where the water was stagnant. It wasn't part of a tide pool that came in and washed the bay every twelve hours. Any body dropped there would rot and bloat and stink to high heaven.
>
> "Very bad place," Musso said.
>
> I couldn't hold it any longer. I felt a rush of wetness on my pant leg. They were letting me piss myself like a goddamn animal.
>
> The rage just welled up in me. I felt degraded. I was screaming at the pirates, just cursing them and telling them they were going to die.[1]

For three of the four men, Phillips's morbid prediction came true. On April 12, believing Phillips's life to be in immediate danger, Commander Frank Castellano ordered the *Bainbridge* forces into action, upon which Navy SEAL snipers killed the three hijackers remaining on the lifeboat. The Leader, Abdiweli Muse (a Puntlander from Galkayo), who had been on board the *Bainbridge* conducting ransom negotiations when the rescue took place, suddenly found his bargaining position shot to bits. He was taken to New York to stand trial, and in February 2011 was sentenced to almost thirty-four years in prison.

Following the *Alabama* attack, Garaad vowed revenge against the Americans, and ordered his organization to retaliate. Two days later, a boatload of Garaad's men sighted the MV *Liberty Sun,* a US-flagged vessel carrying food aid destined for Somalia, which they proceeded to pursue and blast with rocket-propelled grenades; fortunately, neither the vessel nor her crew were harmed. In a subsequent phone interview with the Agence France-Presse, Garaad made it clear that the motive for the attack was anything but financial. "We were not after a ransom," he said. "We . . . assigned a team with special equipment to chase and destroy any ship flying the American flag in retaliation for the brutal killing of our friends."[2]

In February 2009, two months before the *Alabama* hijacking, I had sat across a table from Garaad on the patio of a Bossaso hotel, listening to him discuss his plans to join the Puntland Coast Guard.

* * *

I had been trying to get in touch with him for weeks, but Garaad had exhibited a tendency to disappear for long stretches of time once the initial contact was made. My interpreter Warsame and I had been supposed to meet him the previous day, but after preliminary discussions in the morning, Garaad turned off his phone and we didn't hear back from him. "He's off chewing khat somewhere," Warsame suggested. The next day, Garaad called us with his explanation: "I was busy."

After agreeing to meet us at four o'clock, his phone was off again. It was twenty minutes past four, and I was starting to get worried. I had heard disturbing reports of Garaad's lack of regard for conventional notions of politeness; one of my hosts, Abdirizak, recounted how Garaad had stood him up for a 10 a.m. meeting two days in a row. When one of our party informed Warsame and me that he had recently spotted Garaad near the khat market, chewing with some friends, it seemed that today's rendezvous was destined to share a similar fate. "Forget it," said Warsame, "he's not coming. He won't move for the rest of the afternoon." Soon afterwards, we got a call; despite the hypnotic powers of the khat, Garaad was on his way to the hotel. "His phone must have been off to avoid the people calling him for money," our friend suggested.

At about twenty-five minutes past four, Garaad showed up at the gated entrance to the hotel, and Warsame and I joined him on the restaurant patio. With his freshly ironed dress shirt, pressed slacks, and clean, cropped hair, Garaad blended right in with the crowd of Somali businessmen staying at the hotel. In contrast to his impeccable outfit, his face looked ragged and exhausted for someone in his mid-thirties, his eyes scratched raw by the constant rubbing of his fingers—a textbook case of khat withdrawal. Like Boyah, his face was slightly emaciated, and Warsame suggested afterwards that, like Boyah, he may have also been suffering from tuberculosis—perhaps indicative of a pirate-specific strain of the disease making the rounds. Also like Boyah, the indifference he showed towards me bordered on disdain. He shook my hand with a limp and lifeless motion, barely glancing in my direction. Throughout our meeting, he continually checked his phone, peering around as if hoping for someone to come and take him to the real interview.

Like "Butch Cassidy" or "Billy the Kid," "Garaad" was an outlaw sobriquet that had grown notorious in its own time—at least within the borders of Puntland. Like most pirate handles, his was an assumed name, taken from the Somali word for "clan elder," and was thus a sign of his status amongst his colleagues. In the world of Somali seafaring careers, Garaad had scaled the corporate ladder with remarkable dexterity, rising from artisanal fisherman to fishing vessel hijacker, and finally to one of the most famous pirate organizers and financiers in Puntland.

As I began my questions, Garaad instantly prickled when he heard the word "pirate."

"Illegal fishing ships, they are the real pirates," he rejoined. "I don't know where they all come from, but there are nearly five thousand ships doing illegal fishing in our territory." Garaad's estimate, far more generous than the 200–250 illegal ships projected by the Puntland Ministry of Fisheries, may have been coloured by his strong personal sentiments.

"I was one of the first to start fighting against the illegal fishing, before Boyah," he bristled. So far, his quest against the "real pirates" of Somalia had netted Garaad a total of about a dozen illegal fishing ships. Despite these successes, he assured me that little in the way of ransom money has come his way. "Ransom negotiations over captured fishing ships are very difficult," he said, "because the people you're dealing with . . . drag the negotiations on and on. They don't care how long you keep the ships, they won't pay you anything." But Garaad insisted that his goal was not to make money, but to fight illegal fishing. Aiding him in his crusade, he said, was a pirate army spanning the entire length of the Somali coast.

"I have direct control over a total of eight hundred hijackers operating in thirteen groups spread from Bossaso, through Hafun, Eyl, Harardheere, Hobyo, and Kismaayo," he said. Each of these groups had a "sub-lieutenant" who reported directly to Garaad and did not make a move without his authorization, he claimed. "Independent groups"—those whom he did not control—accounted for an additional eight hundred individuals. To take Garaad at his word, therefore, would have been to give him credit for exerting a half-Stalinist, half-Mafioso grip over half of Somalia's estimated 1,500–2,000 pirates, spread over a criminal empire stretching almost twenty-five hundred kilometres of lawless coastline. Given the decentralized nature of most pirate operations, it was an understatement to say that Garaad's self-portrayal stretched credulity thin.

"If the international community ever pays us our rightful compensation for the illegal fishing," he said, "attacks will stop within forty-eight hours." As to what this compensation might entail, Garaad was less than specific. "Nobody can count it," he answered. "It's a lot of money. The people of the world know how long they have been doing illegal fishing, and from that they can calculate how much they owe us."

* * *

Throughout our interview, Garaad seemed anxious to prove that he was no profiteer. His manner was evasive whenever I asked for specific monetary details, and persistent questioning invariably caused him to retreat. "I've never personally attacked commercial ships," he said. "The only one I've ever captured is the *Stella Maris*, and the reason for it was the financial problems we were having then. At the time, there was a lack of illegal fishing vessels to attack, and we needed money to keep our operations going."

The MV *Stella Maris*, a Japanese-owned bulk carrier, was seized in the Gulf of Aden in July 2008 and held for eleven weeks before being released for a ransom of $2 million, which Garaad reinvested in future operations. His operating expenses since then must have been rather high, because Garaad insisted that he was broke. "I don't have one cent," he said. "I don't even have a house."

Despite his protestations of poverty, the word was that Garaad had been involved with the hijacking of the MV *Faina*, the Ukrainian transport ship laden with Russian tanks that first drew international media attention to the Somali coast. But his level of involvement was anyone's guess, and Garaad himself was not going to provide any clarification. When I asked him about the *Faina*, he immediately tensed up, telling me that he "supported some young guys" for the mission, but volunteering no more information.

There is a credible rumour, however, surrounding Garaad's involvement. In December 2008, Garaad reportedly left Garowe with a cohort of armed men, aiming to relieve the *Faina* hijackers and bring them back to safety in Puntland. They were much in need of his assistance; after forcing the captured ship to anchor at Harardheere, south of the Puntland coast, the US Navy had proceeded to encircle and blockade the pirates on board the *Faina*. On shore, the environment was equally hostile; Harardheere was near territory controlled by the Islamist organization Al-Shabaab, and the group's militias were waiting patiently inland to relieve the *Faina* pirates of their ransom as soon as they dared come ashore.

Into this melee allegedly charged Garaad, his Toyota cavalry gleaming in the sun. His intention, presumably, was to escort the hijackers to Puntland once they had secured the ransom payment for the *Faina*. Unfortunately, on his way to Harardheere, Al-Shabaab militants reportedly ambushed Garaad's convoy, confiscated his weapons and vehicles, and left him, unharmed, to make the long journey back to Puntland on foot. At the first opportunity, I asked Garaad for the truth behind this incredible story. His shields instantly dropped. "No, that's not true, I wasn't involved with that," he said. "I don't have any enemies, only friends . . . everyone is happy with the job I'm doing."

After four months in captivity, the *Faina* had finally been released a week before our meeting, commanding a then-record bounty of $3.2 million. Considering that he had partially financed the mission, Garaad was curiously ignorant of the state of his investment. "I was busy with other things," he said. "I didn't hear about any ransom money." A few moments later, his memory seemed to clear up. "We didn't get that much money," he said. "By the time it finally came down to it, everyone only got a few thousand. A lot of money was spent on that ship, and hundreds of people were involved."

This is one part of Garaad's story, at least, that I was able to verify independently, through a Nairobi source who had been directly involved in the *Faina* ransom negotiation process. As the negotiation dragged on, my source told me, burgeoning expenses forced the original hijackers (Afweyne's group) to approach three or four additional pirate organizations for financial assistance—in effect, issuing stock in their operation. By the time the ransom was delivered, the complement on board the ship had ballooned to over a hundred pirates.

* * *

As the interview progressed, Garaad gradually began to open up.

"Right now, as I talk to you, there are twenty different groups I'm invested in, from Kismaayo to Hafun." He hesitated before continuing. "We control the entire Somali coast." When asked what he thought of Boyah's recent radio-announced ceasefire, a mocking note entered his voice as he shook his head. "My organization is different . . . We're not similar to Boyah . . . We are going to keep going until our seas are cleansed of illegal fishing ships."

When I asked for the names of some of the commercial ships seized by his organization, Garaad deflected my question once more. "I don't know the names of any of the ships my men capture, and I don't care," he said. "The only thing I care about is sending more pirates into the sea.

"Sometimes, the commercial vessels," he continued, "have the same names as the illegal fishing ships. They are owned by the same companies . . . so that makes it legal to capture those commercial ships as well."

Garaad's tenuous justification sounded similar to the Roman emperor Caligula's remark upon being told that he had executed the wrong man for a crime: "That one deserved it just as much." Fishing companies and international shippers rarely share parent companies, but to Garaad, any ship he caught merited equal punishment.

Garaad's vehement quest for maritime justice had recently brought him into the open arms of SomCan, which at the time still had four months remaining on its contract. "Yes, I will be part of

[SomCan]," he said. "If the coast guard is going to stop people from doing illegal fishing, destroying the marine environment, and doing toxic dumping, then we will work with them." In other words, having tried his hand at fishing and piracy, Garaad was looking for a shot at coast-guarding. "The reason I'm with SomCan now," Garaad said, "is because they have special ships that are well-armed with proper guns—with anti-aircraft guns—and their ships are capable of getting close to the illegal fishers." Pressed for specifics about his job description, he continued, "I will be training their marines, and providing them with information and intelligence."

Given his adamant hatred of illegal fishing, Garaad was curiously unconcerned by the fact that his current partners had only recently been in the business of protecting the very foreign ships he vowed to hunt down. "The reason I joined them," Garaad said, "is that they told me that they stopped those practices. If I see that they are still doing that, then we'll have a problem."

As a "reformed pirate," Garaad hoped to be a kind of Hannibal Lecter of Puntland, helping the authorities hunt down the serial hijackers of the Gulf of Aden. But "reformed" might have been a premature descriptor, for Garaad was not about to give up his pirate activities just because he happened to be working as a coast guard. "The agreement I made is to help them fight against illegal fishing," he said. "These days, I'm concentrating on illegal fishing ships. But I will still be doing my other operations on the side."

The exact nature of Garaad's coast-guarding aspirations seemed to vacillate. In one version, his aim was to serve SomCan in a capacity falling somewhere between naval school drill instructor and marine commando; in another, he would use his supposedly massive pirate empire as a paramilitary force to fight foreign fishing in Somali waters, with SomCan tagging along for the ride. His next statement appeared to support this latter interpretation. "SomCan is one of us now," he said, "it is part of our organization." Garaad would not give any more details of the terms of his agreement, other than to say that it would remain in effect as long as illegal fishers trawled

Somali seas. Despite our lengthy exchange, it was impossible to say what he saw as his role in SomCan, and I was beginning to think he had little idea himself.

Hoping to clarify these ambiguities, I brought up the subject of Garaad's employment during my meeting with the SomCan executives the following day. I quickly learned an interesting fact: Garaad was the cousin of SomCan co-owner Said Orey. "Yes," said Orey, "we've been in contact with Garaad. As his relative, it is my duty to stop him from doing bad things." Garaad's role in the company, Orey was quick to emphasize, would be to work on board ship as a marine, "not as a coast guard trainer."

Hiring a pirate to police coastal waters seemed like hiring a bank robber to guard the vault, and, in Garaad's case, one who intended to keep robbing banks during his off-hours. Yet Garaad was not the only pirate SomCan was hoping to work with. What the company had in mind, Orey told me, was a kind of employment retraining program for pirates. "Let us first try and educate these young guys," Orey said, "and if we succeed, then, whoever refuses to cooperate, maybe we can fight against them." At SomCan's behest, Garaad was using his influence to recruit as many pirates as possible into its ranks. According to Orey, many were already lining up to get fitted for uniforms. Yet, if Garaad was any indication, transforming dozens of erstwhile pirates into marine security officers would be a difficult task, especially if many of them also saw their new job as fundamentally identical to their old one.

For better or worse, the end of SomCan's contract quashed its pirate employment experiment in its infancy. Garaad, however, appeared to have seen some limited service with the company before being decommissioned. According to Joaar, SomCan's May 2009 attack on the three ministry-licensed fishing vessels was carried out by a strike team composed of former pirates. "There were sixteen pirates from Eyl onboard, including Garaad," he said. "These [SomCan owners] are crazy people."

* * *

Our meeting over, Garaad got up and silently walked away. An hour after he left, a call came to Warsame's phone: it was Garaad, asking for his help to arrange an interview with President Farole. As with Boyah, his reason for talking to me had been rendered perfectly transparent.

He was, I heard, already back with his friends, chewing khat as the sun set.

6

Flower of Paradise

THE ARRIVAL OF KHAT IN GAROWE IS A CURIOUS SIGHT.
Each day at around noon, the first khat transports begin to
roll in from Galkayo, coinciding with the typical waking hour for
a pirate. The angry honking of the incoming vehicles rouses the
city from its lethargy, bringing expectant crowds flocking into the
streets in defiance of the midday heat. Screaming down the highway at reckless speeds, high beams flashing, guards perched on top,
the transports arrive on the southern road. Turning off the highway and rumbling down the embankment towards Garowe's main
checkpoint, they are eagerly greeted by barking soldiers, who fill
their arms with leafy bundles before waving the vehicles through.
Behind the barrier, a fleet of white station wagons stands ready
to be loaded; hired hands follow behind female merchants decked
in vibrant headdresses, hauling rectangular bushels wrapped in
brown canvas.

As the transports arrive at the khat market, or *suq*, the whole city
begins to buzz with activity. Throngs of shouting men press into the
suq as older children and adolescents mob the transports, hoping to
snatch what they can in the scramble of the unloading. In the poorer
neighbourhoods, barefoot children gather in circles in front of hov-
els, slapping hands and jostling for a few stalks scattered in the dust.
Even the goats respond with Pavlovian consistency to the tooting of

the station wagons, trotting after them in the hopes of nabbing a few fallen leaves.

This is the most significant daily event in Garowe life, repeated with unfailing precision every single day of the year. Steadily increasing in popularity in recent years, khat has become—along with livestock and fishing—one of Puntland's most lucrative economic sectors. As a Puntland cabinet minister once told me: "In Somalia, there are two industries that work: *hawala* [money transfer] and khat." If so, piracy has certainly made the khat trade work even better—since late 2008, the *suq* has been awash with the freshly minted bills of pirate ransoms, threatening to turn a tolerable vice into a national addiction.

* * *

Across clime, culture, and continent, people will find some way to intoxicate themselves. In Somalia, a uniformly Islamic society where alcohol consumption is highly taboo, the intoxicant of choice is khat, an amphetamine-like stimulant consumed either by chewing the plant's leaves or by steeping its dried leaves to make a tea.

Khat—which the Arabs nicknamed the "flower of paradise"—has for centuries been used by Muslim scholars to assist the performance of their intensive day- and night-long studies (and, in more modern times, by Kenyan and Ethiopian students cramming for exams).[1] Growing up to twenty metres high, the plant is extremely water-intensive and better suited to altitudes of 1,500–2,500 metres, giving the Ethiopian highlands and the provinces of northern Kenya a strong natural advantage over Somalia. Once confined to East Africa, the demand for the drug has been globalized over the last twenty years by refugees from conflicts in Somalia and Ethiopia; facilitated by modern transportation technologies, khat can now readily be found on the streets of London, Amsterdam, Toronto, Chicago, and Sydney.[2]

A social drug, khat is usually chewed for hours on end by groups of friends in picnic-like settings. Owing to its bitter taste, it is often accompanied by a special, heavily sugared tea or other sweet beverage, such as 7-Up. Once harvested, the plant retains its potency for only a short time and must be consumed fresh—the plant's active chemical, cathinone, breaks down within forty-eight hours after its leaves have dried—a fact that explains its previous lack of international distribution. Shipments to Puntland are flown three times daily from Nairobi and Addis Ababa into Galkayo airport. As is often the case with products designated for export, the khat that finds its way into Garowe is reputed to be of the lowest quality.

One company, SOMEHT, is responsible for importing virtually all of Puntland's khat, around seven thousand kilograms per day as of 2006.[3] According to Fadumo—a Garowe khat merchant whom I interviewed—each plane is greeted at the airstrip by large numbers of independent distributors, who deploy a network of transports for the slow and bumpy 250-kilometre journey from Galkayo to Garowe. Such is the addiction inspired by this delectable plant that crowds of youth throw up improvised roadblocks composed of small rocks or metal drums at frequent intervals by the sides of the road. At these unofficial checkpoints the young men, often armed with Kalashnikovs, clamour for handouts of the shrub. The drivers are happy to mollify their dangerous fans, throwing offerings of khat out the window at the outstretched hands as they pass. On rare occasions, these self-appointed tax collectors become too persistent, and are shot at, and sometimes killed, by the security guards stationed atop the trucks. Nonetheless, the khat trade generates relatively little attendant violence; Fadumo had never heard of a shipment being hijacked.[4]

Once the transports arrive at the main checkpoint outside Garowe, individual merchants meet them and transfer the cargo to their own cars. Fadumo's arrangements were informal; she tended to buy from a regular distributor, but would sometimes go to other suppliers for smaller amounts, or if her supplier was out of stock.

Though khat has long been a facet of Somali life, the last decade has seen imports into the country soar, and Puntland's piracy explosion in late 2008 brought consumption levels onto a whole new plane. Outside of cars and khat, there is not much available in Puntland on which to spend tens of thousands of dollars, and pirates are famous for the almost religious fervour with which they chew the drug (though they seem to lack the corresponding devotion to Koranic study). So overblown is the pirates' infatuation with khat that at times it approaches comical proportions; there are stories, from the early days of multimillion-dollar ransoms, of recently paid pirates rushing to the khat *suq* and spending their US hundred-dollar bills as if they were thousand-shilling notes (which are worth about three cents).

Even without this absurd level of reckless spending, the money disappears remarkably quickly. A successful pirate is expected to share his good fortune with his friends and relatives; the moment he steps off the ship, his money begins to diffuse through an endless kinship network, ending only when the last of the khat leaves have been chewed up and spit out.

* * *

In its short-term effects, khat resembles its South American equivalent, the coca leaf, causing mild euphoria, heightened energy, garrulousness, and appetite loss. Another effect is the belief in one's own invincibility, which many Somalis view as a factor contributing to the endemic conflict plaguing their country; like pirates, Somali militants are renowned for their rampant khat use, and the drug is thought to help fuel the violence (albeit to a lesser degree than in Liberia, where warlords reputedly rubbed cocaine into the open wounds of their soldiers before sending them into battle).[5] As Jamal, my neighbour during the last leg of my flight into Somalia, eloquently explained, "When people chew khat they believe that they have superhuman strength. They would even think they could lift this plane," raising his arms above his head in a hoisting motion.

Despite such inestimable benefits, the deleterious health effects of khat are both abundant and unpalatable. Short-term withdrawal symptoms include depression, irritability, nightmares, constipation, and tremors, while long-term use of the drug can lead to ulcers, decreased liver function, tooth decay, and possibly some forms of mental illness. The physical ills of the drug are compounded by its social ones; the UN World Food Programme, for example, has reported that in some areas of Puntland the high costs associated with khat consumption are the main reason for not sending children to school (primary school fees are about eight dollars per month) as well as for high divorce rates.[6]

There are also some not-so-scientifically-documented effects. My Somali host, Abdirizak, claimed that khat causes sperm to leak into men's urine—eventually rendering them infertile—which he humorously cited as the principal reason that frustrated wives try at all costs to keep their husbands away from it. Like many folk-medicine theories, Abdi's may have had a basis in truth; there is some evidence that long-term khat abuse can lead to a diminished sex drive. In the short term, conversely, it can have quite the opposite effect.

"When some men chew khat, they need to have a woman immediately," Abdi once explained to me. "They can't control themselves." Indeed, those who prepped me for my own khat experience agreed that the drug would bring about one of two scenarios: I would either become relaxed and talkative, or a sex-crazy maniac bent on immediate satiation. But after all the buildup, I didn't feel much of anything. Four hours of chewing the bitter filth made me sweaty, jittery, sick to my stomach, and, finally, mildly contented. It did not strike me as an equitable trade-off, yet those who can afford it spend their days chewing khat leaves like a cow on her cud.

In the end, I chewed khat six or seven times during my visits to Puntland, out of perverse pragmatism. In spite of a lifetime of exposure to anti-drug public service ads, I continued chewing simply to fit in. More accurately, I discovered that khat was an incredible interviewing tool; it rendered my interviewees relaxed and talkative, with a compelling urge to express themselves. Interviews could go on for hours so long as the khat continued to flow.

* * *

There are few comprehensive academic studies of the Somali khat trade, and any attempt to obtain accurate information on the khat economy suffers from the general dearth of official statistics about Somalia. The latest government figures come from a 2003 report by the Puntland Ministry of Planning and Statistics, which devotes less than one of its sixty pages to the topic. Concluding with the vague assertion that "khat trade and consumption play an adverse role in the Somali economy in general and particularly in Puntland," the report nonetheless provides some concrete figures (see Table 1).[7]

Table 1: Estimated Imports of Khat to Puntland, 2003 (Kilograms)		
Type	Per month	Per year
Mirra, imported from Kenya	90,700	1,088,000
Hareeri, imported from Ethiopia	121,300	1,456,000
Total	212,000	2,544,000
		Source: Puntland Ministry of Planning and Statistics

These statistics are enough to construct a rudimentary sketch of the Puntland khat industry of eight years ago. Urban street prices for khat, according to my sources, have remained fairly steady at twenty dollars per kilogram over the last decade (in remote areas the price can be almost double), suggesting that total revenues in 2003 fell just short of $51 million. Using the UN Development Programme's 2006 Puntland population estimate of 1.3 million, the per capita consumption rate would be around 2.1 kilograms per person. However, khat consumers in Puntland are almost without exception men, and after narrowing the field to males aged fifteen and over,[8] annual per capita consumption climbs to 9.1 kilograms, worth about $180. Other sources support this estimate; for example, a 2001 study by the UN's Water and Sanitation Programme found that poor consumers (the vast majority of Puntlanders) spent an average of $176 per year on the drug.

These numbers, however, are from the pre-piracy era. How might they look in 2011? Attempting to gauge piracy's effect on khat sales in Puntland, I spoke to three Garowe-based merchants. The first was the aforementioned Fadumo, a bored-looking middle-aged woman with stylish beige sunglasses pushed up on the headdress of her fuchsia *guntiino* (a garment similar to a sari). My second conversation was with a pair of close friends in their late twenties, Maryan and Faiza, who owned side-by-side stalls in the khat *suq*. (I later discovered that Maryan—probably the most stunning Somali woman I had ever seen—was a member of Garaad's rumoured harem of wives, a fact she admitted with an embarrassed giggle, asking how I had learned of it.)[9]

Fadumo worked long hours, from ten in the morning until ten at night. Her most profitable period was from one to three in the afternoon, when government employees got off work; four o'clock, the time that construction workers finished their day, heralded another mini rush hour. Her best days came at the end of the month, when soldiers were paid, and the two or three times per year that Puntland's parliament was in session. "When there's an election, that's the very best time," she said, because each candidate would arrive with a large entourage in tow, filling Garowe's hotels to capacity.

When asked how piracy had affected her sales, Fadumo shot me an incredulous look, as if the answer were self-evident. "Most pirates spend money on three things: khat, alcohol, and women," was her reply. "Also, very young people chew it now," she added.

Fadumo estimated that the booming khat *suq* provided a livelihood to over two hundred vendors. One reason for the abundance of merchants is that launching a khat business requires no capital outlay; distributors are happy to supply a new vendor on consignment. "Only one and a half years ago," Fadumo said, "khat suppliers were coming and knocking at our doors, begging us to be sellers.

Now there are too many dealers . . . the market is flooded with them."
Back then, there would be days when she would only earn 20,000
to 30,000 shillings ($0.60–$0.90) profit, and occasionally she
would not have any customers at all. At the time I interviewed her in
June 2009, her gross revenue for an average day had risen to about
$550–$600, of which Fadumo kept $100–$110 of profit. There was
so much competition, she told me, that in order to get a high-quality
product she had to be proactive; on many days she would travel up
to thirty kilometres outside of Garowe to intercept the earliest shipments before they reached the city.

Kenyan khat was far more popular with her customers, and Fadumo did not even bother to stock the Ethiopian variety. The same
went for Maryan and Faiza. "People say *mirra* [Kenyan khat] gets
you in a better mood," explained Faiza.

Piracy had also made a big difference to Maryan's and Faiza's
balance sheets.

"The men have more money," Maryan said. "They buy larger
amounts and they don't ask for loans."

"We've had a lot of problems with loans in the past," said Faiza.
"They take the khat from you when they can't afford it, and they
won't pay you back."

"The pirates pay in cash, nothing less," said Maryan, smiling
broadly.

While men are the exclusive consumers of khat, those who sell
it to them are almost exclusively women. According to Maryan, the
collapse of the central state had forced Somali women to be more
self-reliant. "The men are mainly unemployed," said Maryan, "and
the women have been forced to earn money to pay the bills, school
fees, and things like that. They have to work to survive. Khat is a very
reliable source of income."

Perhaps one reason for its reliability is the fact that its price
remains remarkably stable. But in a city where a cappuccino costs
twenty-five cents, and where the majority of residents have no steady
job, the twenty dollars required to maintain a steady high over the

course of a day makes khat as expensive and luxurious a plant as medieval saffron. So prohibitive is the cost that I was continually baffled by the round-the-clock crowds chewing in the streets, against a backdrop of poverty and squalor; the steady influx of pirate dollars in recent years seemed the easiest explanation. Indeed, piracy has weighted so much of the daily economic life in Puntland towards the buying, bargaining, and bartering of khat that Puntlanders would perhaps do well to junk their near-worthless currency and adopt one based on the "khat standard."

On top of its numerous other negative effects, khat is a huge drain on Somalia's foreign exchange holdings, sending hundreds of millions of US dollars per year to Kenya and Ethiopia at the expense of domestic investment;[10] it was for this reason that former dictator Mohamed Siad Barre tried extensively (and hopelessly) to stamp out khat use in the 1980s. Piracy, which is one of Puntland's best foreign exchange earners, ultimately does little to improve economic opportunity on the ground, because pirate ransoms are continually recycled back into international markets via khat and Land Cruiser purchases.

* * *

Though ubiquitous amongst the local people, khat use is generally viewed by Somali expats as a sordid and disreputable activity, and many consider it a national shame. President Farole's virulent hatred of khat is well known, and he has been heard to vow that one day Somali men will feel shame at ever having chewed the plant.

Medically speaking, khat may be less physically harmful than many other legal drugs—such as alcohol and tobacco—but its social impact is another matter. Because of the many hours required to feel its full effects, chewing khat is a time-consuming activity, necessitating a large portion of the day. While a six-pack after a hard day or an occasional smoke break can fit into the restrictions of a nine-to-five schedule, a society-wide khat addiction seems unsustainable in a modern economy. So long as the majority of Puntlanders remain un- or underemployed, khat will remain a second-tier scourge. But if and when Puntland—and Somalia in general—rejoin the rest of the world, the increasing trend of khat consumption will present a serious public policy problem for the future government.

One need only look across the Gulf of Aden for a preview of Somalia's potential fate. In Yemen, 40 per cent of the country's precious groundwater is devoted to growing khat, Yemeni men routinely take their families on "khat picnics," and it is not unusual for government ministers to chew the plant continuously in their offices. Commentators often speak of the "oil curse" that stunts the political growth of many Middle Eastern and African nations; perhaps Puntland is lucky to have avoided the "water curse" that would have permitted widespread domestic cultivation of the crop.[11]

Jamal, my plane companion, described how he once saw a billy goat munching on a bundle of fallen khat leaves. When he had finished, the goat went trotting after the nearest female, attempting to mount her several times before giving up; the khat had evidently rendered him temporarily impotent. Jamal laughed: "It's the same with humans." If the problem is not addressed, Puntlanders might find that the khat epidemic poses a similarly vexing impediment to their nation-building goals.

*   *   *

For all of khat's sundry evils, it is the way to a pirate's heart. One June day during my second visit to Puntland, Boyah and some of his former gang agreed to spend the afternoon with me, for a small price: an all-you-can-chew khat buffet. As soon as the midday transport trucks had coming rolling into Garowe, Colonel Omar Abdullahi Farole—my host Mohamad's cousin—headed to the khat market with my eighty dollars in his pocket, enough to buy roughly four kilograms of the plant, which was to last us the day.

My translator on this trip, Omar, who was another of President

Farole's sons, and I picked up Boyah just outside his house, on a rundown street littered with old tires and scrap metal. I had not seen him since our meeting four months before, but he remembered me, acknowledging my presence with a brief nod and a half-smile before turning and climbing into the Land Cruiser's passenger seat. The Colonel, meanwhile, busied himself across town rounding up a few of Boyah's former colleagues into an old station wagon; with his arms overflowing with khat, it was not a difficult assignment.

Soon we were tearing along the main road out of Garowe, breaking off after ten minutes to join the dirt trail leading to the cooperative farm where I had first met Boyah. A short time later the station wagon pulled up and parked alongside the Land Cruiser; inside were Colonel Omar and two of Boyah's former running mates: Momman (a nickname) and a man I will call Ali Ghedi. The gathering soon assumed the atmosphere of a picnic, with eager hands offloading the day's supplies: *dirins* (woven mats), thermoses of sweet tea, bottles of water, packs of cigarettes, and the half-dozen black plastic shopping bags containing the khat. We unfurled the *dirins* in the shade of a broad-limbed acacia tree and settled down, tossing our sandals into the dirt. A short distance away, a dishevelled young farmhand sat in the shade of a wooden shack, absorbedly chewing a few stems of khat that one of the pirates had handed him.

As soon as we had settled down on our *dirins*, I reached into my bag and pulled out the thank-you gift I had brought for Boyah, in appreciation of his willingness to be open with me: an Alex Rios Toronto Blue Jays T-shirt. He broke into a broad grin, immediately removing his own shirt and putting it on. "Is it official?" he asked, and I answered that it was. "How much did you pay for it?"

The Colonel laid his mat a dozen paces distant and flopped down on it, the crook of his elbow covering his eyes. He had been khat sober for thirty-two days, part of an all-around cleansing policy that granted few exemptions: "Only in wartime, when things get a little stressful," he explained. Colonel Omar, I had learned weeks ago, was not really a colonel. A battle-hardened militiaman, the Colonel had fought in the south alongside former Puntland president Abdullahi Yusuf against the Islamist militant group Al-Shabaab, one of three conflicts he claimed to have participated in; after each, he said, he had promoted himself by one rank. "I'm going to Ethiopia soon to receive training," he had told me. "When I get back, I'll be a general."

The sun was mild and a light breeze was blowing, a pleasant change from the gale-force winds constantly sweeping Garowe. Taking periodic breaks from the khat, Boyah opened a small plastic bag and removed a pinch or so of chewing tobacco, depositing it gingerly into his mouth. The conversation turned to sundry topics: women, Omega-3 fatty acids, naming customs. The pirates collectively warned me that the khat would make me sexually aroused, to the point that my urge for a woman would be unbearable; I informed them that I had chewed it before, experiencing no such effect. "The white people we see in porn movies are always so horny," said Momman. "So how is it that you're not?"

Mobile phones chimed like persistent alarm clocks every few minutes, each member of the circle splitting his conversational energies between his phone and the people around him in almost equal measure. One particularly harsh voice blaring from Momman's phone, allegedly belonging to a member of Al-Shabaab, piqued my attention. My interpreter Omar summarized the exchange: the caller expressed displeasure that Momman's pirate earnings, in his opinion, had gone not to support the Somali people but to fund President Farole's political campaign, and he warned Momman that he might have to forfeit his life to atone for these sins. Momman remained curiously calm throughout the call; when I expressed my concern, he waved it off with one hand and told me that these threats happened daily as a matter of course. Shabaab apparently conducted its terror campaigns not only through assassinations and suicide bombings, but over the airwaves of Somali telecom networks.

Omar selected one of the half-dozen Kalashnikovs lying scattered around us—which he had recently purchased for the high-end price of $600—and declared that it must be tested. I jumped to my feet and eagerly volunteered for the assignment. Omar and I moved past the hedge marking the boundary of the farm to the banks of the trickling Nugaal River, which was struggling with its last rebellious spurts against the encroaching dry season.

Countless hours of news footage of obscure post-Cold War insurgencies had not prepared me for the raw, ear-shattering power of the AK-47. The two shots I fired into the river's embankment seemed to make the whole earth boom and shake, until I realized that it was my own body being contorted by the force of the recoil. By comparison, the faint bursts of dust marking where the bullets hit were sadly anti-climactic. I returned to the gathering with a stupid grin stretching across my face, and was greeted by an array of patronizing smiles from the circle of pirates—the look of hardened veterans at the overzealous enthusiasm of an amateur.

I didn't bother with any interview questions that day, but chatted amiably and did my best to blend in with the boys. My goal was achieved when, late in the afternoon, the pirates began discussing something between themselves in hushed voices. They appeared to reach a consensus, at which point Momman turned to me: "We've decided that you're a cool guy," he said.

It had been a day well spent.

*   *   *

Two days later, we returned to the same spot, arms weighted down with even bulkier bags of khat—and thus with a commensurately larger pirate gathering in tow. Boyah, when we picked him up on the side of the road, let us know that he had had a rough night. "I was terribly sick with a kidney problem," he said. "I thought I was going to die, so I said goodbye to my kids. But I'm feeling much better today." He hopped into the 4x4 and waited patiently for us to get under way.

Two other cars joined us, bringing the total gathering of pirates to seven: Boyah, Momman, Ali Ghedi, Mohammad Duale (I have changed his name), Ahmed Jadob, and two others to whom I was not properly introduced. Much like last time, we rolled out the *dirins* and flopped down, propped up on our elbows. Pulling two bundles of the wilting leaves out of the bag, Boyah offered me my pick. I hesitated for a moment before I remembered an earlier crash course in khat quality given to me by the Colonel. Quickly scanning the bundle, I chose the bunch with the greatest abundance of red-tinged stems. Boyah smiled, laughed, and slapped my leg playfully, uttering some words of praise. He was still wearing the Blue Jays shirt, evidenced by the powder-blue collar poking out from under his cotton overshirt.

The reason these men were so willing to talk to me went beyond the complimentary khat. When I had last seen him, four months ago, Boyah had been on a personal quest to atone for his past misdeeds. Now, it seemed, his feelings of remorse had spread to his former colleagues: each of the men around me claimed to have renounced piracy, never to return to his former trade—and they wanted people to know it. "It wasn't good, either for us or our country," explained Boyah. "It's cursed money—it only made our lives worse. So we quit. We don't want to get a bad name in foreign countries."

When I suggested that the recent proliferation of warships off the Somali coast had provided an equally compelling reason to turn in one's rocket-propelled grenades and grappling ladder, I was met with a round of scornful laughter. "Don't think that we're scared," said Boyah. "Piracy is just not good for us. We're quitting so that Somalia can get its nice name back. Seven months ago . . . French and US forces were killing us, and we didn't stop then."

As had been the case two days ago, my companions fell into relaxed conversation, hardly conscious of my presence. For people who had never set foot outside Somalia and had access to no more than a few local TV stations, Boyah and his entourage were surprisingly worldly: Momman and Ali Ghedi engaged in an animated debate about whether France or Brazil boasted the most beautiful women.

There was a lull in the conversation, and Ali, having just learned that I had fired a Kalashnikov for the first time two days ago, turned and brazenly challenged me to a shooting contest.

"*Laag?*" For money? I asked, showing off one of the few Somali words I knew.

"Yes, for money," he replied, with a crooked grin. I gestured to the backgammon board I had brought along with me, and asked him if he would match my wager on the gun with his own wager on the dice. He meekly demurred.

* * *

Since giving up the piracy trade, Boyah and his men had put their time to good use. Garaad, whose dealings with SomCan had begun some months earlier, had spread his career ambitions to his former colleagues—or so my sources said; the rumours were that Boyah's gang had also recently entered a partnership with the SomCan Coast Guard. But I soon discovered that the rumours were out of date. "We used to work with them, but that's all over," said Boyah. "What they wanted and what we needed were totally different." What Boyah's men had needed, apparently, was a fresh start.

"We want to start our *own* coast guard," he said. "In fact, we've already started." Their efforts to date, however, had not extended much beyond signing up the men presently lounging around me. "We're hoping the Puntland government will give us the job," said Boyah. "Once they do, we'll get the ships and weapons we need from them." Until then, it seemed, Boyah's coast guard would remain landlocked. His confidence, nonetheless, was unshaken.

"We know how to fight with pirates," he said. "You can't teach us anything about hijacking ships." But immediately his bellicose tone softened: "Of course, we would never kill anyone, even the pirates. There are other ways—peaceful ways—we can get them to release the ships. Before you shoot someone, you can talk to him. If we were in charge, no one would ever have to pay any ransoms, nor would anyone ever die on those ships. We would work it out some way." Despite my pressing, Boyah and his colleagues would not be more specific about what their method would entail.

In defiance of Boyah's optimism were the two ships currently being held hostage at Eyl, their hijackers unreceptive to his efforts at moral suasion. For these men, Boyah had a simple explanation. "They still have the old system in their heads, and they don't want to let it go. Plus, they've already spent so much money while waiting for the ransom. If they leave it now without being paid, there are thousands of people they owe money to who will kill them. Maybe when they get off they'll change their minds, and not return to piracy."

For all his talk of persuasion, Boyah believed that a military solution would be just as effective. "If a warship attacked them, they would run, just like we would have," said Boyah. "These people are not Al-Qaeda; they just want money. They don't kill people."

On land, Boyah claimed that his group was already making a difference. Under the guidance of preeminent Muslim scholar (and Puntland's unofficial grand mufti) Sheikh Abdulkhadar Nur Farah, Boyah's gang of reformed pirates had taken on a role similar to the ex-convicts who speak to high school student assemblies; along with Sheikh Farah, Boyah and his men would drag groups of misguided youth to mosque, where they would make them swear on the Koran to live piracy-free for the rest of their days. According to Boyah, his group had helped reform seven hundred pirates and would-be pirates from around Puntland (though the BBC, which had run the story three weeks earlier, reported the number of rehabilitated pirates at around two hundred).[12] Altruism was probably not Boyah's sole motive, however; in exchange for their efforts, the Puntland government had granted Boyah and his associates full legal amnesty for their past crimes.

Their services as coast guards, on the other hand, were not being so eagerly sought. President Farole was on his own quest to rehabilitate Puntland's damaged international reputation, and commissioning an ex-pirate brigade, composed of his own clan members, as his coast guard would not serve the image he was seeking. Though their redemption movement had been used as PR fodder by the Puntland government—as evidence of measures the new administration was taking to combat piracy—Farole had no plans to unleash Boyah and company once more onto the sea.

* * *

Up to this point, Boyah had been the only member of the gathering to answer my questions, while the others nodded along complacently as he talked. "Boyah speaks for all of us," Momman responded, when I commented on this fact. In an attempt to engage with someone other than Boyah, I directed my questions to Ahmed, who was atypically dressed in a glaringly bright yellow soccer jersey. Beyond his attire, Ahmed also stuck out in another way: he was from the Hawiye clan, whereas all the others assembled were Darod. Originally from the southern city of Baidoa, he had emigrated to Eyl in 2002 and become a successful fisherman. Despite the historical animosity between the Hawiye and the Darod—which came to a head with the brutal clan pogroms of the early 1990s—history seemed to have been forgotten amongst this group of friends. "We pirates have no clans," said Boyah. "We fight together as Somalis."

At my urging, Ahmed began to relate his story. "I was happy with my life," he said. "One day, we were fishing some distance away from shore when we were attacked by some big fishing ships, who stole all our fish." This event was repeated, he said, at least ten times. "They had big guns, and we would be forced to jump overboard. Sometimes, they would destroy our boats and we would have to swim all the way back to shore." According to Ahmed, the culprits were most often Thai or Korean fishing vessels. In what was by now a common story, Ahmed had banded together with similarly aggrieved fishermen along the length of the Puntland coast and beyond to fight illegal fishing.

Groups like these resembled troops of revolutionaries more than criminal gangs, yet Western media sources invariably associated

Somali pirates with a glamorous lifestyle akin to that of gangster rap stars, replete with lavish parties, mansions, luxury cars, drugs, alcohol, and beautiful women. But other than their habitual khat binges, little evidence of this stereotype was to be seen in the sedate, stoic (and now resurgently pious) figures of Boyah and his men. Each of them, as far as I had been able to discover, had but one wife. So what was to be said for the stories of "pirate wenches"?

"There are some women like that . . . the drug addicts, the bad ones," said Boyah. "The ones interested in money." These pirate women, according to Boyah, were not local, but came from outside Puntland. Indeed, a roadhouse on the outskirts of Garowe—one that I had passed many times—had reportedly served in the past as a major transit hub for transporting women to Puntland's coastal areas. But in Boyah's estimation, the women were more than able to find their own way. "They follow the money," he said.

Mohammad turned to Boyah with a quizzical look. "I haven't even seen the women you're talking about," he said.

The same incredulity greeted my question about pirates and alcohol consumption, and generated a round of unmistakably hostile murmurs and head shakes.

"We're Muslims, so we don't do that," came the answer.

"Some of them do—the young guys." Boyah clarified. "They try it because it's something new that they haven't experienced before."

Such may have been the case on board a Russian-crewed hostage vessel, on which the pirates reportedly drank the ship's entire store of vodka, stunning even the Russians with their debauchery. When I brought up this rumour, I again witnessed a round of shaking heads.

"No, no. They drank a little bit, but not to that extent," said Boyah. "They had a job to do. If they had gotten drunk, do you think they would have done it? Anyone who gets drunk, they kick off the ship."

Colonel Omar, lying on his back apart from the main circle, suddenly chimed in with his own version of events. "There *was* one boat with a lot of alcohol on board," he said. "So the pirates threw it all into the sea, and when the crew asked for it, they told them that they had drunk it all." Mohammad nodded his assent to the Colonel's account.

We continued chewing our khat as the sky grew dark, faces fading into the twilight until only the glowing points of cigarettes marked their locations. Abruptly, the Colonel roused himself from his nearby reverie and declared that the time had come to leave—the heightened risk of kidnapping made my presence a security liability at nighttime, even at a location as remote and isolated as this farm.

As we rolled up the *dirins* and collected our garbage—to be dumped by the side of the main road—Boyah admonished me to tell the story of him and his men exactly as they had given it to me. "Something good has to come back to us from all of this," he said.

By the time we had pulled back onto the road it was fully dark. The white outline of the pirates' Mark II station wagon was visible ahead of us, growing closer as Omar gunned our Land Cruiser towards it. The needle on the speedometer pushed past 140 kilometres per hour before we overtook the Mark II, passing it with a few fist-widths to spare. If this was the typical driving style on this unlit, steeply embanked roadway, the stripped chassis and blackened wrecks I routinely saw by the side of the road needed no explanation. We left the Mark II behind as we barrelled towards the lights of Garowe.

7

The Land of Punt

IT WAS JUNE, AND GAROWE WAS IN THE MIDST OF THE HAGAA, the second of Puntland's two dry seasons. It had been a month since rain last fell, and it would be three months before the next rain would come. The bridge over the Nugaal River spanned a vast, rocky emptiness; further down its course, the last vestiges of the wet season had dried to isolated, listless pools. In the evenings, the haunting refrains of *Allahu akbar* drifted from the muezzins over a ruddy landscape strewn with rusted cans, broken glass, and camel tracks. Garbage carpeted the streets; at an improvised dump at the outskirts of town, thousands of plastic bags caught in thorny shrubs formed a vast artificial garden.

Since the collapse of the central state, the city has sprawled outwards, unchecked; over the last two decades Garowe's population has multiplied eightfold, swelled by the influx of Darod clanspeople fleeing the violence in the south. Virtually ignored under the dictatorship of Mohamed Siad Barre, the returning migrants inherited no infrastructure, financial base, or skilled bureaucracy, and were forced to build a functioning polity out of an empty desert.

With a paltry $20 million annual budget that often fails to include items as basic as civil service salaries, it comes as no surprise that Puntland officials at all levels have been accused of systematically accepting bribes and payouts from pirate gangs in exchange for turning a blind eye. My own impression, however, was that there were few local officials actually worth bribing. State power was extremely decentralized and diffuse, and the military forces were highly immobile and mostly confined to garrisons in the large cities. In the smaller towns the government had virtually no presence, and certainly no armed force capable of matching firepower with even the smallest of pirate gangs.

Yet, in spite of the logistical difficulties it faces—not to mention the suspicions about its own complicity—the Puntland government appears bent on proving to the world that it alone is capable of neutralizing the pirates on land.

* * *

Officially, the government of Puntland has advocated a strict policy of non-negotiation with pirates since the very beginning of the crisis. Former president Mohamud Muse Hersi, though himself accused of receiving ransom kickbacks, blamed the piracy problem on the willingness of international shippers to accede to the hijackers' demands. "Can you reward a thief who mugged you?" said Hersi in an interview. "This money makes them stronger and encourages them to carry out more operations. We should never give in to their blackmailing." [1]

Hersi's words were not empty. Where his government was given permission to act, it did not hesitate to confront the pirates head-on. In April 2008, for example, one hundred Puntland soldiers in several armoured boats stormed the UAE cargo ship *Al Khaleej* near Bossaso, capturing seven pirates, who were eventually sentenced to life in prison. Two soldiers and three hijackers sustained injuries, but the hostages were unharmed. A similar incident occurred in October of the same year, when (as described in Chapter 4) the Panamanian-flagged MV *Wail* was freed by the Puntland Coast Guard. In both cases, the ships had been contracted by local businessmen and were carrying consignments destined for Puntland.

Judging from the Puntland government's press statements, it is more than willing to send its security forces to storm every ship being held in its waters. The decision to employ force, however, lies with the vessels' owners, most of whom have no interest in authorizing a potential bloodbath on the decks of their ships.

Abdirahman Farole, who took over from Hersi as president in January 2009, was even more outwardly committed to cracking down on piracy, describing the practice as a black mark on Puntland's international reputation. Three months after his election, Farole launched a grassroots counter-piracy program spearheaded by Sheikh Abdulkhadar Nur Farah. In what was described as an "educational and spiritual campaign" to discourage new recruits, the government offered total amnesty to any former pirate agreeing to give up the trade.[2]

In the mosques, Muslim clerics decried the litany of social ills that piracy had supposedly introduced to the local community: alcohol, khat, sexually transmitted diseases, adultery, and fornication. To kick off the campaign, Puntland security forces conducted a highly publicized raid on two houses in Garowe, confiscating four assault rifles, 327 bottles of Ethiopian gin, five mobile phones, and approximately $900 in cash.[3] Spectators cheered as soldiers hauled away suspected pirates.

Farole's religious campaign has not been an isolated media exercise. Since coming to power, he has tried his best to promote his administration as a fresh break from the one previous, which was widely perceived by international observers as weak and ineffectual. The media wing of the Puntland government has issued a constant stream of press releases detailing raids, arrests, and imprisonments of active pirates—part of a sustained publicity campaign to market the administration abroad as a reliable ally in the war on piracy.

At home, Farole has relied on a network of local police commissioners and office holders to carry out his campaigns. One of these instrumental figures was Garowe's long-serving mayor, Abdulkhadar Osman Fod'Adde.

* * *

Garowe's mayoral office was situated in a rundown complex at the centre of town. A bare flagpole stood by the entrance to a crumbling courtyard; on the steps of the building, a small congregation of clan elders lounged in their *ma'awises*, idly discussing the matters of the day. Inside, the scene was markedly different: Abdulkhadar Fod'Adde sat behind a heavy cherry desk in a tidy and orderly office, dressed in a trim suit and tie. The two Omars had accompanied me, and I took a seat between them across the desk, the Colonel on my right, Kalashnikov slung over a shoulder, and Omar Farole to my left, serving as my interpreter.

"I worked for the previous government for two and a half years," Fod'Adde began. "It was the worst job I've ever had. That was a really bad government to work with; this one is much better. Security was really bad, especially last December," he continued. "There were a lot of pirates, and we couldn't do anything about it . . . we weren't given enough money. Under this government, there are fewer pirates, we have more money, and security is a lot better. We can see things getting better and better every day, and that encourages us to work hard at our jobs."

As Fod'Adde proceeded to draw out his panegyric over the course of several minutes, I was once more made conscious of being under the wing of the Farole family. With the Omars seated on either side of me, it was apparent that much of Fod'Adde's monologue was being tailored for the ears of the president's son and cousin.

Sycophancy aside, the security situation had improved since the days of the previous administration. President Hersi had discontinued the pay of the security forces and civil service in early 2008, a decision that unquestionably contributed to the rise of piracy towards the end of the year. When Farole took power in January 2009, he immediately reinstated civil payrolls and began to reorganize the Darawish, Puntland's security forces. Even in the three-month interval between my first and second visits to the region, the improvements to security had been remarkable: soldiers positioned at regular checkpoints throughout the city checked every passing vehicle, tinted windows had been prohibited, and there had been a successful campaign to get guns off the streets. At night, security patrols swept through the city and the surrounding desert, combing them for pirates and weapons smugglers.

The change, based on the stories I had heard, had been monumental. Garowe in late 2008 had been, by all accounts, practically run by pirates, with opulent weddings attended by processions of 4x4s and khat-fuelled festivities a common sight. It was an assessment that Fod'Adde corroborated.

"Once they got the ransom money the pirates would come to Garowe," he said. "Then they'd get drunk, start gunfights in the street, things like that. Things very much against our culture."

On what did they spend their money? I asked.

"Ladies," Fod'Adde instantly replied. "They ruin families by stealing women away from their husbands. The women can smell the money . . . A lot of the women come from Somaliland, Djibouti, and other places in Somalia, so they bring a lot of diseases."

The view that outside women were somehow tainted—which seemed to be based solely on raw clan prejudice—was shared by many of Garowe's leading citizens; at the beginning of Farole's anti-piracy campaign, one cleric strongly warned his Friday congregation against the spread of HIV/AIDS in the community, as "prostitutes from everywhere" had been drawn to Puntland by the pirates' money.[4]

Piracy, nonetheless, represented a massive injection of foreign exchange into the Puntland economy, and it was hard to imagine that there had been no positive trickle-down effects. Fod'Adde shook his head vigorously. "That money is *haram* [religiously forbidden]," he said. "As Muslims, we believe that money earned in that manner can never do any good . . . not for the economy or anything else. The moment they get it, they waste it on women, drugs, khat . . . *haram* money never stays in one's pocket for long."

Nor could the new houses springing up atop the carcass of the former airport, providing a boost to Garowe's already booming construction industry, convince him that pirate dollars would bring any benefits. "The pirates had all this money, but no experience with business," he said. "So they pay the workers five hundred dollars per day, when normally they might be paid fifty. And so the workers themselves start chewing khat all the time, and they get used to the high pay and now are no longer happy to take regular jobs. You know, the more money you get paid, the lazier you get."

In any case, said Fod'Adde, the reports of pirate construction sprees had been grossly overstated. "That's not the way that most of them spend their money," he said. "I'd say that only one in a hundred actually builds a house. As for the houses that they do build, they can't rent them and no one buys them, because they're *haram*. So the pirates are stuck with them."

At this point, my interpreter Omar could not resist interrupting with his own anecdote. "Even the cars they buy are *haram*," he said. "If we see one driving by, my dad says, 'Don't buy that one. It's a *haram* car . . . a pirate car.'"

As proof of the curse of pirate cash, Fod'Adde brought up the case of Kadiye, a famed pirate leader who had recently returned from a Kenyan hospital after reportedly breaking both legs when he crashed his 4x4. Kadiye's house, a sprawling structure by the side of the road at the northern outskirts of Garowe, suggested an eviscerated corpse, the whitewash of its outer walls terminating around gaping holes of exposed brick. "Look at Kadiye. He earned about three million dollars, but he didn't have any plan," Fod'Adde said. "He spent seventy thousand dollars on that house, but couldn't finish it. He blew all his money on girls, and now he doesn't have one cent left."

As I prepared to leave, Fod'Adde seamlessly resumed his earlier extolling of the present government's efforts to combat piracy: "Some of the pirates have been killed, some have no money left, and some have gone overseas. But we're always looking around for them, and if we catch any we send them to the prison in Bossaso.

"We don't even see them anymore. We ask ourselves, were they ghosts or human beings?" he said, laughing.

* * *

Bossaso prison lies a kilometre down a bumpy path jutting off the main road at the southern outskirts of the city. The square fortress-like structure with outer walls of pale yellow stands alone in an empty expanse, with nothing in the vicinity but stony rubble and the distant outline of the Karkaar Mountains. At opposing corners of the building stand two monolithic guard towers, whose sentries shout out demands for identification from the occupants of any vehicle passing within range of their assault rifles. Like runway markers, lines of carefully placed stones trace out the correct approach vector to the prison's imposing blue gateway.

Built with UN Development Programme money, this is one of two prisons serving a population of 1.3 million; the other, 250 kilometres south in the town of Qardho, is not yet operational. (There are also two rundown jails, located in Garowe and Galkayo.) With an incarcerated population of about one person per 5,000 (in the United States, the figure is one in 120), the fact that Puntland is not overrun by criminal gangs might seem inexplicable. The simple answer is that clan law (*heer*), not the rule of law, rules in Puntland. The state-administered justice system is, in a way, a last recourse in the event that clan mechanisms of dispute resolution fail.[5] Almost half the inmates of Bossaso prison are pirates, a consequence of the Puntland government's desire to demonstrate to the international community that it is serious about cracking down on piracy. It is unclear, however, under which law the men were charged; Puntland is still technically operating under the decades-old criminal code of the defunct Somali Republic, which lacks specific provisions for criminalizing piracy. Though Puntland's Islamic clerics have interpreted vague proscriptions in sharia law against the setting up of trade-disrupting "roadblocks" as applying to sea piracy, such an approach is hardly a substitute for a modern juridical process.

When I visited, Bossaso prison, meant for a capacity of 150, was jammed to the point of putrefaction with 275 ragged men. They were crammed into a half-dozen cells lining a central court-yard that doubled as an exercise yard. Beyond the chain-link fence surrounding the enclosure, the smell of urine saturated the July air. On the far side of the yard was the prison's approximation of a mental health ward, an orange tarp spread over a few barrels, underneath which a solitary man was shackled to the ground by his ankle. The man introduced himself as Dr. Osman, a "human rights victim" who had once lived in Virginia. A few moments later, a prison administrator introduced Dr. Osman as "a madman" who had been jailed for his own good after falsely claiming to be an Al-Shabaab agent.

At mealtimes, guards spooned helpings of gruel into the prison-ers' cupped shirts, or, if they lacked an intact garment, directly into their hands. On alternating days, half the prison population was let out into the yard to exercise. The atmosphere I observed was remi-niscent of a school playground: some inmates congregated in cor-ners, chatting and drinking milky tea out of plastic water bottles, while others kicked soccer balls across the crumbling concrete or launched basketballs at half-detached hoops. Their less fortunate colleagues pressed up against their cell bars, looking on begrudg-ingly. On the walls above the courtyard guards perched like eagles, rifles laid flat across their squatting legs.

My first of two visits to the prison had taken place on a very special day: a presidential visit by Abdirahman Farole. I had been accompanying the president for over a week as he travelled north from Garowe to Bossaso on his first domestic tour since his election. In each town and hamlet along the way, cheering throngs had wel-comed him with joyous ululations, waving fronds and banging furi-ously on empty oil canisters. As his gold bulletproofed Land Cruiser pulled through the outer gate, he was greeted with even greater jubilation by the prison population, and for good cause: in celebration of his inauguration, about sixty minor offenders were to receive presidential pardons—a necessary measure to free up much-needed space in the overcrowded prison for more serious criminals.

The president did not disappoint; after delivering a speech to an assembly of prisoners, his soldiers, arms overflowing with stacks of bills, doled out release grants to the pardoned men, each of whom received one million shillings (this grant, worth about thirty dollars, was enough to buy about a day and a half's worth of khat in the local *suq*).

As the president's inspection tour moved towards the prison's living quarters, three pirate inmates were brought out to me in the outer courtyard, where we sat down on a set of flimsy plastic lawn chairs. Two wore striped tracksuits, the other, slacks and a blue dress shirt; all three appeared to be in a state of robust health that defied the conditions in which they lived. I soon learned that one of the men, Jamal, was Boyah's younger brother. Like his sibling, Jamal seemed to have a natural inclination towards leadership; seating himself directly across from me, he proceeded to field the majority of my questions. His two colleagues sat calmly smoking on either side of him, occasionally blurting out angry responses. Within a few minutes, a crowd of soldiers and prison officials had gathered around us, and the bodies pressing against my back forced me to hunch over my notebook.

"What we were doing wasn't illegal," Jamal began. "We were chasing after illegal fishing ships. We were defending our seas." Like Boyah, the three claimed to have been lobster divers in Eyl. They had habitually sold their catch to Somali middlemen in Bossaso, they said, who had paid them up to twenty-five dollars per kilogram. One month before, the trio had been caught by the French navy in an act of piracy, and were later handed over to the Puntland authorities.

"We were all sentenced to life in prison without even being given a lawyer," said Jamal. "We want a retrial."

The length of their sentences seemed unbelievable, and I asked my interpreter to confirm that I had understood correctly. It seemed a gross injustice for Jamal to languish in prison while Boyah—who had publicly admitted to hijacking dozens of ships—was free to chew khat with Puntland soldiers.

Shifting tacks, I asked Jamal about the former Puntland Coast Guard's involvement with illegal fishing, but he ignored the question and continued as if he were reading from a press release: "As fishermen, we were victims of every kind of ship crossing this planet: Western, Asian, whatever."

I repeated the question, but the result was the same.

"They dump toxins in our waters, and no one cares," he said. "Hopefully, the new government has some new ideas, and we can talk to them about what's going on and the problems we have." It was a strange attitude for men whose life sentences meant that their future problems would presumably be contained within these four walls.

Neither Jamal nor his colleagues would shed any light on the circumstances of their capture, not even the type of ship they had been pursuing when they were caught. But Jamal's next statement suggested that the gang had not been as focused on illegal fishing as he had initially indicated. "Fishing boats are hard to capture, they have more sophisticated defences," he said. "But the cargo ships are from the same countries and they are the same people. Our enemies are the ones doing the illegal fishing, but we'll take anything we can get. We don't discriminate."

Jamal's attack group had consisted of nine men, a typical pirate hunting party. The gang had employed two skiffs: one, a transport, carried the fuel, food, and water, while the other, speedier boat carried their rifles and rocket-propelled grenade launcher. When a suitable target was sighted, the entire team would transfer to the attack shuttle for the chase.

As I began my next question, the president and his entourage emerged from the inner compound and started to make their way slowly towards the outer gate. Without a word to me, the three rose in unison and rushed to intercept him. The president's security stood idly by as they inserted themselves in his path, performing slight bows as they lined up before him; he responded by shaking each of their hands warmly, almost as if they were prospective supporters on the campaign trail. I could understand nothing of their verbal exchange, but I knew that any hope for a pardon they may have held was dashed when the president turned and continued towards his waiting Land Cruiser.

In all likelihood, they would not have to wait too much longer for an early parole. If their relatives and friends did not manage to get them released through clan or political influence, their places in the prison would sooner or later be claimed by a future wave of offenders, part of the ongoing game of musical cells in the Puntland justice system. It was a problem that the Puntland government itself was aware of. "Every time a suspect is apprehended for a crime, there is a whole clan behind him, paying bribes, lying to officials," President Farole announced in a November 2010 public address. "The question is: who should be arrested then if the clans keep interfering on behalf of criminal suspects. Should only the people from outside [of Puntland] be arrested?"[6]

Even if the government were to release all non-pirate inmates, Puntland simply lacks the capacity to handle a steady stream of detainees from the international naval forces. With no domestic victims, piracy is clearly not a matter suited to inter-clan mediation, and, short of international seafarers' unions agreeing to abide by Somali customary law, Puntland will remain unable to carry its share of the burden without international assistance.

*   *   *

In the case of Boyah and company, of course, the response of the Puntland justice system had been to grant them total amnesty for their past crimes.

One afternoon, as I was chewing khat with Joaar, the director general of the Puntland Ministry of Fisheries (and Boyah's former employer in the lobster business), the subject of Boyah and Garaad's coast guard project came up. "Boyah and Garaad should be behind bars," Joaar declared, around a pulpy mouthful. "The idea of them serving as our coast guard is an insult." Boyah, said Joaar, had tried to meet with him on multiple occasions, but Joaar had refused because he feared that the two might be photographed together.

"Boyah called me just the other day to ask me why I was fighting against him," he said. "I told him: 'I want to eliminate you and all others like you' . . . The young guys can be rehabilitated, but the big criminals—the ones we call in Italian the *grande pesce* [big fish]—should be locked up."

Yet Boyah, Garaad, and other well-known pirate leaders still walked free. I once asked a Puntland government insider why Bossaso prison was overflowing with rank-and-file pirates, while the leaders remain on the outside. "The Puntland government can't arrest people based on rumours," he answered. "Also, because of clan loyalty, no witnesses would come forward. It's like having to make a case against a mafia boss." This explanation was somewhat disingenuous; mafia bosses generally do not publicly admit to their crimes, as Boyah had on multiple occasions.

Some, predictably, have imputed more insidious motives to the Farole government's unwillingness to prosecute past (and present) pirate kingpins, namely that the president himself has been receiving handouts from the very leaders he ostensibly condemns. Since his election, the accusations against Farole have ranged from complicity to profiteering, and even to direct involvement in piracy. My own affiliation with the president's son, Mohamad Farole, has been cited as evidence in the mounting case against him; Mohamad's presence at my meetings with pirates had been referenced in multiple online articles aimed at incriminating him, and, by extension, his father.

Some of the strongest indictments have come from the UN Monitoring Group on Somalia, in language surprisingly impolitic for a United Nations body. Warning that the new administration was "nudging Puntland in the direction of becoming a criminal state," the group's March 2010 report cited evidence from unnamed first-hand sources that "senior Puntland officials, including President Farole and members of his Cabinet, notably the Minister of the Interior, General Abdullahi Ahmed Jama 'Ilkajir' . . . and the Minister for Internal Security, General Abdillahi Sa'iid Samatar, have received proceeds from piracy and/or kidnapping."[7]

Hoping to shed some light on these claims, I spoke with Matt Bryden, the monitoring group's Nairobi-based coordinator. Though Bryden refused to reveal the group's sources, he was adamant that there was little reason to doubt their credibility. "We had a wealth of evidence, both direct and indirect, from eyewitnesses to direct monetary transactions, to testimony from captured pirates themselves," he said. "We saw signed statements from convicted pirates who did not appear to have been coerced and who stood by these statements when we interviewed them. We had sources who were in the room when cash was delivered, and sources party to telephone calls where cash payments were being discussed."

During a videotaped interview with local news agency Garowe Online in late 2008, Boyah had claimed that 30 per cent of all ransom money went into the pockets of Puntland officials—a statistic he had denied to me multiple times since (possibly out of concern for embarrassing his newly powerful co-clansman, President Farole). It was a notion that Bryden endorsed. "Did [Boyah] pay 30 per cent to local leaders in Eyl? I would think not," he said. "It is reasonable to assume that what Boyah was referring to was the payments he made to senior officials."

In the West, a public official receiving money under such circumstances would be labelled corrupt. But in the Somali context, the label is not entirely appropriate. In Somalia, clan and politics are incestuously intertwined, and political life is based on loyalty to one's clan, not the state apparatus. When, as is generally the case, one sub-clan—in essence an extended family—dominates the machinery of government, money changing hands between its members is considered no more illicit than an aunt looking after the children when their parents are away. "From the outside, it's impossible to determine whether Boyah giving money to Farole would be an attempt to sweeten the administration, or simply a contribution to a not-so-distant kinsman," explained Bryden.

On a personal level, these allegations came as a shock; it was difficult for me to accept that a man with whom I had shared a table on multiple occasions, a soft-spoken academic who seemed to have a sincere distaste for piracy, and whom I genuinely admired, could be guilty of such hypocrisy. The behaviour also seemed inconsistent with his political past; while serving as planning minister during the previous administration of Mohamud Hersi, Farole had resigned his post in protest over a shady oil deal that the president had entered into with the Australian firm Range Resources—a contract that would have offered Farole as lucrative a kleptocratic opportunity as pirate handouts.[8]

Despite Bryden's claimed plethora of unnamed sources, there has only been one publicly documented case of a Puntland official, Omar Shafdero, being directly involved in piracy. Shafdero, an employee at the Ministry of Finance and a relative of former president Hersi, was arrested in February 2008 and accused of links to the gang responsible for hijacking the Russian tugboat *Svitzer Korsakov*.[9] Shafdero spent a short time in custody before being mysteriously released, after which he fled into exile in Somaliland.

But pirate cash, argued Bryden, had been particularly instrumental in funding political candidacies in the run-up to the 2009 presidential election. According to the UN Monitoring Group report, a prominent pirate leader, Fu'ad Warsame Hanaano, "had contributed over $200,000" to the election campaign of Farole's foremost opponent (and now interior minister), General Abdullahi Ilkajir—a member of Hanaano's sub-clan, the Warsangali. Farole, the report contends, "benefitted from much larger contributions to his political war chest."[10] During the pre-election period, Bryden claimed, "There was a lot of excitement, a lot of money was changing hands and people didn't worry too much about where it came from. Now, because of international scrutiny, the movement of money is quieter . . . people are much more cautious. But according to captive pirates, the payments to the administration are ongoing."

The accusations surrounding President Farole have been fuelled, in part, by the fact that he is a native of Eyl and belongs to the Muse Isse, the same sub-clan as Boyah, Garaad, and many other Puntland-based pirates. This affiliation with Eyl, ironically, has also placed Farole in a much better position to tackle piracy than his predecessor, General Hersi, whose bumbling efforts to fight piracy were once related to me by a Puntland journalist colleague.

In early 2008, as Hersi—who belongs to the Osman Mahamoud sub-clan—continued to lose local support and credibility, Eyl was steadily establishing itself as Somalia's forefront pirate base. Knowing that to enter Eyl with his Osman Mahamoud militiamen would initiate a bloodbath, Hersi appointed an Isse Mahamoud supporter, Mohamed Haji Adan, to the made-up position of "deputy police commander," with instructions to bring Eyl under government control. On June 11, 2008, Haji travelled to Eyl with an escort of soldiers, leaving them on the outskirts of the town and sending an unarmed representative to demand a bribe from the pirates. The negotiations were brief; one of the pirate leaders asked Haji's man how much he wanted and sent him back with a shopping bag filled with $20,000 in cash. Haji promptly vacated his esteemed position and fled to the city of Galkayo, where he spent the following days and nights chewing khat. He was officially sacked four months later.[11]

Despite being far more capable than Hersi of cracking down on Eyl, according to Bryden, Farole has so far made no effort to impose central authority on his hometown, and has yet to even make a visit since his election. "The reason for him not doing so," Bryden wryly jibed, "is quite obvious."

Yet, according to Puntland government insiders, Farole has established new leadership in Eyl, including a mayor and a police commander equipped with a fleet of technicals (armed flatbed trucks). Since late 2009, Eyl had all but lost its status as a pirate base, with ships hijacked by Puntland gangs being taken to the more southern (and isolated) port of Garacad. Whether the pirate exodus was a result of Farole's leadership, or the general decline in the number of hijackings in the Gulf of Aden, is difficult to say for certain.

Bryden, for his part, was not convinced by the efforts of the Farole administration. "What's alarming," he said, "is how foreign governments have been duped into believing that Puntland is a real partner in anti-piracy, closing their eyes to the complicity."

Under mounting international pressure, said Bryden, there had been signs that Farole was starting to take the piracy issue more seriously—particularly since the US Treasury Department had placed Boyah and Garaad on a sanctions list in April 2010 (the US government, it appears, was not convinced by Boyah's quest for redemption). "Now that the US has designated Boyah and Garaad as wanted men," Bryden said, "he is in a position where he can no longer dodge the issue. If Farole wants good relations with the US, which by all accounts he does, he will need to get serious."

Indeed, Farole has made rapprochement with the international community—and in particular the United States—the cornerstone of his foreign policy. In July 2009, Farole accepted an invitation from the US State Department to appear before the House of Representatives Committee on Foreign Affairs. In his speech, Farole proposed a four-point counter-piracy plan to be financed with US money, which included the establishment of a coastal task force operating out of bases situated in eight towns along the Puntland coastline. So far, this plan has not materialized.[12]

The UN Monitoring Group's accusations elicited a predictably irate reaction from the Puntland government. In a press statement shortly after the release of the group's March 2010 report, President Farole hit back, attacking the credibility of the report's sources as well as Bryden himself. "The report's authors used sources that include politicians who are opportunists or are opposed to Puntland's self-development," he said. "Even some of the report's authors are politically motivated to discredit Puntland as a way of achieving another hidden goal."[13]

This claim was not entirely hollow: Bryden has openly campaigned for the international recognition of Somaliland—with which Puntland has a hostile relationship—indicating a political stance that made him an unusual choice to head up a UN body. Nor was it the first time that Bryden, who has familial ties to Somaliland politicians, had been accused of partiality: the pro-Somaliland reports he issued while director of the International Crisis Group's Africa Program in the mid-2000s earned him the criticism of the Intergovernmental Authority on Development states (Djibouti, Ethiopia, Eritrea, Kenya, Somalia, Sudan, and Uganda), while the Puntland government declared him a *persona non grata*. This order was still standing as of 2010; the group's March report had been compiled without Bryden ever having set foot in Puntland.

*   *   *

Though the Puntland government, as Bryden suggested, has become increasingly willing to pursue the pirates on land, enthusiasm alone may not be sufficient to offset its lack of capacity. With an annual budget in the range of $20 million, derived almost exclusively from Bossaso port taxes, the Puntland government cannot afford an effective police force, let alone a justice system capable of processing hundreds of suspected pirates.

With such meagre resources at his disposal, Puntland's president can perhaps be better described as an inter-clan mediator than as the leader of a modern state. Even to fund basic state services, the president is routinely forced to beg for handouts from unconventional sources. Addressing an assembly of Bossaso businessmen at a dinner one evening, Farole appealed for donations to pay for a list of absurdly modest projects: replacing road signs, long ago stripped bare for the valuable metal; building a six-kilometre road from the livestock inspection station to the port; constructing a small hospital.

Given Puntland's capacities, the counter-piracy potential of the local military forces is limited. The Darawish's five to six thousand soldiers are garrisoned at Garowe, Bossaso, and Qardho—far from the locus of pirate activity—so any land operation against the pirates involves transporting troops hundreds of kilometres across roadless terrain. The logistical difficulties in deploying such a response make successful results extremely rare, and almost entirely dependent on timely local intelligence gathering.

One such operation occurred when I was with the president's entourage in Bossaso. Acting on a tip-off, Farole led an impromptu raid on the village of Marero, a well-known human trafficking and piracy launching site just east of Bossaso. In what was more a public relations exercise than a model for future action, Puntland security forces captured two speedboats, several outboard motors, barrels of fuel, food, and ladders. The seized equipment was proudly displayed to local media in lieu of the would-be pirates themselves, who had absconded in a speedboat as the troops approached.

If provided with sufficient financial and technical support from the international community aimed at overhauling its police and justice system, the Puntland government would be in a good position to tackle piracy on land. Like other kinds of undesirables who move and find shelter amongst civilians—militants, revolutionaries, even common criminals—the pirates' success depends on the goodwill and protection of the local people. Though initially welcomed as heroes, they have become increasingly unpopular amongst the local inhabitants due to their perceived un-Islamic influence.

It was perhaps with a view to mending community relations that Boyah's redemption movement had proved so popular amongst his former colleagues. Of these ex-pirates, perhaps none had expressed a greater desire to reform than Momman, a taciturn and thoughtful man whom I had first met at the khat picnics outside Garowe. Two weeks after the picnics, in July 2009, the two Omars procured me an invitation to visit Momman at his home.

8

Momman

MOMMAN'S HOUSE STOOD ALONE AMID A FIELD OF RUBBLE ON THE outskirts of Garowe, past the ruins of the long-abandoned airport, a vast tract of stone and concrete slabs struggling to poke through decades of layered dust. Nearby was a Japanese-funded settlement for internally displaced persons, ramshackle rows of tent-like structures cast in cracking concrete and tin—a damning testament to what a million dollars buys with Somali contractors. The only human activity in the early afternoon heat was a lone woman labouring over a wash bucket with a few haggard, half-naked children scampering in orbits around her.

As with many upscale Somali dwellings, the wall ringing Momman's compound was a vibrant sky blue, decorated with brilliant yellow and red circles and triangles, like a child's finger painting. We parked outside the walls beside another 4x4; this area of town was so deserted that there was no serious risk of theft. We had come directly from the khat *suq*, where, as a friendly offering, I had financed the purchase of several hefty bags of the drug.

Momman had once been Boyah's running mate, a founding father of the core group of Eyl fishermen-cum-pirates, before he split off to form a group of his own. Judging by the size of his house, he had enjoyed a fair measure of success prior to joining the recent pirate redemption movement.

We moved through the gate and into a courtyard carved up by weeds and empty except for a lonely gazebo. My two Special Police Unit guards secured themselves a ration of khat and found a spot under the gazebo to settle down and chew. We were told to wait outside as Momman prepared the house for us.

After about five minutes we received permission to go inside. The dim hallway leading into the house hit my eyes as a formless smudge of black and blue as I left the bright sun of the courtyard behind. Following the Omars' example, I slipped off my sandals and stepped barefoot into a low-lit, spacious room serving as a joint dining and living space. The cloying smell of Arabian perfume hung heavily in the air, reminiscent of the scented tissues provided at Somali restaurants following a meal. To my immediate left a sleek stainless-steel fridge and freezer rested flush against the door jamb; further down the adjoining wall, a brand-new twenty-one-inch TV and DVD player shared a beige wall unit with neat stacks of china. At the room's midpoint it cast off its modernist airs and morphed into an approximation of a sultan's tent: a three-piece divan framed an ornate crimson carpet, itself encircled by thick crimson drapes that blocked the daylight struggling through the barred windows behind them. Reddish, gold-tasselled bolsters sat propped on the floor against the base of the divan, while a few smaller similarly coloured pillows were scattered on the cushions above.

This was one of the nicest houses I had yet seen in Somalia, and I paid Momman the compliment. He was quick to correct me. "This is not my house." he said. "It belongs to my wife and kids." I felt like a tax agent investigating the assets of a mafia don.

Colonel Omar, dressed in his usual striped tracksuit, stocking cap, and scarf, lay staring at the ceiling on the divan across from me. He cradled his AK across his chest, almost caressing it. He was still khat sober: fifty days and counting. On the ground, the smaller Omar reclined against the cushion propped beneath the Colonel's legs. To his left sat his driver, a blithe, lanky man named Mahad.

Momman settled at the head of the gathering, leaning on the

floor against a bolster. Behind his head on the divan lay a loaded Belgian semi-automatic pistol—the little brother, around these parts, to the AK-47. Momman was flanked on either side by two of his former foot soldiers, Mohamed and Abdirahman (not their real names), who casually lounged, fastidiously picking at khat stems.

Momman, like Boyah, looked to be in his early forties, with broad shoulders that gave him an air of great physical strength. But in place of Boyah's free-flowing goat's tuft and traditional elder's garb were a meticulously trimmed goatee and an equally dapper combo of striped red dress shirt and olive slacks. His face was hard, his eyes old and almost fatigued, their gaze producing the impression—impossible to feign—that he did not care at all what I thought of him. He studied me intently, his eyes tracking over my face, and I found it difficult to meet them. His rare smiles slipped by with obvious reluctance, as if his facial muscles had briefly triumphed over his brain for control of his expression.

His austere gaze remained unchanged even when I produced the copious bags of khat I had brought with me. We dropped the black plastic bags in the centre of the carpet and clustered around them, like children around a campfire, an atmosphere that was instantly dashed when Momman rose and threw open the drapes, flooding the room with daylight. I settled back against the cushions, letting my *ma'awis* cascade comfortably over my folded legs, and picked apart the binding of a bundle. Selecting a stalk, I stripped away the tough, leathery leaves until only the soft shoots remained. As I lifted it to my mouth, the hint of bitterness hitting my nostrils carried with it a vision of the day to come: the stomach pains, the nervous chain-smoking, the tossing and turning until the early hours of the morning. Time itself doesn't seem quite real when you're chewing khat; the activity is perfectly in tune with Somalia—the slow, lethargic chewing keeps pace with the plodding of the days, lives measured out in pulpy mouthfuls. "Khat days" are endless, and there was no rush to begin the interview. I relaxed and waited for tongues to loosen.

In the meantime, I produced my backgammon set and played a few games with my interpreter Omar. Mohamed and Abdirahman glanced over as we played and asked some idle questions, but before long Colonel Omar descended from his perch on the divan and snatched the board away from his cousin, pulling it close to him where the others were unable to see it. He pointed aggressively at my chest, indicating a challenge.

The Colonel's militaristic philosophy on life was nowhere better expressed than in his backgammon game. He hit checkers in a mad frenzy whenever it was possible to do so, bellowing in victory each time. I tried to explain through Omar why restraint was necessary, but my interpreter lacked the translational nuance to properly convey backgammon strategy. I did what I could, uttering the Somali word for "dangerous"—*khatar*—after each ill-advised move, but it was of little use. After each inevitable loss, the Colonel scowled and half-jokingly accused me of cheating, wagging his finger.

Ignoring our game, Momman remained fixated on the television set, which was showing the latest Somali Broadcasting Corporation footage of Mogadishu in flames, the result of yet another Al-Shabaab suicide bombing. The conversation somehow turned to the multiple foreign journalists who had been kidnapped in Puntland, some by their own guards. "Here, in the Nugaal valley, we don't kidnap people who are working with us," Momman said, smiling at me for the first time. "It's not our culture."

Someone produced a tall thermos containing the saccharine tea that traditionally accompanies khat to counteract its bitter taste, and I poured a small helping into a cup. Every so often, Momman's wife wandered into the room, arranging the already tidy chairs or checking the placement of the immaculately stowed chinaware.

Momman picked up his handgun and absently began to toy with it. Bored and anxious to develop some kind of rapport, I nonchalantly requested to see it. He removed the clip and passed it through an assembly line of hands until it reached me. I fiddled with the safety for a few seconds and examined the barrel, then cocked the hammer a few times for good measure, nodding approvingly.

An hour and a half on, heaps of discarded khat stalks joined ciga-rette butts in mounting piles next to half-drained teacups. Attention turned to the TV as a procession of images of Somalia's past leaders began to scroll across the screen. Abdirahman and Mohamed excit-edly named each one for me as his photo appeared. Momman sat in silence, watching the television and chewing ponderously.

Enough time had passed for the khat to take effect, so I decided to ask Momman some questions. The tale he began to recount was by now familiar to my ears. "Boyah and I used to fish together," he said. "At first, we operated together in the same group, but later we split into different ones. There were a lot of independent groups . . . around fifteen of them. We used to only go after illegal fishing ships," he explained. It wasn't until 1999, according to Momman, that Boyah attacked his first commercial ship. "We started attacking them when we realized we couldn't fight against fishing ships any-more," owing to the improved state of their armament. "Commercial ships go into our waters, and they don't pay any fees."

Momman's success soon elevated him, as with Boyah, to the position of financier: "I was the one who bought everything for the missions," he explained, sometimes for his own group, but also for others. "We helped each other out."

Boyah had taken credit for hijacking dozens of ships, but when asked for his own tally, Momman hesitated. "I can't tell you that," he said, "it's a secret." He paused, musing. "I got a lot of good ones."

I decided to change tack. Boyah told me that his favourite ship was the *Golden Nori*, I said, referring to the Japanese chemical tanker he had steered into Bossaso port, What's yours? The attempt met defeat against Momman's hard eyes.

"I don't want to talk about that," he answered. "I'm ashamed of what I did."

I pressed further, desperate for any scraps of information he could give me about the ships: the nationalities of the crew, their cargos or destinations.

"No, I won't give you any of those details," Momman said, "because you'll be able to figure out the names of the ships later on."

"He's not stupid," Omar interjected.

Momman invariably hijacked any question aimed at illuminating his buccaneering past and steered it back to the topic of his redemption. "I want to have a good career, and not have it ruined by my past deeds," he said. "I want to be another man." He gave April 20 as marking the beginning of this new life, which he insisted was before the redemption movement had come into fashion. "I renounced piracy before the Sheikh [Abdulkhadar] started taking people to mosque and making them swear off piracy. I made the decision on my own.

"I know it's bad to be a pirate, but at least pirates never kill anyone," he said. "What warships do, especially the Indian ones, is really bad. When they run into a pirate boat, they will kill them, or take their food and fuel and abandon them until they eat one another." He added, in a disgusted tone, "It would be better to just kill them." Even in the international media, the Indian navy had earned a reputation for heavy-handedness; perhaps most infamous was the November 2008 incident in which the Indians blew a Thai fishing ship out of the water with all hands on board, later claiming they had mistaken it for a pirate mothership.

"The Americans, they are the nicest ones," Momman said. "The rest of them just want to do their job—they don't care who dies."

Momman's warm feelings towards the Americans had come from personal experience, like the time they responded to the SOS of a ship he had hijacked—the name of which Momman naturally refused to disclose. "About forty minutes after we boarded the ship, the Americans appeared and started shooting at us," he said. Like Boyah, Momman could recall with surprising accuracy the designations of the warships hemming him in: B135, B132, 125, 128. "The numbers kept changing" as ships arrived and retreated, he said.

"The Americans were talking at us through the ship's loudspeakers, but we just ignored them and moved the ship to Eyl. They were warning us to leave the ship within twenty-four hours, or they would attack," he said, smiling. "Twenty-four hours later, they repeated the same message."

Gunfire from the American ships raked the cliffs overlooking the beach at Eyl. "Then they shot at the fishing boats on the beach," said Momman, "because they thought they were going to bring us supplies. They fired near to the boats as they tried to approach us from shore. They stopped them from bringing us food." It was then, according to Momman, that the ship's owners requested that the Americans back off, paving the way for a painless ransom negotiation.

Reminded of these glory days, Momman began to speak more freely of his past life, sounding almost nostalgic. "We used to take a lot of dry food with us, extra sugar, a little flour. Enough for seven days. We would cook on board," he said.

"It was never that hard to climb up onto the deck—it depends on how high up the ship is, how fast it's going, but usually it's very easy. Personally, I've never seen the crew fighting back. Most people would go and lock themselves inside, some would come out with their hands out, saying, 'What do you guys want?'"

And was the crew ever afraid?

"Definitely, they would freak out. But we tried to calm them down, saying, 'We're not going to hurt you if you take our orders.' We would tell them, 'You'll be all right . . . we're not here to kill you.' We never had to kill anyone."

Momman lamented that things had gotten much more dangerous since those days. Many of his former colleagues had disappeared without a trace in recent times. "Some of my friends are still missing," he said. "About two months ago, some of them washed up dead on the coast, near Garacad," presumably either drowned or killed by the international naval forces. "The families of the missing boys are really upset about it; they don't know where they are or whether they're dead or alive," said Momman. "It's starting to create a lot of anger. Who knows what their families will do.

"Also, some of these young boys have gotten twenty years in

Bossaso jail," he said. "That angers their families too, but at least when they are in Somalia they can go visit them."

*   *   *

It is not only foreign navies that are responsible for dead Somalis in the surf, but possibly the pirates themselves. The stretch of the Gulf of Aden linking northern Somalia and Yemen is one of the world's busiest human smuggling routes; often when travelling from Garowe to Bossaso, I would see dozens of Oromo migrants alongside the road, staffs in hand, walking the hundreds of kilometres from the highlands of Ethiopia to Bossaso under the burning sun. Many I later observed camped in huddles outside the Bossaso compound of the UN High Commission for Refugees, but many others undoubtedly joined the thousands of Somalis making the risky dash for Yemen each year.

Tragically, those who smuggle them often do not complete the job, forcing migrants into the water kilometres from shore in order to avoid Yemeni coastal patrols; according to the UN's Mixed Migration Task Force, 1–7 per cent of those making the journey from 2007 to 2009 died in the attempt.[1] Pirate groups, other UN agencies have claimed, are directly involved in human trafficking. It makes sense: pirates already use Yemeni ports to obtain smuggled weapons, and pirate organizations could use their equipment and smuggling networks to achieve a perverse economy of scale by bridging the piracy and human smuggling "industries."

Momman agreed, but made it clear that his generation had never been involved in such activities. "The pirates operating now are definitely doing that," he said, "but it wasn't going on earlier." According to him, the going rate for a trip to Yemen was $200 for a spot in a "small boat"—holding about thirty people—and $100 for a place in a more crowded "big boat"—one carrying eighty to a hundred people. The business had a dual purpose that went beyond the money: the pirates, said Momman, used the migrants as a cover to conceal their activities from both the Puntland government and international naval forces. Unlike piracy, transporting people is not a crime, at least until an attempt is made to enter a foreign state illegally.

"They don't want the government to see that they are pirates," he explained. "They drop off [the migrants] and then go about their pirating." The idea was not completely far-fetched. During President Farole's impromptu raid on pirates in the village of Marero, his soldiers captured documents conclusively linking the gang to human smuggling.

Whether pirate gangs are amongst the many smuggling groups guilty of murdering their charges is unknown. But Momman doubted it: "They always deliver the people on time."

* * *

The desire to trace the poorly marked money trail always led my interviews to one central question: How do pirates spend their cash? Judging from Momman's response, it was the wrong question to ask. "I told you before," he said, "this house is not mine, it's my wife's. I never used any piracy money to live on—it's *haram* to do so. We used that money to fund new pirate operations and to buy weapons. That's all. We don't build houses with it." Indeed, the like-minded devotion by other pirate headmen to continual capital reinvestment had allowed piracy to develop into a self-sustaining industry.

The fleeting Somali dusk had come and gone, and the strips of sky poking through the bars of the windows were now a deep navy blue. Colonel Omar roused himself from the couch and headed off to meet some visiting Kenyan documentary makers being hosted by the Farole family. The hours of continual chewing had taken their toll on me: gut rot was gnawing at my stomach lining and an indefinable pain was pounding my brain, but my body was taut with nervous energy, my jaw clenched. Omar and I were also scheduled to meet with the Colonel's Kenyan journalists, and his phone chimed every few minutes with the Colonel's insistent reminders. After about the seventh call within a quarter hour, I decided that the interview had reached its natural conclusion.

I picked up my half-finished bundle of khat and tossed it gently into Momman's dwindling pile. He protested; take it, please, I said, and he accepted.

Throughout the interview, Mohamed and Abdirahman had been content to let Momman act as their mouthpiece, perhaps because their own mouths had been too jammed with khat leaves to be of any service to them. As I was about to leave, Mohamed, who up until now had been fairly reticent, timidly requested permission to ask me a question: What, he hesitantly inquired, do people in the West think about pirates? "They think about people with eye patches," I replied, wondering in what mangled form my meaning would reach Mohamed's brain. The romantic stereotype of the swashbuckling pirate was so foreign to the Somalis' self-image that my many previous attempts to convey it had been met only with bemused glances.

As I got up to depart, blood rushing into my numbed legs, I asked permission to take a photo of Momman and his two colleagues. *Maya*, no, he said, waving away my camera. I reminded him that I had videotaped Momman, Boyah, and the other pirates during our recent khat picnic together. "I couldn't do anything about that," he answered. "Here, I can."

Memory would have to suffice. My last image of Momman, as his wife led us out the door, was of him reclining against a bolster, teacup in one hand, khat stalk in the other, staring pensively into the carpet.

9

The Policemen of the Sea

MOMMAN'S ANIMOSITY TOWARDS THE INTERNATIONAL NAVAL CO-
alitions policing Somali waters was shared by many of his peers.
Boyah, for one, still spoke with anger about the six men he lost,
plucked into the sky by French navy helicopters and transported half
a world away to face eventual trial in a Parisian courthouse. Yet he
was quick to express his contempt for the international naval forces.
"Sometimes, we capture vessels when warships are right around us,"
Boyah had told me during our first meeting. "We don't care about
them. They're not going to stop us."

Though it is tempting to write off Boyah's remarks as empty blus-
ter, the facts are harder to dismiss: the deployment of three multinational naval task forces beginning in late 2008 has done little to
halt pirate attacks. Conversely, from 2008 to 2010 the number of
hijackings continued to rise, and the trend had not abated as this
book went to press.

When the Somali pirates exploded onto the scene following the end
of the summer monsoon season in 2008, the world was caught unpre-
pared. The only naval presence in the region was Combined Task Force
150 (CTF-150), a multinational coalition built around the US Fifth
Fleet whose primary function was counter-terrorism. Following the
sharp increase in the pirate threat, counter-piracy was hastily tacked
onto CTF-150's mandate, though clearly only as a stopgap solution.

In October 2008, NATO finally announced plans to deploy a seven-warship task force by the year's end. Two months later, the European Union added its own flotilla to Somalia's increasingly congested waterways, EU Naval Force Somalia (EUNAVFOR, also designated "Atalanta"). And in January 2009, the United States proclaimed the creation of Combined Task Force 151 (CTF-151), a multinational fleet tasked with taking over counter-piracy operations from CTF-150. Independently operating navies from countries as diverse as China, India, Iran, Russia, and Malaysia also joined the fray, with the clear priority of defending their own nationals and flag vessels. As individual warships have come and gone at the behest of their home governments, the combined strength of the international coalition has varied between twenty-five and forty vessels, at an estimated annual cost of $1–$1.5 billion.

For many countries, the piracy crisis provided an ideal opportunity to flex naval muscles: Operation Atalanta was the very first maritime mission under the EU flag, China's deployment of three warships was its first overseas mission since 1949, and Germany's and Japan's respective contributions to Atalanta and CTF-151 exemplified the two nations' gradual movement away from five decades of dogmatic pacifism. The Somali pirates seemed to be an enemy that the whole world could agree on.

Yet these three fleets, the collective product of an unprecedented level of international naval cooperation, have been unable to stop a motley assortment of half-starved brigands armed with aging assault rifles and the odd grenade launcher. Many find it incomprehensible that, despite bristling with state-of-the-art weaponry and detection systems, Western warships have allowed the pirates to continue to hijack ships with seeming impunity.

Such an attitude fails to appreciate the sheer size of the area that international forces must cover. From the time the crew of a targeted vessel spots the oncoming hijackers and sends out a distress call, a nearby warship generally has a window of fifteen to forty minutes in which to respond before the pirates manage to board the vessel.

Assuming the ship is outfitted with a helicopter (which has a maximum speed of about 320 kilometres per hour) ready for immediate launch, it must be within about eighty kilometres of the scene of attack in order to have a realistic shot at mounting a successful rescue operation. Yet Somali pirate attacks have occurred along an east–west axis 3,000 kilometres wide, from the depths of the Indian Ocean to the Red Sea, and along a north–south axis ranging the 3,700 kilometres from Oman to Madagascar—an ocean surface area two-thirds the size of the United States. For the crews of the warships in the combined international naval effort, struggling to contain an estimated 1,500–2,000 pirates operating in small groups of six to twelve, hunting pirates must seem like playing a losing game of Whac-a-Mole. In fairness, controlling such a vast area is not quite as hopeless as I have made it out to be; pirate attacks tend to cluster around shipping lanes, and by patrolling these routes warships greatly improve their odds of disrupting pirate operations. But it is generally accepted that no purely military solution exists to the problem of Somali piracy—at least none that is both economically and politically feasible.

* * *

When EUNAVFOR warships sailed into the Gulf of Aden in December 2008, they came with a plan. In cooperation with the other naval forces, NAVFOR established the Internationally Recommended Transit Corridor (IRTC), a heavily patrolled safe zone running 650 kilometres along the Yemeni side of the Gulf of Aden. In conjunction with regularly scheduled convoy escorts, the IRTC was immediately effective in restoring some order to the stretch of water that wary mariners had nicknamed "Pirate Alley." But though the statistics show that the IRTC was initially effective in reducing the success rate of pirate attacks, the absolute number of hijackings steadily rose. In 2008, there were 134 attacks, mostly concentrated in the Gulf of Aden, resulting in 49 documented hijackings. In 2009, the number of attacks increased to 228, with 68 successful hijackings.

The next year saw 74 hijackings for 243 attacks, and as of February the figures for 2011 stood at 14 hijackings for 40 attacks—on pace to exceed the 2010 total.[1]

These numbers reveal a small drop in the hijacking success rate (37 per cent to 30 per cent) from 2008 to 2009,[2] corresponding to the increased naval presence towards the end of 2008 and the creation of the IRTC. Though the hijacking success rate has remained between 30 and 35 per cent since 2009, the economic incentive—as measured by ransom amounts—has been steadily increasing. In 2008, the average pirate ransom fell in the range of $1.25–$1.5 million, which grew to $2–$2.5 million in 2009 and to $3–$4 million in 2010, highlighted by the record $9.5 million bounty paid to release MV *Samho Dream*, a South Korean oil tanker commandeered in April (the vessel earned her hijackers more than three times the amount garnered by the headline-grabbing supertanker *Sirius Star* merely a year earlier.) In 2008, the pirates earned a total of $25–$35 million, a figure that shot up to $70–$90 million the following year. Yet in 2010, as average ransoms spiralled upwards, ransom revenues surprisingly fell slightly, to $65–$85 million. With the number of hijackings continuing to rise, this seemingly paradoxical drop in earnings was explained by lengthening periods of captivity, as avaricious pirate bosses began to drag out negotiations for months longer in the hope of securing themselves premium ransoms. As a consequence, the majority of vessels hijacked in 2010 were not ransomed until well into 2011.

Of course, not every hijacked ship is a multi-million-dollar lottery ticket; many are dhows or small fishing trawlers manned by poor Yemeni or South Asian crews. Lacking the defence of being worth ransoming, the fishermen are often set adrift or even killed, their vessels converted for use as pirate motherships. Beginning in 2009, the proportion of fishing dhows as a percentage of total hijackings increased, probably to meet the soaring demand for motherships required by the pirates' Indian Ocean expansion. Exactly how many poor fishermen have fallen victim to Somali pirates will likely never be known; often neglected or abandoned by their parent companies, attacks against fishing vessels frequently go unreported to the International Maritime Bureau or other authorities. The untold brunt of brutality borne by Yemeni fishermen has prompted Puntland expert Stig Hansen to call these attacks "the hidden tragedy of piracy."[3]

* * *

Unlike rival street gangs, pirate groups do not have formally demarcated "turfs" that they jealously guard from their enemies. Yet the geographical locations of hijackings have correlated with remarkable accuracy to the geographical origins of the hijackers. All ships known to have been seized in the Gulf of Aden, for instance, have ended up in Puntland ports, while the vast majority of those hijacked in the far south, near the Seychelles and Madagascar, have been taken to Harardheere. Thus, as the choice pirate hunting ground shifted from the Gulf of Aden to the Indian Ocean, Puntland's strategic importance waned. Many pirate groups continued to operate out of the region, but they mostly used the southern port of Garacad, which had the dual advantages of being more remote and isolated than Eyl, as well as closer to the Indian Ocean shipping lanes.

Perversely, the constant naval pressure may also have bred a higher class of pirate, because the groups operating upwards of 1,500 kilometres into the Indian Ocean required a much higher level of sophistication—in terms of boats, supply logistics, navigational skills and equipment, and perhaps intelligence networks—than those who had previously floated in the Gulf of Aden, waiting for any target of opportunity to come along. The forces of artificial selection meant that only the most advanced pirate gangs were likely to survive in the new reality created by the Gulf of Aden safety corridor.

The pirates' Indian Ocean expansion did not go unnoticed by the international naval forces. In April 2010 I spoke to Commander John Harbour, the media spokesman for EUNAVFOR, via telephone from his London office. According to Harbour, the upper echelons of

EU leadership had vigorously debated how to respond to the pirates' change in tactics. Some voices, he said, had argued for a complete blockade of pirate ports along the entire length of the Somali coast, an approach that he viewed as unrealistic: "The Somali coast is over a thousand miles long, and although it's got maybe six or seven main [pirate] ports, we haven't even got enough ships to cover those. What we can do, with good intelligence, is find the pirate camps and sit off of them. These camps can be anything from a mothership, a couple of skiffs, and a few barrels on the shore covered by a tarpaulin, to ten motherships and thirty skiffs."

Locating and blockading these floating bases, often through information gathered by maritime patrol aircraft, formed the first pillar of the EU's latest counter-piracy strategy; by interdicting suspicious craft before they reached the international shipping lanes, NAVFOR hoped to contain the problem at its source. In many ways, NAVFOR's vessels had begun to operate like the defensive line of a football team, concentrating their forces at the line of scrimmage but positioning safeties further afield to intercept any opponent slipping through the perimeter. "The new strategy was basically to take the fight to the pirates," Harbour explained. "First, interdict them off their bases. Then, have ships available in a second layer, maybe one to two hundred miles off the coast, who can respond to attacks. Finally, have maritime patrol aircraft and ships in the deeper Indian Ocean, who can visit the scene after an attack has occurred."

Over the previous month, he estimated, NAVFOR had disrupted twenty-five pirate "attack groups"—each consisting of a mothership towing two skiffs—half of which had been intercepted before reaching open ocean, and half captured in the wake of attempted hijackings. The success of their shift in strategy, said Harbour, had provoked yet another tactical adaptation by the pirates. "They've discovered that we're sitting off the shore," he said, "so therefore they've started to throw their skiffs behind their 4x4s and go find a bit of deserted beach where they can launch the operation. We've also seen far more launches done from southern Somalia."

The pirates also responded to the NAVFOR crackdown by pushing ever deeper into the Indian Ocean. With attacks occurring over 1,500 kilometres from the Somali coast, they had struck as far south as Madagascar and almost as far east as the Maldives—closer to India than Africa. Six months to one year previously, said Harbour, things had been different. "The pirates tended to get out with enough fuel to take them maybe a hundred miles offshore, then they would switch off their engines and drift with the currents for days and days until they found a target of opportunity. And of course their plan was to find a target, take it out, and use it to get themselves back to the coast. But inevitably we would find small skiffs, adrift with no food, no fuel, and no water, and people dead in the bottom of the boat. They were probably pirates, but at that point it's a humanitarian mission to rescue these guys."

In more recent days, the pirates' deep-sea missions had stepped up the demand for more far-ranging and sophisticated motherships. Over the previous month alone, said Harbour, NAVFOR had documented ten cases of fishing dhows or small coastal traders commandeered for this purpose, compared with a total of twelve to fifteen cases during the previous twelve months. "The advantage of that is that they've already got a hijacked crew on board, and that makes it a lot more difficult for us to find them and take them out," he said.

As an example of the pirates' recent ship-hopping proclivity, Harbour launched into the story of the ML *Arzoo*, a small transport seized after developing engine problems off the Somali coast while en route to Mogadishu. Realizing that the *Arzoo* was damaged and low on fuel, the nine hijackers called in reinforcements from Somalia, who duly arrived in a commandeered Indian trading dhow. After taking the captors aboard and leaving the *Arzoo* and her crew dead in the water, the group proceeded to hijack a third vessel, the Seychellois fishing boat *Galate*, which they in turn used to hijack an Iranian merchant ship, *Al Abi*, transferring the *Galate*'s six crew members aboard and abandoning the vessel. At this point, the Seychellois coast guard caught up to the pirates and brought their joy ride to an end; believing the hostages' lives to be in danger, the coast guard opened up on the vessel with its machine guns.

"They started firing at the *Al Abi*'s waterline, to such an extent that they hit the engine and it caught fire," said Harbour. "There was a fireball, and eventually the damn thing sank, leaving twenty-seven people in the water, plus nine pirates, who were duly picked up. The incident showed the pirates that we won't always stop because there are hostages on board."

Despite Harbour's attempt to claim collective credit for the Seychellois coast guard's action, NAVFOR's rules of engagement have so far prevented its members from launching a comparably audacious rescue operation. During the one commando mission conducted by EU forces—the rescue of the German-flagged MV *Taipan* by the Dutch warship *Tromp*—the *Tromp* was forced to circumvent EU rules by temporarily removing itself from the Atalanta fleet, striking its NAVFOR colours and raising the Dutch flag.

Understandably, NAVFOR has drawn criticism for its perceived softness, which is underscored by its consistent practice of freeing captured pirates after confiscating their weapons and paraphernalia. One of the reasons behind this "catch and release" policy is that the EU, NATO, and CTF fleets have been operating under procedures more befitting a civilian police force than a military. Just as it is unacceptable for police officers to make arrests based on shades and hooded sweatshirts, naval personnel are not allowed to detain any AK-47-toting "fishermen" they happen to find floating in the Indian Ocean. But Harbour was quick to dismiss the notion that NAVFOR was hamstrung by its procedural rules.

"It's not true that we have to catch pirates in the process of an attack. We can catch them well afterwards, as long as there's clear link of evidence," he explained, proceeding to describe an incident where EU maritime patrol aircraft had tracked a pirate attack group from the scene of an attempted hijacking for twelve hours before a warship caught up and took them into custody. "Of course, if we catch them in the act, that's great, because we'd be killing them . . .

we'd shoot them down," he said. "Normally, they're not that stupid; they usually try to break off, and even scatter." Indeed, when catching pirates in the midst of an attack, NAVFOR has not hesitated to respond with deadly force. From August 2008 to May 2010, the combined international naval forces killed at least sixty-four pirates and wounded twenty-four.[4]

The blame for the typically lenient treatment of arrested pirates, according to Harbour, lay squarely with the domestic legal systems of the nearby countries—such as Kenya—to which the pirates are sent for prosecution. "EUNAVFOR forces are the policemen of the seas; our job is to gather the evidence to present to the court, but it's up to the judge to decide whether to prosecute," he said. "What we'd like to see is countries develop laws on *conspiring* to piracy. To use the police corollary: if a policeman catches some bloke walking down the road with an unlicensed gun in his pocket, then he is conspiring to commit a criminal act. He should be taken to court and given a very long sentence just for carrying the gun."

The metaphor was not entirely apt; unlike the streets of London, on the high seas it is not a crime under international law to carry firearms, even when they consist of a rather suspicious assortment of Kalashnikovs and rocket-propelled grenade (RPG) launchers. The United Nations Convention on the Law of the Sea (UNCLOS) permits the seizure of "pirate ship[s] or aircraft" without actually catching the occupants in an act of piracy but also without clarifying what constitutes adequate grounds to do so. This omission is especially problematic given that a Somali fishing boat with a few Kalashnikovs stashed in the bottom could as easily contain legitimate fishermen as pirates. The danger is that by prosecuting suspects for "conspiracy to commit piracy," countries would be giving an unprecedented interpretation to UNCLOS, one that unfairly targets all seafaring Somalis. So far, the Seychelles has been the only country to pass such a law.

The international naval effort, Harbour conceded, represented only part of the solution to the piracy crisis, which in the end had to be resolved on the ground. "It's important to remember that we are the military arm of the European Union, which is spending $250 million on trying to stabilize that country by supporting the Transitional Federal Government (TFG)," he said, referring to money pledged at an April 2009 donor conference in Brussels. "We look upon ourselves as part of that political grouping, and that is why we differ from NATO and [CTF-151], which are purely military forces conducting a particular job, i.e., anti-piracy or anti-terrorism."

But with the TFG currently in control of only a half-dozen neighbourhoods in Mogadishu, I asked Harbour whether funnelling money to such a "government" could realistically make any difference to the anti-piracy effort. "A bit of optimism is required there," he conceded. "But by stabilizing the TFG, by supporting it, that's going to defeat piracy . . . The fact that you've currently got eight huge cargo or oil ships sitting at anchor off the coast of a country controlled by a bunch of criminals, who are demanding huge ransoms from the international community, is just appalling. Can you imagine that happening off Brighton, or Portsmouth? It's just unthinkable. We're trying to approach the problem from the other side, to explore the issue politically and help build a legitimate country, which will eventually bring Somalia's own forces to bear to defeat this utter scourge of criminality."

* * *

While pirate gangs have proven remarkably adept at outmanoeuvring the international naval armada, they have no monopoly on the ability to adapt tactics. The Panamanian-flagged cargo ship *Almezaan* had been hijacked twice, most notably in November 2009 while transporting a consignment of small arms—in contravention of the UN embargo on Somalia—intended for a Mogadishu businessman.[5] In the early morning of March 23, 2010, as the *Almezaan* steamed once more towards Mogadishu, the pirates struck again. On this occasion, however, she was ready to meet them on their own terms, with armed private security personnel stationed on her deck.

When the pirates opened fire, the guards responded in kind, spraying the attackers with their automatic weapons. Initially repulsed, the pirates came about for a second assault and were repelled in the same manner, following which they fled towards the open sea. When a helicopter from the Spanish warship *Navarra* caught up with them, the two skiffs were riddled with bullet holes and a pirate was shot dead in the bottom of one. It marked the first time that a pirate had been killed by private security guards.

Within the international shipping community, the *Almezaan* shooting stirred up an already ongoing debate over the use of armed guards on commercial vessels. The standard concerns surrounding private military contractors—their accountability and the rules of engagement under which they operate—are considerably magnified when they are engaged on the high seas. Complicated questions arise over which country has jurisdiction over the contractors: the flag state (in the case of the *Almezaan*, Panama), the owners (United Arab Emirates), or the nationality of the contractors themselves (undisclosed). These issues are especially worrisome when the victims are Somali citizens, who lack a functioning state to defend their rights. In addition to the legal and moral concerns is the more pragmatic fear that arming the merchant marine will provoke the pirates into increasingly violent behaviour.

"While we understand that owners want to protect their ships, we don't agree in principle with putting armed security on ships," International Maritime Bureau director Captain Pottengal Mukundan told the BBC following the *Almezaan* incident. "Ships are not an ideal place for a gun battle."[6]

For a high-risk target like the *Almezaan*, running guns into Somalia, armed guards were perhaps a prudent choice. But for most shippers, the risk of escalating an incident typically makes hiring private security a poor business decision. No shipping company wants to make headlines because of the body count on the deck of one of its vessels. The added possibility of a firefight resulting in a serious financial or environmental disaster—in the case of expensive or sensitive cargo, such as crude oil or volatile chemicals—makes the potential cost of violence extremely high. Indeed, the risk assessments carried out by marine insurers are as likely to judge the presence of armed guards as a net liability rather than a reason to reduce premiums. "From our point of view, unless you can really guarantee the quality of the armed guards put on board, you're probably increasing the risk of the total loss of a vessel," said Neil Smith, head of underwriting at Lloyd's Market Association, which provides member support to Lloyd's of London, the largest marine insurance market in the world. "In fact, it could cause the shipowner's premiums to go up."

Low-cost measures, such as barbed wire and high-pressure water hoses, Smith argued, are usually the wiser course. "At the moment, the pirates can still be dissuaded relatively easily," he said. "They're opportunistic, and if there's a vessel they can get onto with reasonable ease, they'll go after it, as opposed to a vessel that shows any signs of defending itself against attack—even using relatively low-tech measures. It's always about not wanting to escalate things," he added.

More basic, however, is the fact that maritime shipping is an extraordinarily competitive global business, and hiring private security is simply not in the average shipowner's budget. Engaging a team of armed guards costs in the range of $10,000 per day ($30,000–$60,000 for an escort vessel), and given that it takes three to five days to pass through "pirate waters," the added security bill would destroy the profit margins of all but the most lucrative consignments.

Similar reasoning explains why shipping companies do not simply arm their own employees. Neither shipowners nor their insurers wish to risk escalating a piracy incident, especially as a result of inexperienced sailors-cum-mercenaries, fresh out of a crash course in marine combat. Second, shippers already grant hazard pay ranging from 25 per cent to 100 per cent for crew members serving in high-risk piracy areas, and would likely have to offer an even greater pay hike in order to convince their employees to double as armed guards. More significantly, shipowners mutually insure one another for liabilities not covered under standard marine insurance, such as loss

1. An Antonov prop plane operated by Jubba Airways, Djibouti. Next stop: Somalia.

2. The author's house during his second trip to Puntland, a self-governing region in northeastern Somalia.

3. Boyah, who has claimed to have hijacked more than twenty-five ships, with a Toronto Blue Jays T-shirt slung over his shoulder.

4. The view from the mayor's office, Garowe.

5. A Toyota Surf, the vehicle of choice for pirates. The "18" on the licence plate indicates that it has been recently registered.

6. House of a pirate, Garowe.

7. President Abdirahman Farole (right) and Vice-President Abdisamad Ali Shire (centre) in the village of Dangorayo, the first stop on President Farole's visit to Bossaso, February 2009.

8. The presidential convoy stops for a rest.

9. The author with residents of Dangorayo. The beard stayed in Somalia.

10. Qardho prison: much-needed, but not yet operational.

11. Puntland Finance Minister Farah Ali Jama (left), Interior Minister General Abdullahi Ahmed Jama Ilkajir (centre), and Vice President Abdisamad Ali Shire (right) discuss politics over lunch, Qardho.

12. Elders in Armo gather to bring an inter-clan dispute to President Farole's attention.

13. Schoolchildren greet the president's arrival in Armo.

14. President Farole greets an officer during an inspection of a police academy, Armo.

15. President Farole greets the media upon arriving in Bossaso.

16. Presidential palace, Bossaso. The Italian architecture harkens back to Somalia's colonial period.

17. The presidential convoy on the road to Bossaso.

18. The inner sanctum, Bossaso prison. The only functional prison in Puntland, it held more than a hundred pirates when I first visited in February 2009.

19. A pardoned prisoner receives 1 million Somali shillings before being released. The same day, I interviewed three inmates sentenced to life in prison for piracy.

20. A village on the road to Eyl, a modest fishing town that in 2008 earned worldwide infamy as Somalia's foremost "pirate haven."

21. The second of three flat tires we suffered during the bumpy drive to Eyl.

22. The redoubtable Colonel Omar, dressed in his characteristic striped track suit, on the beach at Eyl. The Colonel served as my guide (and unofficial bodyguard) during my second trip to Somalia.

23. Eyl Dawad, June 2009; reports of pirate mansions have been greatly exaggerated.

24. The Puntland Coast Guard during the tenure of the Hart Group.

25. The author's bodyguard Said, on the beach at Eyl. The MV *Victoria*, a German-owned cargo ship hijacked on May 5, 2009, is just visible at the horizon.

26. The MV *Victoria*, being held at Eyl in June 2009.

27. Minions of the pirate leader Computer, a reported psychic, load the day's supplies for the *Victoria*.

28. An abandoned Soviet fish-processing facility, Eyl. Many pirates blame illegal fishing by foreign ships for the area's economic collapse, a fact they often cite as a justification for their actions.

29. A broken-down refrigerated transport container, indicative of the state of Eyl's fishing economy.

30. Former Eyl residence and command post of Somali freedom fighter Mohamed Abdullah Hassan, known as "The Mad Mullah."

31. Dhanane: a pirate town that, under different circumstances, might have served as a prime location for a tourist resort.

32. The MV *Marathon*, a Dutch-owned cargo ship captured on May 7, 2009, being held at Dhanane.

33. One of the *Marathon*'s hijackers (left), chewing khat and chatting with Ombaali, a former pirate who has claimed involvement in three 2008 hijackings.

34. Bushmen in Dhanane. The pirates in the town, they explained to me, were outsiders who sometimes stole their goats.

35. The half-finished house of the pirate leader Kadiye, on the outskirts of Garowe.

36. Abdiwahid Mahamed Hersi, known as Joaar, director general of the Puntland Ministry of Fisheries, enjoying a break from the office.

37. Wanini Kireri, the warden of Shimo La Tewa prison in Mombasa, Kenya, where over a hundred suspected pirates currently await trial.

38. The booming Nairobi suburb of Eastleigh: a little slice of Somalia.

39. A busy market street in Eastleigh.

of life and injury to crew members, through associations known as protection and indemnity clubs. In the event of a pirate encounter, the shipping industry itself would be responsible for paying compensation for any crew members injured or killed—a far more likely occurrence if they are engaged in combat.

Rerouting their vessels around the Cape of Good Hope, the southern tip of Africa—thereby bypassing the Suez Canal as well as the Somali pirates—is another alternative open to shipowners. Few, however, have exercised this option; as well as additional crewing and fuel costs, the delays inherent in the detour may result in ships arriving late to port—extremely problematic in the case of time-sensitive cargos, such as high-value consumer goods (for example, the latest car models) or just-in-time manufacturing inputs. According to a report by the US Department of Transportation, routing an oil tanker from Saudi Arabia to the United States around the Cape of Good Hope adds 4,300 kilometres to the trip, and reduces the tanker's round-trip annual voyages from six to five, at an additional yearly fuel cost of $3.5 million.[7]

And while sailing via the Cape of Good Hope virtually eliminates the chance of running into pirates, the marine navigation hazards are amplified. "If you go around South Africa, you're facing a much more exposed sea route," explained Smith. Thus, while shippers could save money on war risk insurance—which often subsumes acts of piracy—they would face increased premiums on hull insurance, which covers loss due to marine perils, such as running aground and hazardous weather.

The fact is, piracy just is not enough of a bother to cause most shipowners to change their plans. As we saw in Chapter 3, in 2008 the average vessel passing through the Gulf of Aden faced only a 0.17 per cent, or 1 in 550, chance of being hijacked. In the unlikely event that a ship is captured, the owner (or, as is more likely, the owner's insurance provider) is forced to pay a ransom generally not exceeding 2–5 per cent of the worth of the vessel and her cargo—an annoyance, to be sure, but not a particularly uneconomical one.

Most owners, in the end, are content to string up some barbed wire, buy an insurance policy, and pray.

* * *

One defensive option that was considered in the early days of Somali piracy was the long-range acoustic device, or LRAD, a non-lethal sonic weapon described as a "bullhorn on steroids" that is capable of inflicting excruciating pain on its targets. Alas, the arguments for the LRAD turned out to be nothing more than a lot of noise. On November 28, 2008, the chemical tanker *Biscaglia*—equipped with an LRAD operated by three unarmed guards provided by the British private security firm Anti-Piracy Maritime Security Solutions (APMSS)—was assaulted by six pirates wielding the standard AK-47s and RPGs. After forty minutes of ineffectual resistance using the LRAD and high-pressure water cannons, the guards abandoned their posts and jumped overboard.

It is hard to fault the *Biscaglia*'s guards for choosing to save their own lives rather than dying in a senseless last stand—they were, after all, involved in a gunfight armed with nothing more than a glorified bullhorn. LRADs, it turns out, are far more suited to crowd control than repelling armed sea bandits; they have an effective range of less than three hundred metres—inferior to that of an AK-47—and the fact that they can be trained on only one target at a time is a serious limitation when the standard pirate attack pattern involves a two-skiff team. Luckily, the three guards were eventually rescued by a German naval helicopter. The crew of the *Biscaglia* were not so fortunate; they spent the next two months in the company of their Somali captors.

The *Biscaglia* spelled the death of the LRAD as a valid counter-piracy defence, as *Lloyd's List,* the world's forefront maritime trade journal, published an article blasting the device's effectiveness.[8] It was also the end for APMSS; after the embarrassing incident, owner Nick Davis dissolved the company.

* * *

Individual crews have occasionally come up with their own creative methods of dealing with pirate attacks. When seven pirates armed with heavy machine guns and RPGs boarded the Chinese fishing ship *Zhenhua 4* on December 17, 2008, they probably thought that the difficult part was over. Instead, the *Zhenhua*'s thirty-member crew unleashed a ragtag assault, blasting the invaders with water cannons, improvised Molotov cocktails, and even beer bottles.[9] After half an hour, the cowed pirates signalled for a ceasefire, barely making it back to their skiffs before a Malaysian warship appeared on the scene and opened fire. No members of the *Zhenhua*'s crew were injured during the battle.

The *Zhenhua*'s crew were likely aware that only their own reckless courage would save their ship from becoming the latest addition to the pirates' fleet of motherships, and themselves from indentured servitude or worse. Most shipping companies, however, would expressly forbid their sailors to escalate the situation through active resistance. Passive measures, on the other hand, such as barbed wire, electric fences, blocking stairwells, and barring windows, have all been employed at various times, with differing degrees of success. But two defensive techniques have stood out above these others, owing to their relatively low cost, simplicity, and high degree of effectiveness.

The first is merely the stationing of extra watches on deck. On most commercial vessels, it is standard to have the officer of the watch on the bridge, and perhaps one additional lookout to assist the watchkeeper. This status quo puts crews transiting through pirate-infested waters at unacceptable risk, according to Andrew Linington, a UK spokesman for the international maritime union Nautilus. Due to the intense cost competitiveness of the international maritime shipping industry, he says, crew sizes have been significantly reduced over the last thirty years; in the 1970s, medium to large container ships commonly had crews of twenty-five or more, but recent years have seen many vessels reduced to running on skeleton crews of eleven to fifteen. "Manning levels have been reduced so much, and workloads have been increased so much, that people struggle to do their jobs as it is," he told me. "One of the biggest problems we have at sea today is simply fatigue."

Linington was adamant that early detection is the single best method of deterring pirate attacks. "Talk to any naval officer," he said, "and they will all tell you the same thing: the ships that are most successful at resisting attacks are the ones who spot the pirates coming early . . . Often if the pirates recognize that they've been detected early on, and they see the ship taking evasive action, they will not even bother to attack. And the key to early detection, we believe, is having enough people on board the ship. All the best management practices recommend an increase in watches and patrols, but the shipping companies don't add any additional crew members to carry out those duties."

The second successful measure is a tactic that I call the "turtle defence," which involves the crew barricading themselves in a secure area of the vessel—typically the engine room—in the event that pirates manage to get on board. With foreign warships bearing down on their position, pirate boarding groups often have only a short window to seize control of the ship (and more importantly, the crew). With the crew safely out of the line of fire, international forces would be free to retake the vessel with less risk of civilian casualties. Deprived of access to their human shields, most pirates would flee back to their skiffs before the cavalry arrives.

The turtle defence has been successful on multiple occasions. In February 2010 the Danish warship *Absalon* became the first vessel to stop a hijacking once it was already in progress, its appearance causing such a panic in one automatic-weapon-wielding pirate on the deck of the MV *Ariella* (an Antigua and Barbuda–flagged cargo ship) that he jumped into the sea. A more noteworthy incident occurred two months later, when Dutch marines abseiled onto the German cargo ship *Taipan* and arrested ten pirates, whom they subsequently extradited to Germany to face trial.

The turtle defence, according to International Maritime Bureau manager Cyrus Mody, is not without its drawbacks. First, the threatened vessel must be in prior contact with a warship with the resources to launch a commando assault—a capability that many in the international fleet do not possess. "If a crew in the middle of the Indian Ocean broadcasts that they're going into lockdown," Mody told me, "and there is no naval asset in a hundred-mile-or-so radius—which is basically VHF [high-frequency radio] range—then no one's going to hear them."

Second, if help does not arrive soon, the pirates may try their hand at cracking the safe room using the only tools they have available. "There was an incident some time back in which there was a crew in lockdown and the pirates started firing, and a couple of bullets went through the bulkhead and injured a few crew members," said Mody. "That is one scenario; the other scenario is that the shooting causes a fire to break out. What happens then? There has to be an escape route for the crew."

In spite of these potential risks, the turtle method has been effective even when a warship was not in the immediate vicinity. In a May 2010 incident, the Russian destroyer *Marshal Shaposhnikov* was over twelve hours away from the oil tanker *Moscow University* when her crew went into lockdown. For unknown reasons, the pirates remained aboard for an entire day as the *Shaposhnikov* bore down on their position, then engaged the Russian special forces in a suicidal shootout while the crew was still safely out of harm's way. Whether stubborn or reckless, the pirates paid for their error in judgment; after killing one pirate during the rescue operation, the Russian commandos probably summarily executed the remaining hijackers, later concocting a story that they had perished at sea.[10]

* * *

With \$1–\$1.5 billion per year being spent to clamp down on a piracy "industry" worth not more than \$90 million, it is hard to argue that the international naval armada has provided a good return on investment. When hijackings fail (60–70 per cent of the time), it is usually because of early detection, increased speed, and evasive measures—not because of warships or navy helicopters saving the day. In 2009, *fewer than one in six* unsuccessful pirate attacks were stopped by the direct intervention of coalition forces, with only two of these rescues occurring in the Indian Ocean (out of fifty-three failed attacks).[11] All told, in 2009 the coalition probably saved the world something in the range of $80–$100 million in potential ransoms—less than one-tenth its operating budget.[12]

But to judge the effectiveness of the naval forces based solely on the number of attacks prevented is not entirely fair, as the statistics do not reflect the coalition's multifaceted deterrent effect. First, the forces indirectly prevent attacks (for instance, pirates breaking off pursuit because they fear a response from a warship). Second, they reduce the overall number of attacks by maintaining the Gulf of Aden safety corridor, by interdicting pirate groups before they have a chance to carry out hijackings, or by simply discouraging potential pirate recruits from taking up the trade in the first place. But the failure of the coalition forces to react to actual attacks in progress is disappointing. Though their numbers have mounted steadily since 2008, the warships are still spread far too thin—particularly in the vast Indian Ocean—to consistently respond in a timely manner.

Despite hundreds of millions of dollars in annual net operating losses, the international fleet is unlikely to sail away anytime soon. The naval presence is a classic exercise in defence theatre; for political and humanitarian reasons, home governments must demonstrate that they are making an effort to protect their own nationals, as well as to safeguard international commerce. The optics, in short, are more important than the results. Meanwhile, the vast majority of masters and crews charting the boundless reaches of the Indian Ocean will remain on their own, with only their own vigilance and courage to save them from becoming the latest victims of the Somali pirates.

10

The Law of the Sea

TO DATE, CAPTURING PIRATES HAS PROVED FAR EASIER THAN deciding what to do with them afterwards. The laws of foreign nations have treated Somali pirates as another group of "boat people," that is to say, illegal migrants. The largely Western countries that patrol the Gulf of Aden and the Indian Ocean understandably desire to avoid the costs associated with transporting captured offenders and processing them in domestic courts. In some nations, such as the United Kingdom, arrested pirates would even be within their rights to claim asylum (the UK Foreign Office has voiced concerns that the pirates may face the Islamic punishments of beheading or amputation should they be returned to Somalia).[1] Although in rare instances national pride has prevailed over fiscal sense—Boyah's six unfortunate compatriots, for instance, as well as five pirates turned over to Dutch courts by the Danish navy in January 2009—prosecuting pirates through Western institutions is not a feasible long-term solution.

So labyrinthine is the legal maze that many foreign navies have opted simply to release suspects after confiscating their weapons and destroying their ships, thereby drawing attacks from media outlets. Such criticism is not entirely fair. Pirates operating out of a failed state are unprecedented in modern times, and the existing international legal machinery is simply not suited to handle them.

International law, fortunately, is continually being reinvented as needs dictate, and in no case is this fact better demonstrated than in the legal dilemma posed by the Somali pirates.

* * *

Since ancient Rome, pirates have been labelled as *hostis humani generis*—"enemies of all mankind"—and piracy has been considered a crime of universal jurisdiction, giving states the right to arrest and prosecute suspected offenders outside national boundaries, such as the high seas. Two principal instruments of modern international law define the procedures for exercising this jurisdiction: the 1982 United Nations Convention on the Law of the Sea (UNCLOS) and the 1988 Convention for the Suppression of Unlawful Acts against the Safety of Maritime Navigation (SUA Convention). Of the two, the SUA Convention is considered to be the more robust, as it contains a broader definition of piracy and includes explicit instructions for extraditions amongst its signatories. In practice, this permits the master of a ship to deliver captured pirates to another state party, thereby theoretically allowing nearby acceding countries like Kenya, Djibouti, Yemen, and Tanzania to prosecute offenders.

However, the SUA Convention is unsuited to the Somali pirate situation for two reasons. First, the terms of the convention permit only the arresting state party—or another state with a demonstrable interest in the offence (for example, if its own citizens are the victims)—to assume jurisdiction over the accused. As a result, the home government of a given warship should usually be stuck with the responsibility of prosecuting. In theory, this obstacle could be overcome through the use of "shipriders," officials from a third state brought on board a foreign warship in order to conduct the arrest and subsequent judicial process under the laws of their own country. This arrangement, which would legally authorize neighbouring countries (such as Kenya) to step in as the prosecuting authority, has yet to be put into practice.

Second, as an international treaty the SUA Convention applies only to the high seas and has no effect in the territorial waters of a state, which extend twelve nautical miles from its base shoreline.[2] Somalia has no functioning government to administer justice in its seas, but the state remains a legal entity, and its phantom rights persist; by entering Somali waters, foreign navies are technically in breach of international law. In an effort to address this problem, in June 2008 the UN Security Council passed Resolution 1816, a stop-gap attempt to use the moral stature of the United Nations to patch the obvious cracks in the existing legal structure. The resolution decreed that states authorized by Somalia's figurehead Transitional Federal Government (TFG)—a collection of former warlords and self-styled moderate Islamists controlling a few checkpoints in Mog-adishu—would be allowed, for a period of six months, to enter the territorial waters of Somalia and use "all necessary means" to repress acts of piracy and armed robbery at sea.[3] The token permission of the TFG was allegedly granted through a letter delivered to the Security Council by the UN permanent representative to Somalia, Ahmedou Ould-Abdullah, though this mysterious document was never made public.[4] In reality, Resolution 1816 merely legitimized the status quo, wherein foreign navies routinely violated Somali waters when neces-sity demanded (on occasion, states have sought the TFG's explicit permission, as when French forces pursued Boyah's gang inland fol-lowing the Le Ponant hijacking). Six months later, Resolution 1851 went as far as to authorize the use of ground forces on Somali soil; not surprisingly, no country has volunteered its troops.

In a world without failed states, any Somali caught in the act of piracy—whether in international or Somali national waters—would be handed over to the government of Somalia for prosecution. As noted in earlier chapters, many piracy suspects are turned over to the government of Puntland, and occasionally that of Somaliland. Yet, for just cause, international actors doubt the will and capacity of these makeshift governments to seriously prosecute the offend-ers; furthermore, there is the problem of what to do with suspects originating from southern Somalia, who would undoubtedly go free if returned home.

Since late 2008, the long-term solution has been, in effect, to "rent out" the Kenyan justice system in order to process the backlog of pirate detainees captured by Western warships. In December 2008, Kenya signed a memorandum of understanding (MOU) with the United Kingdom to receive and prosecute pirate suspects apprehended on the high seas, and it entered into a similar agreement with the European Union in March.[5] In the same month, American forces handed over seven pirate suspects to the Kenyan authorities, inaugurating a bilateral pact signed two months earlier.[6] In essence, these agreements amounted to extradition treaties where there existed no legal reason why the capturing states could not prosecute offenders in their own court systems.

With one of the most overcrowded prison systems in the world and institutional problems ranging from underpaid personnel and staff attrition to a lack of cooperation between the police and prosecutors, Kenya's legal system may seem a strange choice to assume the complicated burden posed by Somali piracy.[7] However, following the refusal of Mauritius to lend its soil to an EU-funded prison, as well as the hostility of Somalia's other neighbours to the concept of local trials, Kenya, in the words of E. J. Hogendoorn, the International Crisis Group's Horn of Africa director, was "the last country standing."[8] Nonetheless, Kenyan minister of foreign affairs Moses Wetangula made it clear in a statement that the MOU was not "an open door for dumping pirates onto Kenya [sic] soil because it will not be acceptable."[9]

The problem was that it was not clear whether Kenyan law allowed the country's courts to try non-nationals for crimes committed extraterritorially, and pirates' attorneys were quick to argue that it did not. A test case had occurred in 2006, when ten suspected pirates were arrested by the US Navy three hundred kilometres off the coast of Somalia and turned over to Kenyan authorities. In the country's first piracy trial, a Mombasa court convicted the accused of hijacking the Indian trading dhow *Safina Al Bisaraat* on the high seas, and each was sentenced to seven years in prison. Subsequent to this ruling, the pirates' defence lawyer filed an appeal, which was ultimately rejected, arguing that Kenyan courts had no jurisdiction over crimes committed by non-nationals on the high seas.[10]

In the maximum security prison at Naivasha, a booming town on the very edge of Kenya's Rift Valley, I managed to track down four of the ten men convicted in the *Al Bisaraat* incident. Shackled in irons and dressed in black-and-white striped jumpsuits reminiscent of an old convict movie, they shuffled in silently and took their seats across the wooden table in front of me. Hassan, an abrasive early-thirtysomething with yellowing teeth, sat directly opposite me, assuming the role of the group's mouthpiece; the other three stared despondently at their handcuffs, occasionally rousing themselves to shout an answer in Hassan's direction. Though their broken English testified to the language lessons they had been receiving at the prison school, a Somali-speaking Kenyan inmate acted as our interpreter. The meeting took place in the officer's lounge, and it quickly became clear that Naivasha's governors had no intention of relinquishing their territory; the prison's entire senior staff sat in a row over my left shoulder, overseeing the meeting like diligent chaperones.

The hijacking of the *Al Bisaraat* was one of the best-documented early cases of a pirate band seizing a dhow to use as a mothership. On January 16, 2006, two days after loading its cargo at the southern port of Kismaayo, the *Al Bisaraat* was attacked by three small speedboats carrying the ten hijackers, members of Afweyne's pioneering Harardheere-based pirate group, the Somali Marines.

After assuming control of the vessel, the pirate leader ordered the crew of the *Al Bisaraat* to take the group's attack skiffs in tow and set a course for the open sea, towards the international shipping lanes. For the next three days, the pirates took the *Al Bisaraat* and her crew on a hunting spree, unsuccessfully attempting to hijack a container ship and a tanker, and registering a direct rocket-propelled grenade (RPG) hit to the bridge of one of their fleeing victims in the process. The gang's third target, the Bahamian bulk carrier MV *Delta Ranger,* proved to be their downfall; responding to the *Ranger*'s report to the International Maritime Bureau, the destroyer USS *Winston Churchill* was dispatched to the area. After shadowing the pirates with one of its attack helicopters, the *Churchill* twice fired warning shots at the *Al Bisaraat,* following its failure to respond to hails. A three-hour standoff ensued, at the end of which the hijackers panicked and initiated standard pirate operating procedure when faced with superior force: some threw their weapons overboard, while others, strangely, decided to hide them on the ship itself. Shortly afterwards, US naval personnel boarded the *Al Bisaraat* and arrested the pirates.

Given that the men sitting before me had been caught aboard a foreign vessel, using her crew as the modern equivalents of galley slaves, the standard protestations of innocence rang remarkably hollow. "We were fishermen," said Hassan. "And we were fishing when we were captured. But the Americans destroyed all the evidence: our boats and our nets."

After investigating them as possible Al Qaeda agents, said Hassan, the Americans turned them over to Kenyan authorities, who charged them with piracy. He said they had been railroaded by a court system of which they were entirely ignorant: "We were in the dark. We weren't even given a lawyer." Although the public record shows they had an attorney who not only defended them against the charges but launched an appeal on their behalf, Hassan painted himself and his co-accused as the victims of a show trial. "There was no evidence brought against us," said Hassan. "And no witnesses, either." The BBC's account of the trial tells a different tale: not only did members of the *Al Bisaraat*'s Indian crew testify before the court, they claimed that they had been "tortured" by the defendants.[11] For his part, Hassan remained steadfastly unconvinced. "We were not proved guilty beyond a reasonable doubt," he said.

Hassan insisted that he and his co-defendants should have been tried in their homeland, where they would have been able to call defence witnesses. When I related to him the horrors of Bossaso prison, the hundreds of ragged prisoners crammed into urine-soaked cages, many serving out life sentences for piracy, he was unfazed. "In Somalia, at least we would have gotten a fair trial," he replied. Just as likely, they would have been let go—and Hassan knew it.

Hassan and his colleagues had served more than three years of a seven-year sentence, and expected to see another full season at Naivasha prior to their early release at the beginning of 2012. They had no intention of returning to Somalia following their parole. "What we want is to be granted refugee status, or residency permits," said Hassan. "Whatever we need to stay in Kenya." Many Somalis would undoubtedly judge Kenyan citizenship a far better prize than the most overloaded oil tanker; in an ironic twist, their utter ineptitude as pirates may have inadvertently granted Hassan and company a way out of their dead-end career. As for their future employment plans, Hassan shrugged matter-of-factly. "We're Somalis, we'll be businessmen," he said. "All we need is a little capital to start off with."

As if deciding to end the interview with this pronouncement, Hassan abruptly cut off my next question. "We have nothing more to discuss," he said, pushing himself away from the table. But as I rose to leave, he stopped me with a parting comment. "I hope that by the time we get out of here, piracy in Somalia has stopped," he said. "Since being put in jail, I've come to understand that it's a really bad thing." It was probably the closest thing to an admission of guilt that anyone was ever going to get out of Hassan.

* * *

Although his appeal was rejected, Hassan's lawyer raised an interesting legal challenge. At the time, the Kenyan penal code contained no explicit provisions specifying how to treat suspects captured on the high seas; in essence, Kenya had never implemented its obligations under UNCLOS and the SUA Convention in its domestic legal system.

This all changed in February 2009, when the Kenyan parliament passed the Merchant Shipping Act. Adopting the UNCLOS definition of piracy, the legislation explicitly assumed jurisdiction over piracy offences regardless of "whether the ship . . . is in Kenya or elsewhere," whether the offences were "committed in Kenya or elsewhere," and irrespective of the nationality of the person committing the act.[12] By unilaterally extending its extraterritorial jurisdiction over non-nationals, argues Kenyan legal scholar James Gathii, the Kenyan government "exceed[ed] the bases for jurisdiction in the SUA Convention."[13] It was precisely to avoid this kind of conflict that the UN had advocated the shiprider option; with Kenyan law enforcement representatives posted on foreign warships to arrest pirate suspects at the source, Kenya's jurisdiction over them would not be in question.

Following the Kenyan parliament's elimination of the legal hurdles, the pirates have come sweeping off the Indian Ocean like the monsoon winds. After being handed over to Kenyan authorities they are transferred to Mombasa's colonial-era Shimo La Tewa prison, an institution whose living environment was condemned in 1995 by local journalist Mutonya Njunguna as "belonging to a horror film," with thirty-five hundred inmates forced to sleep on the floor in sweltering and unhygienic conditions.[14] Perhaps the criticism had an effect, because Shimo is now touted by the Kenyan prison service as one of the most progressive and modern prisons in the country.

As of my visit, 107 suspected pirates were awaiting trial in Shimo, and the number is certain to increase faster than Kenya's beleaguered legal system can process their cases. Shimo's indefatigable warden, Wanini Kireri, embraced the challenge despite her limited resources. Built for a thousand-prisoner capacity, her maximum-security facility was crammed with twice that number, and the added responsibility of becoming the world's foremost pirate warden came as a shock.

"I wake up one evening and they tell me that I have fifty pirates to take care of," she said from across her office desk. "I didn't know what to do. There were security issues, questions on how to treat them—whether we should mix them with the Kenyan prisoners, how we were going to communicate with them, and so on. We didn't know how to handle them at first. There was a lot of talk from different quarters, about whether Kenya should really be taking the Somalis, if our prison conditions were good enough for them," she added.

The culture shock, said Kireri, went both ways. "At first, we saw a lot of anger from [the Somalis]," she said. "They said, 'We've done nothing to wrong the Kenyans, so why are we here?'" Many, according to Kireri, had wished to face trial in the home countries of the ships that captured them—a demand entirely justified under the SUA Convention. "By six months, they had settled in," she said. In the end, Kireri decided to give the pirates their own prison block, with a few Kenyans mixed in to fill up the remaining space. Despite their cultural differences, conflicts with the Kenyan inmates were rare—though friendly competition abounded.

"They love football," she said. "The pirates have a team, and the Kenyans have a team, and they play against each other." Temporarily discarding the neutrality required of a prison warden, Kireri had no problem letting me know where her loyalties lay. "They can't beat the Kenyans," she said, laughing. "The Kenyans have been playing football for years, while the pirates say that they have been at sea, so they haven't had much time to practice."

Although the Kenyan authorities lacked the ability to notify most of the prisoners' relatives of their situation (or even locate them), the populous Somali community in Kenya ensured that the pirates received visits from their countrymen every weekend, though not always from members of their own families. "Even when there are only one or two people visiting, they'll bring things like soap and clothes for all the Somali prisoners," Kireri said. "I don't know if they're all cousins, or they just behave like they are." Through this close-knit network, she figured, her prisoners were able to send messages that would eventually find their way back to their relatives in Somalia.

Though accommodating her Somali charges had been difficult at times, the extra work had brought its rewards. As partial compensation for the Kenyan government's willingness to serve as a dumping ground for the world's piracy problem, the United Nations Office on Drugs and Crime (UNODC) stepped in with a $12 million EU-funded counter-piracy program aimed at strengthening the country's overburdened justice system.

"The way I look at it, it was a blessing in disguise," said Kireri. "Since I took over in 2006, nothing had been done to improve the conditions here until UNODC came in. Since then, the prisoners have been given blankets and mattresses, our kitchen has been upgraded, the prison has been painted, and there have been improvements to the water and sewage systems. Before, I didn't even have a computer," she said, pointing to her glossy new desktop monitor and laughing. "This came with the program." Her prison was not the only beneficiary of the UNODC's largesse, she said; its mandate included improvements to the entire justice system, including the police and courts.

Kireri admitted that she enjoyed some other perks that had come with the media spotlight, including the chance to give a personal tour to Hollywood celebrity Nicolas Cage, who had visited the prison the previous month, ostensibly to draw attention to the problem of Somali piracy. "He was so nice, and such a humble man," she said. "He was very impressed with our prison." Cage's five-minute meet-and-greet with the remanded pirates, media cameras in tow, had played out in the familiar pattern. "They told him they were fishermen," said Kireri, pausing to recollect. "Yes, that was their story."

* * *

If there was a man likely to believe these tales of innocence, it was pirate defender Oruko Nyawinda, a suavely attired Kenyan attorney currently representing sixteen of Shimo La Tewa's hapless denizens. Perched behind the desk in his deserted office in downtown Mombasa, two days before Christmas, Nyawinda launched into an impassioned defence of his clients worthy of a crowded courtroom. "Our constitution is very clear," he declared. "If a person is charged with a bailable offence, that person must be given bail and bond." As piracy is a bailable offence in Kenya, he said, there was no reason that he should have to visit his clients behind bars. "They are actually serving a sentence while being tried," he said. "To me, denying them bail is an abuse of their human rights."

Their right to a state-appointed counsel had also been violated, according to Nyawinda. Despite EU funding, the windfall from the UNODC program had all blown in one direction, he said: towards the prosecutors, the prisons, and the attorney general's office. He and his fellow defence lawyers were receiving payment neither from the state nor from UNODC, and Nyawinda had been forced to lean on his destitute clients to raise funds. "They told me that to get money they had to send word home for goats and sheep to be sold," he said. "We had to talk to the Red Cross, who sent their people into Somalia and finally tracked down some of their parents. In the end, I received a small payment."

This service was not performed out of a concern for Nyawinda's bank balance. The International Committee of the Red Cross had been saddled with the thankless task of tracking down the relatives of *every* pirate in Kenyan custody—even, as was often the case, when the pirates themselves were unable to point out their homes on a map.

In addition to the cost of the pirates' defence, said Nyawinda, the EU had promised to fund new courts and new prisons to handle the pirate influx, none of which had materialized. And he said the EU had failed to take into account a plethora of future costs: "Not every suspected pirate brought here is guilty, so we can expect some of them to be acquitted and set free. The question is, who will finance their going home? Who will finance their temporary stay before they go home? Or do we give them homes here?"

But whether the majority of suspects were guilty or innocent was beside the point, Nyawinda argued. Piracy, he said, had become a full-time criminal enterprise—but instead of targeting the heads of the cartel, the police were going after the street dealers. "You hear every day about the millions being paid out [as ransoms]," he said. "The question is, are these wretched ones being brought to court the ones receiving the millions? They are arresting the workers, the employees. If the international community were serious, they would go after the pirate lords, the ones financing the activities. Otherwise, we'll just continue trying these poor guys, and the trials will go on and on." Unfortunately for these "pirate employees," they were the only ones the international naval forces could get their hands on; short of an international invasion of Somalia, Nyawinda's "pirate lords" would remain safely beyond the reach of justice.

Nyawinda's clients had not been so lucky. One group of his defendants claimed to have been migrant workers in transit from Yemen to Somalia when they were accosted by an Italian warship and taken into custody. "There was a video-conferencing trial on the ship broadcast from a courtroom in Italy," said Nyawinda. "There was allegedly a lawyer representing my clients, whom they did not know." With barely a pause for breath, he fired off an accusatory barrage: "If the trial began on this ship, why not complete it in Italy? Why is Italy not competent to try them?" Any conscientious reader of the SUA Convention would be hard pressed to answer these questions.

Given the existing tensions between native Kenyans and the Somali community in the country, Nyawinda also worried that these pirate trials could strain relations even further. "Imagine an innocent Somali, arrested as a pirate. He spends two years on trial, stuck in our prison system, eating that food, sleeping in those conditions," he said. "He's not being offered a fair trial, his family is not there to support him, and his advocate is not being paid. What's the difference between that and Guantanamo Bay?" As with Guantanamo, Nyawinda feared a backlash over the potential perception of injustice. "We are going to create very bitter persons," he lamented.

His confidence in the judicial procedure was not bolstered by the quality of evidence brought against his clients, which Nyawinda claimed had consisted of nothing more than footage of a fleeing skiff and a single loaded gun; there had also been an alleged RPG launcher that, he scoffed, "no photograph or video camera could capture." It was not only the evidentiary support that Nyawinda found suspect, however, but the legal process itself. "Kenya didn't arrest [the alleged pirates], they were just brought here by people who purportedly found them in the act of piracy," he said. "People who give their evidence and run away."

Not surprisingly, Nyawinda already had a remedy in mind. "This is my proposal: create a proper group of international investigators to deal with any arrested pirate," he explained. "The moment so-called pirates are arrested, this group should rush to the scene and take charge. Identify the alleged pirates and find out where they come from; then notify their relatives. Inform the detainees within twenty-four hours which country is going to charge them, and then take them there. The way it is now, the person testifying in court as the investigator is a Kenyan police officer. They were not there during the arrest, and they have never visited the scene of the crime."

The solution, in Nyawinda's view, was for the international community to fund specialized tribunals tasked solely with processing suspected pirates. "These people are a special group, and should be treated in a special way," he said. "They shouldn't be mixed up with other cases, and their trials should take no more than a week to one month."

If Nyawinda's vision had a fault, it lay with its naive optimism, not its core prescriptions. With international tribunals established to resolve issues ranging from war crimes to bilateral trade disputes, it is inexplicable that an issue of such obvious global dimensions as high seas piracy should have been relegated to Kenyan courts.

168 DEADLY WATERS

Lacking even a home government to defend their rights, Somali detainees are amongst those most in need of international protection—a view that Nyawinda echoed in his closing arguments. "It is them against the entire international community," he implored. "No one is standing by them."

* * *

Like a tattered quilt that has been patched too many times, the international legal framework governing piracy is worn and inadequate, with legislative stitching like Resolution 1816 and the Merchant Shipping Act barely keeping it from coming apart at the seams. Still, given an array of imperfect solutions, the "dumping ground" option may be the best choice for the present. For all the flaws of its legal system, Kenya is a relatively stable, democratic country. It possesses a large and vibrant Somali community that can lend its support to detainees during the trial process, provide links to their families, and aid in their possible integration into Kenyan society following their release.

In September 2010, hopes for a permanent Kenyan solution were dealt a setback. After months-long wrangling over what the Kenyan government deemed to be unsatisfactory financial assistance from the international community, Kenya barred its prison doors to future waves of captured pirates. Two months later, a senior Kenyan judge issued a controversial ruling ordering the release of the approximately sixty suspected pirates brought into custody prior to the passage of the Merchant Shipping Act.

Spurred by Kenya's increasing unreliability as a partner, Western countries have since begun to take justice into their own hands. In the first trial of its kind in almost two centuries, on November 29, 2010, a Virginia judge sentenced one pirate to thirty years for his involvement in a (clearly confused) assault on a US warship; five of his colleagues will face possible life imprisonment when they are sentenced in March. At around the same time, Germany announced that it was to try ten pirates captured in an attack on the German cargo vessel MV *Taipan,* and the following month both Spain and Belgium revealed their intentions to follow suit. In December, the Netherlands became the first European country to prosecute pirates who had not been involved in an attack on its own nationals, agreeing to try five Somalis captured by the HNLMS *Amsterdam* following an attack on a South African yacht. In January 2011, South Korea joined the fray; following a commando raid on the commandeered oil supertanker MV *Samho Jewelry*—the first of its kind on a vessel whose crew had not retreated to a secure area—the Koreans flew five surviving pirates back to Seoul, where they were charged with attempted murder (soon after, Somali pirates began appearing as characters on Korean television shows). At present, these à la carte prosecutions seem more piecemeal reactions to specific incidents, rather than a true indication of the "global diversification" of pirate justice. Whether a consistent alternative to the Kenyan solution will be necessary will depend on the outcome of its government's ongoing feud with the international community.

With all these prosecutions, there is the danger that the defendants' rights surrounding issues like family access, evidentiary rules, and reintegration following acquittal or release may not be adequately protected. While Nyawinda's Guantanamo Bay parallels may be alarmist or extreme, a similar kind of legal purgatory could be created by current practices. James Gathii, for instance, warns that the "huge militarization of combating piracy is likely to create large numbers of suspected pirates being held in undisclosed locations inconsistently with their rights to process under international law."[15] The creation of international tribunals composed of representatives from a cross-section of countries—Somalia included—would go a long way towards ensuring that suspected pirates receive a fair trial.[16] Some of them, after all, may just have been fishing.

11

Into the Pirates' Lair

THERE WAS A TIME WHEN THE PIRATES' OFT-INVOKED FISHING defence was more than mere self-exculpating propaganda. The defence originated in Eyl, among the fishermen-pirate pioneers of the 1990s, born out of just indignation over the abuses of foreign fishing vessels. Since then, what was once a justification has become a rationalization. Successive waves of pirates, attuned to the international media sympathy the fishing story generates, continue to rail about the plunder of Somalia's waters, while pushing over 1,500 kilometres into the Indian Ocean in search of ever-increasing ransoms.

In the middle of June 2009, halfway through my second visit to Puntland, I finally found my way to where it had all begun: the infamous "pirate haven" of Eyl, the small fishing village that had launched a new breed of pirate into the modern world. We left Garowe at quarter past six in the morning, the sun hanging distorted and brilliant on the horizon. Colonel Omar, dressed in jungle combat fatigues, turned to me and locked my eyes in a menacing stare. "I am in command during this trip," he said. "You take orders from me. Understand?" I nodded.

Our convoy consisted of two Land Cruisers, the first holding me, the two Omars, and Mahamoud, our driver. The second contained the cavalry: Said and Abdirashid (my two Special Police Unit guards) and three Puntland government soldiers (including Ombaali, the former pirate), led by a grizzled veteran named Yusuf, whose fingers on one hand had been partially shot off. A few kilometres outside of Garowe we stopped at a squalid roadside restaurant to stock up on water bottles and quickly eat a dubious breakfast of *sukaar,* a goat stew that I managed to hold down for only a few hours on the road.

After about a quarter hour of speeding along the deserted high-way, our driver abruptly slowed and struck off-road, creeping down the steep embankment. I was uncertain what reference point on the uniform landscape had identified the turnoff, but after a few min-utes across open terrain we joined the path running eastward to Eyl. There was nothing but empty land ahead and empty sky above, and a twin set of sandy tire tracks leading into the Wild West.

The constant passage of pirate vehicles over the last few years had worn multiple tracks into the ground that continually diverged from the main path, weaving around obstacles before rejoining it several hundred paces down the road. In spite of the frequent traf-fic, the behaviour of the local herd animals resembled that of wild-life on a game reserve. Herds of grazing sheep and goats, caught on their haunches with hooves tangled in the upper reaches of bushes, careened wildly into the bush as we passed. Even the camels were more vigilant, watching us from a distance with wary eyes, while their solitary human guardians, staffs in hand, waved friendly greet-ings. Occasionally the igloo-shaped dome of a *mudul,* the traditional bush hut of the Somali nomad, poked through the shrubbery.

Our two vehicles descended into valleys and mounted plateaus, the vegetation changing as quickly as the terrain. We passed under the outspread canopies of thick-trunked trees hanging over the desiccated beds of dry rivers, then onto powdery red sand cutting through a virtual desert of ground-hugging shrubs and acacia trees, our four-wheel drives fishtailing through every high-speed turn.

We stopped for lunch in Hasballe, a bush town situated at roughly the halfway point of our journey. The corridor running from Garowe to Eyl is almost exclusively populated by the Isse Mahamoud, and Hasballe is home to Nugaal region's clan chief, or *islaan*. He had recently inherited this title from his father, who was rumoured to have lived over a hundred years and had been so influential that his standing threat to curse errant hunters had singlehandedly rescued the threatened local population of dik-diks from extinction. It is said that two men who had insulted his name were swallowed up by the earth.

We were ushered into an amalgam of a *mudul* and a pavilion, constructed around a single living tree. It was covered with the traditional woven grass mats of the Somali nomads and lined with aluminum panels onto which rudimentary algebraic equations had been scratched. The gathering quickly turned into a family reunion, friends and relatives shaking hands and hugging over plates of spaghetti and cups of *shah*. My entire party was of the same sub-clan as the inhabitants of Hasballe, which meant that virtually everyone present was at least second or third cousins.

Colonel Omar introduced me to the townspeople as "the son of Levish," a local man renowned for his light skin. The Colonel had taught me to recognize the Somali question "Which clan are you?" and to respond with Reer Jarafle, the name of his own sub-clan, five levels deep on the Somali clan tree. I performed the routine repeatedly, like a jester, to great acclaim; it invariably provoked hearty peals of laughter from the assembled crowd. So amused was he by his joke that from time to time the Colonel would elbow me, winking and exclaiming, "Eh, Levish? What clan do you belong to?"

As we were preparing to leave Hasballe, an old man approached the car window. "Please don't kill the pirates," he pleaded. "You need to give them jobs."

From the townspeople in Hasballe, we had learned that the *islaan* was currently residing in his bush hut, some distance down the road. My interpreter Omar made it clear that passing by without stopping was not an option. "It would be the ultimate show of disrespect," he said.

Three-quarters of an hour later we turned off the road and crossed a lush plain of green grass, towards a *mudul* no different in size from the others I had seen along the road, amidst a herd of grazing camels. One of the *islaan*'s wives informed us that he was napping and would be out shortly. Wiping the sleep from his eyes, the *islaan* soon emerged dressed in the simple nomad's attire of a shawl and *ma'awis* and exchanged warm greetings with the two Omars, as I stood awkwardly by. Just when I was starting to think that he had not noticed my presence, the *islaan* turned to me with an expectant glance.

"Do you have anything to say to him?" Omar asked me.

For the first time in my life, I found myself completely tongue-tied, frozen under the spell of pomp that Omar had lent to the meeting.

Mercifully, Omar stepped in. "He thanks you for welcoming him to the homeland of the Isse Mahamoud," he said, relaying my phantom message.

"I thank you for coming to visit us," the *islaan* replied in Somali. "Foreigners are always welcome here." Omar stood between the two of us, hands solemnly folded in front of him as he translated. I requested to take a photo with him, but the *islaan* demurred.

"I will gladly take a photo with you, but not here. Wait until I am in Garowe, when I'm dressed properly."

The last stretch of the journey took us across a sparse plateau where the only sign of human presence was a curious sequence of pipes punctuating the road every few kilometres, from which arrow-straight dirt trails jutted at right angles into the distance—the long-abandoned boreholes and service roads set up during Conoco's oil exploration in the 1980s, before the company declared *force majeure* and departed Somalia in the wake of the civil war. Colonel Omar pointed out a landing strip, now little more than open bushland, which British forces had used to transport supplies during a nine-teenth-century siege of Eyl. From this escarpment, said the Colonel, colonialist forces had unleashed their bombardments on the town below. As if in silent testament to his statement, we passed by a crumbling graveyard containing the remains of Somalis killed during the anti-colonial struggle.

It was three o'clock in the afternoon when we finally reached the outskirts of Eyl. It had taken us seven hours to cross 220 kilometres.

* * *

The town of Eyl is a historic place. Long before it became known to the world in 2008 as the infamous "pirate haven," it had served as a base for an equally notorious character, anti-colonial freedom fighter Muhammad Abdullah Hassan, nicknamed the "Mad Mullah" by his British adversaries. A warrior-poet in the purest sense, the beauty of Hassan's verses attracted a diverse following to his Dervish movement, which for twenty years successfully held off British colonial expansion into the Somali interior (notwithstanding their common association with dancing and whirling, the Dervishes also knew how to fight). Despite considerable brutality towards his own people, Hassan remains a nationalist hero to Somalis and a point of pride for the people of Eyl. His residence-cum-fortress still stands on a summit overlooking the town, built with camel milk mixed into the mortar in order to render it invulnerable to attack. Hassan reputedly severed the hands of the structure's Yemeni architect after its completion, to ensure that it would be the last he ever built. The architect's descendants, it is said, still live in Eyl.

Today, Eyl can boast of another prominent son, President Abdirahman Farole, who was born and grew up in the town. Along with Garowe, Eyl is one of the principal strongholds of President Farole's Isse Mahamoud sub-clan, a fact that made the area a virtual no-go zone for the previous Osman Mahamoud–dominated administration and thereby allowed the town to flourish as an autonomous base of pirate operations.

Eyl is actually two distinct towns separated by several kilometres. The first, Eyl Dawad, meaning "lookout," is the seat of local government. By far the more populous of the two settlements, Dawad contains roughly ten thousand people, living in a collection of box-like buildings grafted onto the sloping wall of a yawning gorge carved by the Nugaal River. Halfway up the slope a natural spring bubbles forth, creating a localized jungle of towering trees along the course of a canal running down to the riverbed below.

Moving quickly through Dawad, we proceeded along a craggy path hugging the northern wall of the defile, a track whose name in English translates as "rocks, wait until I pass before you fall." At rare intervals the dirt and rubble gave way to ten-metre stretches of concrete, the beginnings of some abortive NGO project to pave the entire roadway. It was the onset of Puntland's second dry season, the *hagaa*, and much of the river had dried to solitary pools of water, but a verdant belt of vegetation along the bank still marked its course. A single goat was drinking from one of these oases, not even bothering to look up as we passed.

If one parallel could be drawn between the pirates of Puntland and those of Western storybooks, it is the tales of buried booty. Omar pointed to the opposite side of the gorge, high above us. "The townspeople say that there is pirate money hidden in those hills," he said.

After a quarter hour crawling up and down this roller coaster of a road, we sighted the Indian Ocean for the first time, a slice of brilliant blue framed by the gorge's gaping mouth. After a final bumpy downhill stretch, we passed under an unmarked, dilapidated arch flanked by an empty guardhouse and into Eyl Badey, or "seaside." Reggae-inspired Somali tunes blasting from our speakers, we sped past houses of thatched branches and grasses, orange tarp fused with the odd piece of cardboard or corrugated metal to provide skeletal support to the walls. Even the whitewashed cement of the more upscale buildings was chipped and faded. Dented oil drums, pieces of refuse, and loose building materials were strewn haphazardly in the streets. A few fishing nets were stretched to dry in the sun.

If Eyl was awash in pirate cash, its inhabitants were certainly hiding it well. As a pirate haven, it was a profound disappointment; conspicuously absent were the opulent mansions, wild parties, and drug-fuelled binges that the international media coverage had led me to expect. The town was a fraction of Dawad's size and seemed even poorer—not much more than a shanty village on the edge of the water. Beyond the village lay an expansive beach of white sand running kilometres in either direction, onto which spilled a small settlement built by refugees from the south, their dwellings little more than pens cobbled together out of driftwood. Lining the edge of the beach for several hundred metres was Eyl's most imposing structure, a Soviet-built fish processing centre now crumbling into disrepair. Five-metre fishing skiffs lay idle in the sand, rendered useless by the overpowering winds of the *hagaa*, while refrigerated trucks that had once transported the day's catch to Garowe and other inland markets were now broken-down heaps ensconced in tarps and cinder blocks, their tires shredded.

For some, however, Eyl's economy was thriving. Floating beyond the surf, in plain sight, was the MV *Victoria*, a German-owned freighter hijacked on May 5 while transporting rice to the Saudi port of Jeddah. The recent onset of the monsoons had heralded the end of "pirate season," and the *Victoria* was the sole remaining hostage vessel of the fleet that had once jammed Eyl's harbour. Another ship was being held a few kilometres down the coast in an inlet known as Illig, or "Tooth"; its jittery hijackers had reportedly moved it there on account of hostility from the local people.

We turned northwards and within two minutes were out of Eyl on a path running along the beach towards a large walled house rising out of the dunes. A vacation home for the Farole family, the compound had also been an abortive experiment in fisheries development; the seaward-most building in the compound was in fact a small-scale seafood processing plant, its breeding tanks and refrigeration units now empty. Before the project could get off the ground, much of its infrastructure had been destroyed by the 2004 Indian Ocean tsunami, a fate also suffered by Eyl's fishing industry as a whole. Since then the compound had been virtually abandoned; the wires that had once led from the generator to the main residence were severed, and a nearby well lay in ruins. Sand deposited by the wind in sweeping dunes had half reclaimed the compound, spilling over the wall and into the courtyard.

* * *

Following a quick late-afternoon nap, I was taken back into town to meet the village elders. As we sipped *shah* around a listing wooden table in the centre of town, Omar introduced me to Abdirizak, a stout man with a crooked smile and yellowing teeth, whose official position was something resembling a town sheriff. Beside him was a lanky man with gold-rimmed glasses, Abdul, another of the town's leading citizens, who I was told spent much of his time combing the hills for diamonds and precious metals. The exotic sweetness of the tea cascading over my tongue, against the backdrop of the setting sun, brought me a feeling of tranquillity I had not experienced in a long while.

"Look around you," Abdirizak said. "We have nothing. Do you even see any two-storey houses? There is no pirate money here; it all goes to Garowe."

"This is not a pirate town," Abdul added. "It is safe and peaceful here; even foreigners, like you, can walk around at midnight with no problems."

"We appreciate that you've come here with so little security," said Abdirizak. "It shows that you trust us, that you respect the people of this town." Though I had not considered a carload of AK-toting soldiers to be "light security," my retinue was apparently meagre compared to the veritable invasion forces marshalled by BBC and Al Jazeera reporters during their recent visits to Eyl.

"We're not criminals. No one here likes the pirates," Abdirizak said, gesturing in the direction of the ocean. "Those two ships are the last ones here, and I think they are very close to being freed. Everyone in Eyl will be happy to see them go."

Hawa Abdi Hersi, a middle-aged woman with a black headscarf and a leathery face, joined us at the table; consistent with the trend of unofficial titles, she was introduced to me as the "spokesman for the women of Eyl." The three spoke eagerly about the problems facing the women of the town, the need for education, and democracy. I listened in silence.

At my request, the two men agreed to convene a town gathering on the following day.

* * *

Back at the guest house, dinner consisted of tuna canned in Las Qoray—one of the few products bearing the exceedingly rare stamp of "Made in Somalia"—and plain spaghetti, which we scooped off a communal platter with our hands. A few of the soldiers had managed to hook up a small generator, which emitted a soothing half buzz, half hum. Daylight was quickly supplanted by the pale hue of two flickering bulbs.

Half a kilometre distant, two generator-powered floodlights illuminating the centre of town were all that saved Eyl from total darkness, while the blackness enveloping the ocean was broken only by the distant lights of the *Victoria*, gently moving back and forth like a floating lantern. As I gazed over the wall of the compound, I spotted the tail lights of a four-wheel drive tracking across the beach, probably delivering the night's ration of khat to a waiting skiff.

* * *

I rose early the next morning to find that a few empty oil containers, fashioned into makeshift wash buckets, had been filled with water from the courtyard well. I emptied a bucket over my head and felt the water begin to melt yesterday's layer of sandy paste off my skin. Grabbing Said and Abdirashid, I exited the compound for a stroll along the deserted beach. The sand was blinding under the early sun; the wind was just awakening, whipping a fresh onslaught of fine grains into the grooves of my camera lens. A few hundred metres away, a fresh cohort of young pirate stevedores had picked up where the night shift had left off; they were loading several fishing skiffs beached near the edge of the surf, outboard motors attached. A lone goat stood tethered to the side of a boat, and a maroon 4x4 was parked on the sand nearby.

Whenever I glanced out to sea, the *Victoria*'s distance from shore appeared to fluctuate, at times so close that I could make out the colour of the deck cranes, other times so far to sea that she was almost lost to the horizon. Whether the ship was adrift and being swept in and out with the tide, or whether it was an optical illusion, I was unable to discern. I was told that the pirates on board had ordered the *Victoria*'s crew to keep the vessel in constant motion, in order to prevent US frogmen or submarines from latching cables onto its hull. The pirates erroneously believed US naval forces had employed these tactics during the *Maersk Alabama* incident to tow the ship's doomed hijackers into sniper range.

In town, Omar, the Colonel, and I ate breakfast in a small lean-to, reclining in bare feet on woven mats. Abdirizak, Eyl's "sheriff," told me that a special meal had been planned in honour of my arrival, a fish caught especially for me late the previous night, when the wind was calm enough for a skiff to manage. A tray containing a single bony fish was brought out, which the four of us proceeded to attack with our *injera* bread. "This is the worst fish," Abdirizak said apologetically. "The good ones all stay away during the *hagaa*. You should come back in December, which is the best time for fishing."

Following our breakfast, I met with the townspeople of Eyl outdoors, on the sprawling veranda of a general store. Seated directly in front of me on plastic lawn chairs were Abdirizak, Abdul, Abdi Hersi, and a new man by the name of Aaul Mohammad, who introduced himself as the head of Eyl's "public relations department." The place of honour was reserved for a withered, silver-haired man said to be the oldest fisherman in the town. For the duration of the meeting, the old man remained placidly rooted to his seat, staring vacantly into space. On the other end of the age spectrum, a large crowd of young men and women formed a ring of spectators around us; their only contribution to the conversation was the intermittent ringing of their mobile phones, as loud as stereo speakers.

Aiming to strike a sympathetic tone, I began with a question about the town's troubles with illegal fishing.

"In 1991, after the government collapsed, ships from all different countries started coming here," said Abdirizak.

"Italians, Taiwanese, Japanese, Koreans, everyone comes here," added Aaul Mohammad. "The trawlers come as close as one mile. Illegal fishing vessels were around here last night, not very far away; we saw their lights. But no one can get close to them, they carry such heavy weapons."

"They use drag nets made of hard metal, and they pull everything off the bottom," added Abdirizak. The result, he said, had been the destruction of the local lobster population. "There used to be a lot, now they're all gone. The trawlers took the rocks off the bottom, and the lobster eggs along with them."

But the lobsters had not been the only victims, Abdi Hersi lamented. "One time, four young men—lobster divers—were caught up in a trawler's drag net. They all drowned. We've lost a lot of boys, about twenty of them. The foreign ships come and run over their small fishing boats. They used to die every day . . . and no one cares about them."

Though small-scale sustenance fishing continued, exports had trickled to a halt.

"We don't even have a market here where we can sell our fish," explained Abdirizak. Referring to the ubiquitous laid-up refrigeration trucks, he continued: "They're all rusted and broken down now. There used to be a lot of business here."

Where were their export markets? "Dubai!" the townspeople enthusiastically exclaimed in unison, where they used to receive a good price for their lobster and shark fins. The 2004 tsunami, they said, had destroyed Eyl's fishing economy, as well as reduced local fish stocks. In the aftermath of the disaster, an immense NGO relief mission had distributed new fishing gear to 105 fishermen, but it was soon destroyed by illegal fishing vessels. This type of hostility had spurred local fishermen to fight back, beginning, if Boyah is to be believed, with his attack on a Korean fishing vessel in 1995. But Eyl's townspeople did not appear ready to take Boyah at his word.

"It was in 1999 that Boyah started attacking ships around Eyl; in 1995 it was a different one—near Garacad," they debated. Each time I had attempted to establish a piracy timeline—whether through Boyah, members of his gang, or the people of Eyl—the dates seemed to change. Only a hatred of the rampant corruption and double-dealing miring the illegal fishing trade united the various accounts I had heard.

"In 1999, we caught an Italian fishing trawler and brought it to court," said Abdirizak. "But a Somali businessman arrived and arranged for its release. There was one Somali stationed on board the ship, who translated for the crew." Indeed, since 1999 many illegal fishing vessels had placed armed Somali guards on their decks, and there was a widespread belief amongst local Somalis that local businessmen in the diaspora were responsible. "Somali businessmen from overseas are organizing it. They call their cousins, some local guys here, and tell them, 'Go on that ship, I'll give you a hundred bucks,'" Abdirizak added.

A voice addressing me in English drew my attention to the periphery of the circle. It belonged to a man by the name of Hussein Hersi, whom I had first met months earlier during my first trip to Puntland, when I had found him sitting by himself on a plastic lawn chair in the middle of Bossaso prison's courtyard. Having spent much of his recent life in self-exile in various cities across North America, Hersi had returned to Puntland some months earlier to visit relatives. His presence in Eyl was no coincidence; I learned later that day that Hersi's cousins were members of the gang responsible for hijacking the *Victoria*.

"Western warships, you know the NATO ships, all the European countries are just here to protect their own fishing ships," he began. "These people are victims. We're seeing a lot of diseases that never used to happen: skin diseases, cancer—Somalis never had that problem." The crowd murmured its assent—yes, yes, cancer, they said.

"One thing we're one hundred percent sure about is that they're dumping a lot of things in the ocean, because every month we find new diseases that we never had before," said Mohammad. "Also, there are a lot of fish and birds dying for no reason all along the coast. It's been getting worse and worse over the last three years."

"Even in Garowe, a lot of people refuse to eat fish from here because they're worried about it being toxic," my interpreter Omar interjected.

These claims were supported by an initial UN assessment mission sent to the Puntland coast in February 2005, which confirmed reports that the tsunami had stirred up tonnes of submerged chemical and nuclear waste, breaking open rusting barrels and washing their contents ashore in northern Somalia. Amongst the local population, the mission had observed far higher than normal rates of ailments consistent with radiation sickness, including respiratory infections, mouth ulcers and bleeding, abdominal haemorrhages and unusual skin infections. Subsequent studies, however, failed to corroborate these findings.[1]

"That's the real problem," Hussein Hersi said. "Fish can be replaced, but twenty years from now these people are going to have a lot of problems. Even if they get millions from piracy, it doesn't pay back what they have lost."

The millions had come recently, though the townspeople could again come to no agreement about when the attacks on commercial vessels began. The numbers flew at me: "'95; no, no, '99," the voices argued. A consensus was reached: by 1999, illegal fishing ships had become too tough to handle, arming themselves with anti-aircraft guns and other heavy weaponry. But it was not until 2007, according to the townspeople, that attacks on commercial shipping began in force.

And was Boyah the leader? A round of laughter rippled through the crowd.

"Yes, yes," many exclaimed in unison, except for Aaul Moham-mad, the sole dissenter: *maya*, no, he said. "Leader, no. Member," he added in English.

"They didn't have a leader at first, but Boyah just naturally took on that role over time," Abdirizak said.

"He's the one who first put the idea in their heads," added Hus-sein Hersi.

In those early days, the pirates had been welcomed in the local community. "They were heroes at that time. We encouraged them. Now it's out of control, and we're not happy with them," said Abdi-rizak. "They drive up all the local prices for everything, especially for food." One *farr*—about half a kilogram—of khat cost twice in Eyl what it did in Garowe.

"Also, it's against our religion. We're too ashamed to support them," said Abdul.

Another reason for the townspeople's recent hostility was that pirate operations had been increasingly taken over by outsiders. "The pirates here now all come from somewhere else," said Mohammad. "They're not allowed to come into the town, or people will get angry. The pirates don't want to study, they just want quick money. People here don't want their children mixing with the pirates, exposed to such bad role models. They want their kids to grow up with good behaviour, to study."

Perhaps they had forgotten, I suggested, about the good example that Boyah had set by giving a portion of his earnings as charity to the local poor. This set off another round of laughter.

"The only person he ever gave charity to was himself," someone said.

"We don't even want Boyah to talk to us," added Abdi Hersi.

"If they had brought money here, you would see it. Take a walk around the town, go into every house if you want," said Abdirizak.

The discussion turned to Boyah's recent coast guard aspirations, and I asked if the people of Eyl believed he was fit for the job. A huge clamour of nos rippled through the crowd.

"But that's not our business. That's up to the government," said Abdirizak.

Was Boyah serious about his desire to reform? I asked.

"Yes, yes, he is serious," came the universal response.

"But we can't give him a job," said Mohammad. "That has to come from the government."

I could not resist asking one final question: What had Boyah been like as a child?

"He was a good boy," said Abdi Hersi, smiling. "He wasn't that well educated, but he was a really good fisherman."

* * *

With my impromptu town meeting accomplished, I decided to turn my attention to another goal: getting on board the *Victoria*. For the past few weeks, I had been shooting footage for CBS News with a small hand-held video camera. No Western journalist had yet been able to get a camera on board a hostage ship, but I intended to try. The difficulty lay in making direct contact with the gang; the pirates, despised by the local community, were lying low. My only potential foot in the door was a pirate who went by the name of "Eighty-nine"—a former friend of Omar's who was holed up on the *Victoria*. But we had no way to get in touch with him.

The pirates may have been keeping a low profile, but their associates were not. Lounging in the courtyard of a whitewashed stucco house, chewing khat in the mid-afternoon heat, were a half-dozen young men dressed in polo shirts, Hussein Hersi among them. These were pirate groupies: friends, cousins, and miscellaneous hangers-on, bumming around Eyl with the sole purpose of begging handouts from the impending ransom money. Their greed was a potential ally in my quest to get on board the *Victoria*.

We returned later in the afternoon to find them rooted to the same spot, lethargically chewing like a herd of pasture animals. I made a simple offer: help me to get on board the ship, and CBS's subsequent news report would put such pressure on the *Victoria's* German owners that they would load the ransom money onto the next available aircraft. My pitch had the desired effect; they immediately roused themselves from their stoned stupor and rushed to their vehicles.

The next hours were filled with fitful anticipation of the decision from pirate command. After another visit by our money-hungry go-betweens, Omar announced the bad news: the gang's Garowe-based leader, a putative clairvoyant known as "Computer," was less than enthusiastic about my proposal.

"He says there's no *way* you're getting on that ship," Omar reported. "They think that you're a CIA spy." Computer would not even consent to allow Ombaali, the ex-pirate, to film the footage. The day's efforts had come to naught, and there was nothing to do but wait for tomorrow to try again.

On the morning of my third and final day in Eyl, I awoke at twenty past five to Colonel Omar, fully dressed in his combat fatigues, obnoxiously snapping his fingers at his cousin in the bed across from me. I had counted on another two hours of sleep, but there was no chance of that; with military discipline, the Colonel had mapped out the day's schedule, and it began now. I sloshed what little water was left in the wash bucket over my face and back, running it through my sand-laced hair. Snatching a rare glance in a mirror, I briefly considered trimming my dishevelled beard.

This early in the morning, the wind was quiet outside, but my soldier escorts were not. Shouting and wildly gesticulating in the direction of the sea, they were trying to draw my attention to a fact that was as plain as the empty water in front of me: the MV *Victoria* was gone. The word was that the ship had weighed anchor late the previous night, as if on one of its routine repositioning manoeuvres. Only on this occasion it hadn't stopped, its lights getting gradually dimmer as it pulled out of the harbour. Where it had gone, no one had any idea. But one thing was clear: they had left because of us. A few uniforms, some innocent inquiries, and one paranoid leader in Garowe were all it took.

The pirates were spooked.

* * *

Rejected by Computer and his underlings, I was forced to turn to an inside source for information about the gang. A few weeks after I returned from Eyl, Hussein Hersi, pirate informant, agreed to visit me at my guest house in Garowe.

12

Pirate Insider

HUSSEIN HERSI WAS NOT A PIRATE. BUT HE WANTED TO BE ONE.
In his early forties, Hersi was tall, with a closely shaved head and a pair of gold-rimmed aviator sunglasses perched high on his face. A black diamond-pattern *ma'awis* hung off his hips, terminating just a few centimetres above the ground, and a crimson shawl was slung over his right shoulder. The latter, he later explained, was not mere fashion. "It's a kind of pirate gang sign, like with the Crips and the Bloods," he said, referring to the infamous Los Angeles street gang rivals. Coiling around his right bicep was a menacing black snake tattoo, a serious transgression under the dictates of Islam. So anathema was this choice of body art that Colonel Omar disdainfully referred to Hersi only as "Tattoo." (Later, the Colonel began repeatedly prank-calling Hersi, posing as a member of Al-Shabaab and threatening to execute him for his blasphemy.)

I met with Hersi in the courtyard of the compound in which I was staying for a leisurely day of khat chewing on the veranda. His local reputation was so unsavoury that my guards, Said and Abdirashid, only begrudgingly allowed him into the compound, and then decided to throw him out about fifteen minutes later; it was only through a combination of cajoling and threatening that I was able to persuade them to allow him to stay. Said's distaste for Hersi came from personal experience: several months before, he had been summoned to help restrain a violently raving, high-out-of-his-mind Hersi, who repeatedly punched Said in the face for his troubles. Said called him a *dhqancelis,* the closest English translation of which is "one who is in need of cultural healing." After spending most of the last twenty years in Ohio and Montreal, Hersi had returned to Somalia two years ago, allegedly (if Said is to be believed) to cure himself of his drug addiction through the purifying power of the local culture.

As Said and Abdirashid watched warily, Hersi and I unrolled a prayer mat onto the whitewashed floor of a westward-facing enclave tucked into the side of the principal residence, as far out of the path of the raking wind as possible. Even so, powerful gusts briefly turned our *dirin* into a billowing sail, upending our 7-Up bottles and sending our stainless-steel water cups clanging down the steps of the veranda. We finally managed to pin a variety of weights onto the corners of the *dirin,* and, pouring cups of sweet tea, we started to chew the khat. A few minutes later, feeling out of place in my jeans, I excused myself and changed into my only *ma'awis,* a cheap piece of fraying yellow and green cloth I had picked up in Bossaso.

When I returned, Hersi was the first to fire off a question. "Is it all right if I borrow a hundred dollars from you, man?" he asked. "I'll send it back to you in a few days, through Dahabshiil," referring to Somalia's largest *hawala* (money transfer) company. I informed him that I would be making a trip to a Dahabshiil branch later in the afternoon to pick up some much-needed cash, and would be happy to give it to him then. He smiled, stuffing another khat stalk into his mouth. Hersi had been spending most of his recent days in Eyl, chewing khat and waiting, quite literally, for his cousins' ransom to fall from the sky. To his credit, he did not wish to remain a welfare case, but was looking for gainful employment as a pirate interpreter—the man responsible for communicating with the crew on board a captive vessel, and often for negotiating with the shipping company. Unfortunately, it was the wrong season for hiring new pirate help; the *Victoria* hijackers had been grounded, along with all other pirate groups, since the monsoons began. That fact, however, had not stopped Hersi from anxiously monitoring the international news in the hopes of catching wind of a hijacking—a ship he could call his own.

Though the *Victoria* remained in captivity, Hersi had temporarily returned to Garowe. Since our encounter in Eyl, he had been calling two or three times daily with one of two invariable themes: arranging a time to chew khat together (at my expense), or asking for a $900 video camera with which to shoot a documentary about pirates. While the latter desire remained beyond my ability or inclination to fulfil, I gladly obliged Hersi's request for a khat picnic. Since my attempts to get aboard the *Victoria* during my visit to Eyl had been rebuffed by Computer—the gang's leader—as the machinations of a CIA spy, Hersi was likely the furthest I would get in my attempts to infiltrate the organization. "They're my cousins," he explained. "I can hang out with them, and nobody can touch me."

Hersi had already succeeded where I had failed. A few days after I returned to Garowe from Eyl, he had called me at three o'clock in the morning from on board the *Victoria*, obviously high on khat. "I need a video camera, man, so I can film what's going on here, so I can show the world!" After I patiently pointed out that his request was impossible, he calmed down and promised to contact me once he was back in Garowe. Sitting with me now, Hersi explained what he was doing that night. "Computer is on [the *Victoria*] now. He offered me some money, but I told him that I didn't need it, but that I did want to chew some *mirra* with them," he said, using the Kenyan word for khat. "So since I am their cousin, they let me come on the ship and chew with them."

Shortly after Hersi phoned me, the Romanian captain of the *Victoria* had reported an unknown vessel approaching on radar, throwing the pirates into a panic. A civilian in wartime, Hersi was ordered back to shore as the pirates prepared for battle. He recalled the scene around him as he made ready to leave the ship. "Boof! [The pirates] ran to the edge of the deck with their weapons raised, ready to fight," he said, pointing an imaginary rifle in my face. "They turned the ship's spotlights on, and cut off all outgoing communications for the next three hours." The *Victoria's* captain then radioed the other ship, warning it to back off. Hersi claimed that the mystery shadow had been an American military ship, trying to catch the pirates off guard under the cover of darkness.

"They're afraid," said Hersi. "Attacks can happen at any time."

I asked Hersi to tell me about Computer, the group's leader and sole financial backer; the nickname was too unusual not to have a good story behind it, and I was not disappointed.

"His name is Abdulkhadar," said Hersi, "but everyone calls him Computer." Once a police lieutenant in Mogadishu, Computer, like many Darod, had returned to Puntland in the wake of the civil war in 1991, where he gained a local reputation as a psychic. Disturbed by his claims, a group of Sufis—Muslim holy men—came and confronted him. "Only God can see the future, not people like you," they said. "If you're a psychic, prove it to us." To test him, they bundled some money and buried it in the desert, far outside of Garowe. "Now go find it, if you can," they told him. As spectators looked on, Computer made a beeline into the bush, right to the spot where the Sufis had hidden their treasure. Combining their ascetic mysticism with a dubious understanding of the capabilities of modern technology, the Sufis reached a startling conclusion: "This man knows everything!" they exclaimed. "He is a computer!"

Following the Sufis' pronouncement, Computer's legend only grew. Pirate leaders began to come to him for advice—whom to choose for their missions, how to avoid foreign warships, which day to depart, even the exact time of day at which to launch their boats. When Computer's advice yielded munificent ransoms, they were quick to show him their appreciation, presenting him with gifts of up to $100,000, according to Hersi. Before long, Computer decided he could make more money as a venture capitalist than as a psychic.

"He called some of his cousins together, and chose ten of them, very carefully," said Hersi. "You, you, you; not you," he continued, pointing his finger in imitation of Computer. "You—you're good." After his team had been assembled, Computer provided them with specific instructions. "Right after you leave, you'll meet a ship. Leave that one alone—it's no good—and pass it on the right side. The second ship you'll see will be the one you want; it will be moving slowly. You'll see it within eight hours of leaving shore. Call me when you're on board."

"It happened just as he predicted," said Hersi. "I'm telling you, man, he's psychic."

The ship was the MV *Victoria*.

* * *

Once Computer had chosen his employees, the gang's next step was travelling to Puntland's northern coast undetected from where they would set sail into the Gulf of Aden. In order to conceal themselves from the Puntland authorities, the pirates travelled alone or in pairs, arranging rides with transport trucks on the route from Galkayo to Bossaso and stashing their weapons amidst the vehicles' cargo. "It's easy to hide there," explained Hersi. "The police don't check those trucks." Such surreptitiousness would not have been necessary in 2007–2008, but since the new administration began to rebuild the Darawish in early 2009, frequent security sweeps had made planning pirate operations a more delicate task.

Once his attacking team was in place, Computer sent money from Garowe to Bossaso for the purchase of various supplies—boats, outboard motors, fuel, and food—as well as for the accommodations and entertainment of his men during this preparatory phase. In order to escape the scrutiny of the Bossaso police and their notoriously tough anti-pirate chief, Colonel Osman Hassan Afdalow, the gang made its way to a location a few hours' off-road drive east of Bossaso—perhaps the village of Marero, a common launch site for pirates, as well as human traffickers.

Within a few days, Hersi said, on May 9 the attack group sighted the *Victoria;* following a forty-minute chase, she was boarded without a fight. "The first one to jump on the ship, his name was Abdi," said Hersi. "Computer bought him a fifteen-thousand-dollar Land Cruiser as a gift."

The bestowing of such gifts on the first to board a vessel—the piratical equivalent of what in more traditional workplaces would be called performance-linked bonuses—is commonplace in many pirate groups, and Land Cruisers are a typical choice. Such incentives must have arisen out of a need to encourage understandably hesitant pirates into climbing up metres of hull on flimsy ladders while carrying out the seaborne equivalent of a high-speed chase. According to Hersi, his cousins were the right type of people for the job.

"They're suicidal," he said. "As they are heading into the ocean, they say to themselves, 'Either I capture a ship, or I die.' One or the other. They say, 'If I don't get a Land Cruiser to drive in Garowe, it's better to be dead.' All of them, except for Computer and the interpreter, are between eighteen and twenty-five years old. This is their mentality."

* * *

Like most eighteen-to-twenty-five-year-olds, Hersi's cousins enjoyed experimenting with mind-altering substances, alcohol included. "When they drink, they go wild," he said. "They start fighting each other. The young guys, they don't know how to drink—they take a bottle of tequila and glug-glug-glug-glug," he said, emptying an imaginary bottle into his mouth. "Then they start shooting." According to Hersi, drunken duelling had cost the life of one gang member and resulted in another being wounded.[1] Unruly behaviour, however, carried consequences.

"Inside the ship they're organized like a military," Hersi said. "There are officers, subordinates . . . everyone has a title. If you refuse to take orders, they take your weapon away and tie you up, hands behind your back, and beat you."

Hersi obliged me with accounts of two incidents that had

resulted in this punishment. He described how one member of the original nine-strong attacking party had been testing out his recently acquired Land Cruiser on the rocky bluff overlooking the Eyl valley. Having drunk large quantities of Ethiopian liquor, he decided that his new prized possession was able to leap the gorge. The next part played out like a bad Hollywood movie: "The guy in the passenger seat grabbed the driver and pulled the hand brake, stopping the car just in time," said Hersi. "It was teetering back and forth on the edge of the cliff." Computer sent eight members of the gang to stabilize the situation (literally), and bring the two joyriders down to him. They were tied up and subjected to a gang beating, as the other pirates encircled and repeatedly kicked them. Still inebriated, they were then locked together in a small room (the *Victoria*'s version of a drunk tank) and thoroughly doused with water. The next day, having sobered up, they begged Computer's forgiveness. He granted it, but declared an era of prohibition, forbidding any member of the group to consume alcohol thereafter.

In Hersi's second yarn, one of the members of the attacking team—having evidently decided that he was above guarding prisoners—refused to serve his scheduled shift aboard the *Victoria*, and conveyed his position to Computer with an obscenity-laced tirade. Computer did not bother to argue; he ordered the man tied up, dropped bodily into a supply skiff and taken back to shore, where he was released, fined $10,000, and told not to return until the ransom had been delivered. Five days later, the man came back to Computer, apologizing for his transgressions and pleading for his old job. Not only was he reinstated—let no one claim that pirate justice is unfair—he was given special consideration for good behaviour: his fine was reduced by half.

Such stories were surely caricatures, but they no doubt somewhat faithfully reflected a highly dysfunctional working environment. Indeed, for all the talk I had heard about mutual affection and solidarity born of a common struggle, the pirates often seemed to mistrust each other as much as they did outsiders.[2]

Hersi confirmed this impression when he steered the conversation back to the forthcoming ransom, a topic that was clearly weigh-
ing heavily on his mind. "After the ransom has been divided, each
pirate has to throw his phone in the ocean before he leaves the ship,"
he said. This unusual divestment of their coveted mobiles ensured
that no member of the gang was able to arrange an ambush for any
of the others once they left the safety of the ship. Once they reached
shore, it was every man for himself, with each pirate attempting
alone the perilous dash from the wilderness of Eyl to the relative
shelter of Garowe. "When you call members of the gang and their
phones aren't working, that is the sign that the money has arrived,"
Hersi explained.

* * *

If the *Victoria* gang was a military hierarchy, then Computer, the
outfit's commander-in-chief, was an armchair general—he rarely
made personal appearances aboard the ship, but issued orders to his
gang from his Garowe hideout. On board the *Victoria*, authority was
exercised by his plenipotentiary, known as Loyan, the group's interpreter. Loyan had been the logical choice for field commander—the
eldest pirate after Computer (at thirty years old), he was the only
one capable of communicating effectively with the crew, and was
also a veteran of three campaigns, coming on board the *Victoria* a
mere two days after his previous interpreting assignment had ended.
Hersi, it appeared, could not resist taking a few shots at his more
successful rival.

"Loyan is a khat addict," he said. "He ran up a $37,000 khat bill
before Computer finally cut him off.[3] He told him to stay on the ship
and shut up." Hersi continued, "He doesn't even speak very good
English. He only knows how to say basic things, like 'We want more
money.'" His statement seemed to imply that Loyan was also responsible for negotiating with the *Victoria*'s shipping company—a position that would have further enhanced his status within the gang.

While pirate organizations often hire outside, professional intermediaries, in less sophisticated operations the interpreter will double as negotiator, engaging in a routine "ask high, settle low" back-and-forth exchange.

Hersi paused, lighting another cigarette, and said, "Once the first ten guys caught the ship and brought it to Eyl, there was another group waiting to relieve them." They were quickly brought on to guard the hostages. "The attackers had done their job, and had earned the right to do anything they wanted. Immediately, they went on land, bought cars, started to party."

Each one of the "holders," he said, would receive $20,000 from the ransom, while each attacker would receive $140,000, which they had begun to spend almost as soon as the *Victoria*'s anchor hit the ocean floor. Their subsequent spending binges—made possible by the almost limitless credit extended to them by anyone with anything to sell—would have made the most reckless subprime mortgage look like the model of fiscal responsibility. "As soon as the ship gets to its destination, the party is already on, the money is already flowing," explained Hersi. "No one knows when the ransom will come. It could take one month, two months, three months. But [the pirates] want to have fun, they want a car now." The value of a ransom-backed IOU, it turned out, was about fifty cents on the dollar. "In the end, they pay double for whatever they buy on credit—a Land Cruiser will cost them $16,000 or $17,000," and, like most luxury goods coming into Somalia, would be imported from Dubai. "If they want a house, the regular price might be $20,000, but for them it's $30,000 or $40,000."

Each purchase was carefully noted by the group's accountant, a man called Mustuku, who acted as a kind of underwriter, assuring understandably wary proprietors that they would eventually be paid for their goods. "If one of the guys wants a car, the accountant will speak to the seller. He'll tell him, 'Okay, give him the Land Cruiser. You're dealing with me now. Just hand him the key and don't worry about anything—I have your money.'"

The next specialized member of the gang was a man to whom Hersi referred only as the "commander of the khat," whose purpose was simply to manage the mammoth logistical task of keeping the pirates on board the *Victoria* amply supplied with the drug. "The gang has one or two Land Cruisers at their disposal at all times to take care of things like that," Hersi explained. "Whatever they need."

Rounding out the crew was the cooking staff. "The pirates have their own cook, plus an assistant, on the ship," said Hersi. "They cook their own food, and so does the crew. The pirates never touch the crew's food, because they're afraid of poison." He claimed that both the cook and the sous-chef would receive $15,000 for their services.

Computer, it turned out, was the gang's big winner. "When I left them, the pirates were coming close to agreeing on a ransom, around $3 million," said Hersi. Computer, he said, would receive half of this predicted amount—$1.5 million—without ever having set foot in a skiff. But he was also solely responsible for financing the gang's operating expenses incurred during the lengthy ransom negotiation period. Like the other members of the gang, he had taken out a loan to help pay the bills.

"Everything is twice as expensive," Hersi explained. "Food, guns, *mirra,* cigarettes, a glass of water, whatever. They pay 100 per cent interest on everything." The credit was issued in two forms, either as deferred payments to merchants—for example, a khat vendor (who in turn would obtain credit from her supplier)—or as direct cash loans from local businessmen. Under such usurious conditions, footing the bill for dozens of men over a period of more than two months added up to a staggering sum, even in Somalia. Hersi guessed that Computer was on track to spend $500,000 on expenses. But if Computer was feeling the pressure of his financial responsibilities, he was not showing any signs of it.

"Once, a woman came crying to Computer, telling him, 'Computer, Computer, I love you,'" said Hersi. "'Why are you crying?' he asked. 'Everyone has a car, I need one too,' she says. So Computer shouts at a young guy driving a white Land Cruiser on the street to stop his car. And he stops. 'How much for this car?' he says. 'Sixteen thousand dollars? Here you go, give me the keys.' And he gives the car to the woman! 'Why are you crying?' he says. 'Take the keys.' I saw this with my own eyes, I swear."

Perhaps because of tales such as this, the pirates—after having successfully avoided the patrols of state-of-the-art warships—later found themselves hunted on land by their own friends and relatives. "Everyone is trying to call them, trying to ask them for money. So they go and lock themselves inside a house and turn off their phones," said Hersi. "Maybe they come out after ten days, when they have to, but then they'll go right back in. Everyone is chasing them."

When they could not stay holed up any longer, the pirates turned their attention to women. With their new-found wealth, they were able to afford to marry younger and more attractive wives; the ten *Victoria* attackers, said Hersi, had already married, and not for the first time. "They used to only have one wife, have a normal life, live in daylight, all that stuff. Once they become pirates they don't go back to their wives," he said. Their lives with their new wives, however, did not typically lead to matrimonial bliss. "They might each have twenty thousand dollars left, and they finish that in two weeks. After that, they start to sell everything back. Then, the women are history. The marriages run until the money runs out."

The short-term marriages Hersi was describing, known in Islamic jurisprudence as *nikah misyar,* or "travellers' marriage," are not unique to Somalia, but are widely used by Sunni Muslims as a loophole to circumvent Islam's circumscription of casual sex. Unlike *nikah,* or traditional marriage, *misyar* does not carry the corresponding burdens of financial responsibility, co-habitation, or inheritance, and divorce can be pronounced simply by verbal agreement. Hersi was not the first Somali adult I had heard sermonize about the pernicious effects of travellers' marriages on Somali society; the practice is becoming increasingly common amongst the youth population as a whole, eliciting the inevitable warnings about the corruption of Somali culture.

"Before, you would come to the girl's family and ask for their daughter, and then give them money, or, if it's a traditional bush family, some camels . . . But these pirates take them from their families. They come by in their Land Cruisers, the girls jump inside and they go get married in a hotel and fuck like crazy. They give them jewellery, introduce them as their wives, and then one month later, everything is done . . . Then they go back to their old wives."

Once the attackers had had ample shore leave (or honeymooning, as the case may have been), they were required to report back to the ship in order to take their turn guarding the hostages. However, each had the option of hiring someone (usually a relative) to take his place on the ship for the duration of its captivity—much like buying one's way out of a draft—in which case he would return only when the ransom was being delivered. In total, twenty pirates remained stationed on the *Victoria* at all times, taking turns guarding the hostages in four-hour shifts.

Hersi's obnoxiously loud cellphone chimed to life, cutting in on our conversation. After a brusque exchange in Somali—of which I picked out one sentence: "What's happened to my car?"—Hersi turned back to me.

"That was the guy in Eyl who's looking after my Land Cruiser," he said. "I'm getting ready to sell it to one of the pirate boys." Then, smiling broadly, "It's an old one . . . it cost me only six thousand dollars in Dubai. He's giving me ten thousand dollars for it. Cool, huh?"

As he was finishing his sentence, Hersi's phone rang again. This time it was his sister, informing him of the repair estimate for his Land Cruiser; evidently, something was wrong with its radiator. Hersi frowned, hanging up, before seamlessly continuing his previous train of thought.

"Imagine these young guys . . . twentysomething years old, no food, no life, with a wife to support. When you're hungry, you'll do whatever job you can get. Many of the pirates used to be police. I know five of them personally; [Mohamed Abdi]—the one who first boarded the ship—was a lieutenant in [former Puntland president] Adde Muse's time, when he was twenty-five. Then they stopped getting paid. In Abdullahi Yusuf's time, things were different. Whatever money he had, he would pay the soldiers first. Puntland was tough . . . security was good; there were no guns in the street, no shootings. Then Adde came along . . . he didn't give a shit who lived and who died. So that's when these guys turned to piracy. If they got good money, they would become police officers again," he said.

If nothing else, this anecdote lent support to the theory that the near collapse of Puntland's governmental institutions in 2008—particularly the security forces—had contributed significantly to the piracy outbreak. Hersi, however, was not short on explanations. "The problem is that they have no education at all," he said. "They take human beings hostage, and for them it's a joke. Only when you're educated do you see that it's a serious crime, that it's real."

It was close to four o'clock in the afternoon, nearing Dahabshiil's closing hour. I was two weeks in arrears with Said's and Abdirashid's wages (twenty dollars each per day), and I had promised them earlier that I would make a cash run before the day's end. I now spotted them wandering around the corner of the house, peering expectantly in my direction. Not wishing to give them any further cause to despise Hersi, I decided to take a break from the khat; for his part, Hersi was also delighted by my decision to fetch some cash. We agreed to reconvene in half an hour.

* * *

As soon as I returned with the money, Hersi picked up where he had left off, beginning a lecture on the Puntland government's total inability to tackle the piracy issue. "At the beginning of this game, maybe fourteen or fifteen months ago, Puntland tried twice to attack Eyl with their military forces," he said. "They came to the town with technicals and almost sixty soldiers, but when they arrived there were three hundred twenty-year-olds with anti-aircraft guns waiting for them. The soldiers came running back."

The incident to which Hersi was referring, Haji's abortive invasion of Eyl, had unfolded much as he described. After their boss had absconded with his $20,000 payoff, the Puntland soldiers had been wise to withdraw; not only would the pirates have defended themselves, but their clan militias—indeed, anyone in the town who owned a gun—would have come to their defence, and the streets of Eyl would have turned into an urban battleground.

"The second thing," continued Hersi, "is that the soldiers are related to the pirates. Farole couldn't attack Eyl. His soldiers would say to themselves, 'How can we kill our cousins?'" There was no better illustration of the problem gnawing at the root of President Farole's attempts to combat piracy. Unlike the army of a mature state, Puntland's security forces (as is the case across Somalia) are not seen by the local population as a neutral entity, but through the lens of clan. Military action is viewed either as a declaration of war by one clan on another, or as an attempt to turn cousin against cousin; in both cases, it is ineffective. Only inter-clan mediation, not a strong central state, has prevented Puntland from Balkanizing into a collection of warring enclaves.

As the sky darkened, we slowly began to collect the discarded khat pulp and empty cigarette packs. Hersi seized the opportunity to remind me of my earlier promise. "Hey, man," Hersi said, "it looks like the repairs to my car are going to cost $140, a bit more than I thought. Can I borrow that much?" As I only had hundred-dollar bills in my possession, I opted to round down his request, and went inside to retrieve one of the crisp bills I had just picked up at Dahabshiil. I handed it to him and he thanked me, promising to pay it back within a few days.

A few moments later, he presented a slightly stranger petition. "Hey, Jay, you know those pants you were wearing when I came in?" he asked.

"You mean my jeans?"

"Yeah. They were really nice, man," he said.

"Thanks."

"Can I have them, man? I'm going back to the coast soon and I need a really good pair of jeans, to protect me from the wind."

Having but three pairs of trousers in my travel ensemble, I was sadly forced to refuse his request, and suggested that he take five dollars out of the hundred I had given him and buy a pair of knock-off jeans at the market.

He sighed. "Those won't be nearly as good."

Under the watchful escort of Said and Abdirashid, Hersi made his way out of the compound, soon to rejoin his comrades on the beaches of Eyl. A few weeks after our interview, on July 18, Hersi's khat-fuelled vigil finally came to an end with the long-awaited delivery of the ransom money for the *Victoria*. It must have been a bittersweet moment—the final ransom turned out to be only $1.8 million, far short of Hersi's $3 million prediction.

At the beginning of September, several months after I had last spoken to Hersi, the monsoons came to a close and pirate season opened again in full force, with almost two dozen hijackings occurring before the year was out. If only one of those many ships had need of an interpreter, perhaps Hersi finally got his big break.

13

The Cadet and the Chief

IT WAS A FROZEN MID-DECEMBER DAY IN THE BLACK SEA PORT OF
Constanţa, Romania. Trudging down to the harbour with Teddy, my
Romanian translator, we were caught in a crossfire of icy blasts of
ocean wind sweeping across the jutting peninsula and through the
deserted streets of the Old Town. A statue of the poet Ovid dominated the central square, surveying with marble eyes the same place
where, two thousand years ago, he had spent his final days lament-
ing the cruel fate that had seen him banished to this backward out-
post at the very margins of the Roman Empire. My first impression
was not much different from Ovid's; after the bustling cosmopolitan
streets of Bucharest, some 250 kilometres away, Constanţa's grey
tones and empty streets conveyed the feeling of a declining province.
But first impressions were misleading: the city is a bustling mercan-
tile centre—the fourth-largest port in Europe, and the biggest on the
Black Sea.

Little about Constanţa, on this cold and sombre day, reminded
me of the sunny desert plains of Somalia. Yet the two places were
connected more intimately than one would expect, by way of the
international shipping routes linking the Black Sea, the Mediterranean, the Suez Canal, and finally the Gulf of Aden and the Indian
Ocean. Indeed, the city's tenuous connection to Somalia had brought
me here, in pursuit of the story of the MV *Victoria*. For Constanţa

was home to seven of the eleven crew members held hostage aboard the vessel for seventy-five days.

In an American-style Italian restaurant, a welcome oasis from the bitter cold, I met with a young man I will call Matei Levenescu. We had never met, but I felt an oddly personal connection to him. Six months earlier, I had stood less than a kilometre away from him, separated by an unbridgeable stretch of hostile water lying between the *Victoria* and the beach at Eyl. For utterly different reasons, we had both ended up in a country that neither of us would have expected to visit in our lifetimes, viewing it from entirely divergent perspectives—I, desperately trying to get to where he was; he, wishing he were anywhere else on earth.

Spurning my invitation to order food, Levenescu contented himself with a Pepsi, which he proceeded to nurse over the course of the hour. In his early twenties, Levenescu was slender and thin-lipped, with eyes that told me he would likely command a ship of his own one day. Still a cadet, he was in the third year of a four-year program at Constanţa Maritime University, soon to complete his studies and become a full-time seafarer. His assignment aboard the *Victoria*, like the cooperative education programs offered by North American universities, had been intended to furnish on-the-job training. Levenescu ended up with far more first-hand experience than he had bargained for.

Almost as soon as we sat down, Levenescu launched into a straightforward warning about the dangers of overly detailed media coverage of pirate operations. "You have to be careful what you write," he said. "The pirates can easily go on the Internet and learn how to adapt their operations based on your reports." In a manner oddly patronizing for his age, Levenescu lectured me on the potential harm of publicly revealing the size of ransom payments. Such open reporting, he feared, would only increase the pirates' leverage at the bargaining table.

"That's what happened to the *Hansa*," he said, referring to the MV *Hansa Stavanger*, another German-owned freighter held concurrently with the *Victoria,* further south at Harardheere. The crew of the *Hansa* suffered through an agonizing four-month ransom negotiation, during which the pirates continually revised their demands upwards. At one point the negotiators on both sides had agreed on $2.5 million, only to see the pirates inflate their asking price once more. Whether this double-dealing was the result of the media creating an environment of perfect information within the "ransom market," as Levenescu suspected, is uncertain. (A ransom of $2.75 million was finally agreed, and the *Hansa* was released on August 2, 2009.)

* * *

Levenescu was lying in his cabin when the attack came. He immediately knew something was wrong when he heard the knocking of the propeller, indicating that the vessel was attempting to turn at top speed. When he heard the pirates on the deck above, Levenescu and seven of his crewmates, all save Captain Petru Constantin Tinu and two seamen, went back into their cabins and locked themselves in.

The attack did not come as a complete surprise, Levenescu told me, since there had been an attempted hijacking in the area only seven hours earlier. Levenescu knew this because it had been his duty to monitor international piracy bulletins and report potential trouble spots to the captain. Before entering "Pirate Alley," moreover, the crew had implemented a series of counter-piracy measures ordered by the vessel's German owners: positioning high-powered water hoses, welding metal plates to the windows on the first and second levels, and blocking the stairwells leading up to the bridge. None of these precautions, however, made much difference to a ship as slow and sluggish as the *Victoria.*

The deck officer and second mate, Ruxandra Sarchizian, spotted the pirates at only six kilometres' distance (the *Victoria*'s radar was blind to the attack craft until it was three kilometres away). "There were nine of them in one ten-metre-long boat," Levenescu recalled.

"They came up fast on our port side, moving at twenty knots." Equipped with two 350-horsepower outboard motors, the craft was carrying about five hundred litres of gasoline—not nearly enough fuel, it must be noted, to get them back to Somalia (Hussein Hersi may not have been exaggerating when he spoke of his cousins' suicidal "capture or die" philosophy).

Even though the *Victoria* had been travelling in the Internationally Recommended Transit Corridor and was in the vicinity of two NATO frigates, Mohamed Abdi and his team boarded the vessel unmolested. When asked how the pirates could have pulled off their assault practically under the gunnels of two warships, Levenescu rolled his eyes. "They're useless," he scoffed. "There was a warship, a Turkish one, fifty miles away when we were attacked. But at the same time, a Turkish cargo ship was also calling for help, and so it chose to help them instead." [1]

Sarchizian raised the warship on radio, but instead of mobilizing a response, the Turks plied her with aimless questions. "What colour is the boat, what speed is it going at, how many pirates, how many guns, what kind of guns, . . . all this shit, you know? *Help us!* Finally, when the pirates were about fifteen cables away, they said a chopper would arrive in thirty-five minutes," said Levenescu. When it arrived, the helicopter circled two or three times overhead as the pirates nervously tracked it with their rocket-propelled grenade (RPG) launchers. "The warships, they don't prevent anything," Levenescu said, with a contempt he extended to the international safety corridor. "That corridor is hell," he said. "It just makes the pirates' job easier, because they know where all the ships will be going. 'Okay,' they say, 'Let's fish!'"[2]

The sea was calm, and with the *Victoria's* thirteen-knot top speed and two-metre freeboard, the pirates had been able to board her with ease; the entire hijacking, from sighting to capture, took less than forty minutes. Once on deck, the pirates fired several rounds from their Kalashnikovs into the air in an attempt to intimidate the crew into surrendering. As the rest of the crew huddled on the lower decks, the captain and two seamen barricaded themselves in the bridge. Using a four-metre aluminum ladder, the attackers climbed from level to level until they reached the command deck. One pirate advanced with his weapon raised, shooting a bullet through the bridge's glass housing and into the ceiling. Before he could decide to switch to living targets, Captain Tinu opened the door to the bridge and pushed the man's weapon down, agreeing to surrender the ship.

Once in control of the *Victoria*, the pirates ordered the crew to hoist their attack boat aboard using the vessel's deck cranes. Lacking the proper cables with which to secure the boat to the crane, the ropes snapped and it fell back into the sea. As the crew looked on in terrified anticipation, the pirates' reaction was remarkably cheery. "No problem," they said. "We'll just buy another one."

And what happened after that? Levenescu shot me a bemused look. "We go to Somalia," he replied in English. For two days the crew stayed confined to the ten-metre-square bridge as the ship made its way to Eyl. Arriving towards the end of "pirate season," they joined a fellowship of three hostage ships already moored in the harbour; for the next seventy-five days the crew watched other commandeered vessels come and go, until, finally, only the *Victoria* remained.

After the first two days, the crew was moved to the captain's and owner's quarters, where they spent the rest of their imprisonment in a world consisting of the two cabins, the ship's mess, and the corridor linking them. The pirates, conversely, came and went freely, rotating between ship and shore in two- or three-week shifts.

* * *

Frequent shore leave was a necessary pressure release valve to prevent tempers on the ship from flaring. Supply boats went to and from the shore two or three times per day, though this ferry service was later reduced to one evening transport as the *hagaa* season wore on and its winds became increasingly merciless.[3] The pirates came and went with the transports, but there was an average of twenty on board at all times. Those not native to the Eyl area rarely left the ship, but the Romanian hostages observed that even the group's Eyl residents were decidedly apprehensive about taking shore leave.[4]

"They had some problems in Eyl," said Levenescu. "There was trouble between the pirates and the government, or other pirates . . . I don't know." Given the anti-pirate hostility I had witnessed from the local people while in Eyl—as well as the recent Puntland government crackdown—the pirates' anxiety was hardly surprising.

The pirates treated him and his shipmates with decency, if not kindness, Levenescu asserted, and never resorted to physical violence against any crew member. All things considered, he was content with the lot that he and his shipmates drew. "The group that captured us was a good one," he said. "In the south, the pirates are terrible. They do much more violent things to intimidate the shipping company into paying." Levenescu's (somewhat accurate) generalization stemmed from the brutal treatment of the crew of the *Hansa Stavanger*, whom the pirates subjected to mock executions in order to pressure the *Hansa*'s owners into paying a higher ransom.

Levenescu had few quarrels with his captors, and recalled that the only woman in the crew, Sarchizian, was treated with more respect than any other crew member. "They would sometimes call her name seductively, but nothing more than that," said Levenescu. Of the *Victoria*'s complement, in fact, it was the Romanians who had the more lascivious inclinations. "We asked them to bring some women on board," said Levenescu, sheepishly. "They said no."

I laughed, and mentioned my own difficulties in dealing with the *Victoria* gang, partly owing to the fact that they had believed me to be a CIA operative. He nodded understandingly, "Yes, they are stupid. They are very stupid."

But Levenescu dashed my solipsistic assumption that the *Victoria* had fled from Eyl, during my second night in the town, because Computer feared my meddling in his plans. By the time I reached Eyl, forty-four days into the *Victoria*'s captivity, the vessel's vital supplies—fuel, water, and food—were critically low. She was completely out of fresh water, and the ship's desalinator functioned effectively only in the open ocean, away from the algae blooms and other contaminants present close to shore. What I had thought of as the gang's flight from Eyl was merely a water harvesting trip, down the southern coast and back.

The ship's fuel woes also explained why the *Victoria*'s distance from shore continually oscillated, giving the appearance—from my vantage point on Eyl's beach—that she was being swept back and forth by the tides. Shortly before I arrived in Eyl, the ship's supply of diesel had run out, and the auxiliary generator, which had powered the ship's lights and mess facilities while anchored, sputtered to a halt. In order to generate electricity, the crew re-engaged the main engine, and with it the main propeller, forcing the *Victoria* to weigh anchor and chart continual circles in the harbour.

Using a four-thousand-kilowatt engine as a generator was an extremely inefficient way of powering light bulbs and kitchen elements, and it was not sustainable for long. Shortly after I left Eyl, on June 20, the ship's reservoir of bunker fuel (the crude oil by-product consumed by the main engine) was exhausted. The prospect of losing the *Victoria*'s floodlights—a critical defensive resource in case of attack—was not an option for the pirates. So they resorted to transporting small amounts of diesel from shore to power the vessel's emergency generator during the night. For the final month of the ship's captivity, the emergency generator provided limited power for its occupants' basic daily needs.

As for the pirates, their daily activities were predictable enough. "They chewed a drug that made their eyes wide, like this," said Levenescu, using his fingers to spread his eyelids in imitation. "They wouldn't sleep for thirty or forty hours at a time. The supply boat came three times per day to bring that fucking khat. There was only one pirate who didn't chew: the cook. But in the end, even he started." The pirates partnered the khat with the habitual hyper-sweet tea, having brought three kilograms of sugar on board with them. One time, said Levenescu, they substituted 7-Up for their tea, but did not alter their routine, heaping spoonfuls of sugar into the soft drink as well.[5] Levenescu had also experimented with the drug. "A bit," he said, gagging at the memory. "They all ate *a lot*."

One pragmatic effect of the khat was its ability to keep the pirates alert and ready. Staying awake late into the night, the pirates would routinely shoot off their Kalashnikovs for amusement. According to Levenescu, their on-board arsenal consisted of two RPG launchers, two Russian standard-issue machine guns (PKMs), and an AK-47 for each man. But the gang did not seriously expect to fight off an international naval assault with this weaponry. "They were more worried about attacks from other Somali pirates, not the navy ships," said Levenescu. Yet again, Boyah's claims of pirate solidarity and mutual affection did not seem to match the reality.

Having heard so much about the eccentric Computer from Hersi, I eagerly asked Levenescu for his impressions of the man. But it seemed Computer was an elusive, shadowy figure even to the *Victoria's* crew. "They spoke a lot about their leader," said Levenescu. "But I don't think he even existed. I think they made all their decisions as a group." On the day the ransom was delivered, however, the entire gang assembled on the deck of the *Victoria*. "There was an older man aboard then, about fifty years," said Levenescu. "He was dressed like a garbage man. If there was a leader, it was him." There is little doubt that the shabby figure Levenescu described was Computer. If, as Hersi claimed, Computer had served as a police lieutenant under the former Somali Republic, he would probably be in his mid-to-late fifties.

When the pirates finally departed, they left the *Victoria* in much worse shape than her crew. "The ship was a mess," said Levenescu. "There was trash everywhere. In the end, they stole everything from us—laptops, cellphones. But they did give us back our SIM cards."

On July 18, the *Victoria* was finally released. But sudden liberty after seventy-five days of captivity was apparently not enough to perturb the stoic equanimity of Levenescu and his crewmates. "We weren't happy," he recalled. "We were nervous. Once we left Somalia, we were really worried about getting hijacked again." The hardest part, he said, was the open-water dash from the Somali coast to the Yemeni island of Socotra, where a tugboat was waiting with fresh supplies, ready to take the *Victoria* in tow. Fortunately, the *Victoria's* crew made the rendezvous, after which they were towed to Salalah, Oman, and from there were flown home via Bahrain.

If Levenescu had been irrevocably damaged by his ordeal, he concealed it well. "It wasn't a difficult psychological experience for me," he said. "Maybe it was different for the others. I don't know. I guess I appreciate life a little more," he added, shrugging.

Levenescu certainly had no plans to abandon his career path; as a matter of fact, I was lucky to catch him a few days before he shipped out on his next assignment. But he made it clear that he would not be returning to Somalia: "No way. Never again."

* * *

The next day, in a diner on the other side of the country, Teddy and I met with Levenescu's commanding officer and the *Victoria's* chief mate, Traian Vasile Mihai—or, as he playfully called himself, "Chief." Mihai looked to be in his early fifties, short and squat, with a drooping moustache and thinning hair. The lines of his face were imbued with mirth, his eyes lively and jovial. Like Levenescu, he declined to order any food, leaving me alone to munch on a chicken and ketchup sandwich between my questions.

Though posted to the same ship as Levenescu, Mihai was born of a different age; lighting one cigarette after another, he wistfully reminisced about the past glory of NAVROM, the state-owned shipping fleet active during the rule of Communist-era dictator Nicolae Ceaușescu. "Romania had a merchant marine of 345 ships at that time," he sighed. "Now, nothing." After about five minutes, I managed to steer the conversation to the subject of the *Victoria's* capture.

Following the pirate takeover, said Mihai, he, Captain Tinu, and the second mate Sarchizian were the only three crew who remained on active duty—though "forced labour" was perhaps a more accurate description. Serving six- to eight-hour shifts, Mihai's principal responsibility was to keep watch on the bridge and monitor the radar for possible threats to the pirates. One night, he detected a small vessel approaching, which he dutifully reported to his captors.

"What is that? What's its name?" they asked him.

"How am I supposed to know?" he retorted, gesticulating at an imaginary radar display. "It's a radar! It tells you the position, course, speed—no problem. But that's it."

Mihai chuckled at the recollection. "Everyone ran outside to the edge of the ship, pointing their guns. 'If they come closer, we'll just kill them,' the pirates said. Then they hailed the ship on the VHF [high frequency radio] in the Somali language, checking to see if it was one of their own," said Mihai. In the end, the situation was resolved without violence. It is possible that this incident was the alleged "American attack" described by Hersi. For his part, Mihai hypothesized that the unknown vessel was a Somali fishing boat— far more likely than an American warship attempting to sneak up on the pirates in the middle of the night.

One night, about a week after arriving at Eyl, the Chief was serving his watch shift on the bridge. At around midnight, several pirates barged in and demanded that he start the main engine and set an immediate course for the south. Mihai hurriedly tried to explain to non-receptive ears that the main engine required half an hour to warm up before it could be engaged.[6]

"'It's not a car,' I told them," he said, miming the act of turning a key in an ignition. "'You can't just start it and go. It's impossible!' 'No, now!' they said." Pleading that he had no authority to order a course change, Mihai hastily summoned Captain Tinu to the bridge. When he arrived, Tinu took an unsuccessful turn at explaining the mechanics of the engine to the pirates. Finding it difficult to get their message across, the two men asked to speak to Loyan, the interpreter.[7]

"'Fuck Loyan,' they said. 'Start the engine!' Then one of them points a gun at my head," Mihai said, raising an imaginary weapon to my temple. "And tells me that if I don't start the engine in five minutes he'll kill me." In desperation, Captain Tinu convinced the would-be absconders to first speak with their boss on the shore. Two or three minutes later, Tinu was on the satellite phone with the group's chief (presumably Computer), who did not prove much more helpful.

"Captain, please start the engine," Computer said through the interpreter. "I can't control these guys, they're crazy. Do whatever they tell you." Faced with no alternative, Mihai contacted the engine room and ordered a cold start-up. Seven or eight minutes later, the *Victoria* weighed anchor and headed south.

"It was a big risk," said Mihai. "The engine could have easily broken down." If the pirates had had a good reason for risking damage to their hard-won prize, the Chief was not aware of it. After sailing south for six hours, the *Victoria* dropped anchor for two or three hours before turning around and heading straight back to Eyl. "I have no idea why they wanted to leave," he said. "Maybe because they were chewing their drugs."

If their khat had more influence over the pirates than Computer, one wonders how strong a leader he could have been. Perhaps he could be better likened to the majority shareholder in a company, whose employees—as is the case in any corporation—sometimes functioned in divergent and unpredictable ways. Of the nine pirates who attacked the *Victoria*, Mihai said, three of them held positions of authority over the others, though the exact nature of their power remained a mystery. "One of these leaders was very dangerous," he said. "Very evil." Mihai described how Mohamed Abdi, the first pirate to board the ship, had approached him as he was eating in the mess hall with three of his crewmates.

"Chief, today I'm going to kill the whole crew," he said.

"Why?" Mihai replied, in a tone of mock incredulity. "Why you gonna kill me? I'm on board this ship working for the German company to make money. I have a wife and children to support, no? You understand?"

"Yes, Chief."

"You are a pirate. Why'd you capture this ship?—For money, no?"

"Yes, Chief."

"Then, Romanian and Somalian, we're the same, no?"

"Okay, Chief. I'll kill the Germans instead."

Mihai burst into hearty laughter, and my interpreter and I could not help but join him.

* * *

With the air conditioning switched off to conserve power, most of the crew was forced to sleep on the floor on mattresses the Chief had managed to beg from their captors, while the pirates slept comfortably in their beds. To pass the time, Mihai and his crewmates watched movies (the *Victoria* had a library of over a thousand DVDs), listened to music, and played cards and backgammon. Cigarettes were ample; at sixty cents a pack, the pirates were extremely liberal in providing them to the crew. The Chief lamented, however, that there had been no alcohol to help them pass the time; the crew had intended to replenish their depleted supply once they reached their destination of Jeddah. Contrary to Hersi's assertions, Mihai never witnessed the pirates consume any alcohol themselves.

"I asked one pirate: Why don't you drink? Because of the Koran?" he said.

"Yes, that's right."

"You read the Koran?"

"Yes, Chief."

"What else does the Koran say? Don't kill, don't kidnap people ... ?"

"Yes, Chief."

The pirates showed as little regard for the Koranic injunctions against theft. "They stole *everything*, even Ruxandra's Tampax and underwear," said Mihai. The pirates' cook had taken a liking to her, and managed to convince his colleagues to return all of her belongings. The Chief was not so lucky: he lost his mobile phone, a pair of shoes, two bags, a set of pyjamas, two sweatshirts, a leather jacket, and around $500 in cash; fortunately, he had managed to hide his laptop. The pirates also helped themselves to communal goods, ransacking the medical stores and stealing, among other things, the defibrillator and emergency oxygen kit—though according to Mihai they had no inkling what the items were used for.

Nor were the Romanian crew members the only victims of the hijackers' seemingly compulsive desire to thieve. "One pirate stole the Somali cook's mobile phone," said Mihai. Wondering where it had gone, the cook did the first logical thing in such a situation: he called his telephone from another line. "The phone rang in the thief's pocket," said Mihai, laughing aloud. Punishment was swift; the pirates tied up the transgressor and sent him to shore, only receiving him back about two weeks later. "That was a unique case," he said.

Not surprisingly, fights involving khat were much more common. "When one of them had greener stuff, and the other had drier stuff, they would fight," said Mihai, throwing a few shadow boxing jabs in my direction.

Unlike his younger shipmate, the Chief had never felt the desire to experiment with khat, and seemed more shocked by the pirates' lack of fiscal responsibility than anything else. "Thirty-eight dollars per kilogram they paid for that stuff," he said. "My God!" Yet, despite their khat-fuelled antics, the Chief had no objections to the majority of his captors. "The three leaders were the worst," he said. "The others were okay."

Nevertheless, the crew and the pirates always ate separately, said Mihai, relating how he spurned the one invitation he received to the pirates' dinner table, extended by the pirates' cook. "They used their hands to eat, and they added a hot green pepper to their food," he said, disgusted. "My God! If I had eaten that I would have had to run right to the toilet."

In a sign of improving relations between hostages and captors, the pirates began to bring goats on board for the crew during the final three or four weeks of their imprisonment. "Small ones, eight or nine kilograms," said the Chief. They had to slaughter the goats themselves, but the meat was a welcome complement to their previous meals, which had been based around potatoes, onions, and flour—as well as an endless supply of rice from the *Victoria*'s ten-thousand-tonne hold, as my translator Teddy lightheartedly pointed out. "Yeah!" Mihai exclaimed. "I told my wife on the telephone: 'Honey, I'm coming home. No rice, please, no rice!'" wagging his finger in mock consternation.

The Chief's loving warning to his wife had occurred during one of only three or four opportunities the crew were given to speak to their families on the *Victoria*'s satellite phone, each call lasting only a few minutes. The exception was Levenescu, once again thanks to the kindness of the Somali cook, who risked his colleagues' wrath by secretly allowing Levenescu to contact his family on his mobile phone.

In addition to the predictable assurances of their well-being, the crew members also urged their loved ones to help bring them home. "We told our families to protest, to talk to the media—anything that could help put pressure on the German company," said Mihai.

*　*　*

The German owners had warned the pirates that no ransom would be agreed upon unless the *Victoria* had enough fuel remaining to reach international waters—twelve nautical miles from the Somali coast—under her own power; in response, the pirates immediately shut down the main engine in order to conserve bunker fuel. The endless circles the vessel had been performing in Eyl's harbour for almost two weeks had taken a toll on its reserves. According to Mihai, the ship had consumed 146 tonnes of oil, leaving a mere 28 tonnes, enough for only a day and a half on the open sea. There was another problem: the heating system used to warm the main engine prior to ignition was diesel-powered, and the *Victoria*'s diesel stores had long since been depleted. Consequently, the pirates began a mass importation of diesel, bringing on board four tonnes, in increments of thirty- and forty-litre drums, over the course of three days.

As the negotiations drew to a close, the pirates started to plan their getaway. Two or three weeks before the ransom was delivered, the supply boats began to bring sets of new combat fatigues and matching boots, which the pirates subsequently used to disguise themselves as Puntland soldiers upon leaving the ship.[8]

By satellite phone, the *Victoria's* owners had kept Captain Tinu and Mihai closely apprised of the status of the ongoing negotiations, and, as a result, the two knew a week in advance when the ransom was to be delivered. When the big day arrived, every leader, attacker, and holder in the pirate operation turned up on the *Victoria*, including, as Levenescu testified, Computer himself; Mihai counted a total of thirty-two individuals, including the gang's accountant. They all waited with anticipation for a small eight-seater aircraft en route from Kenya, loaded from the vaults of a Nairobi bank.

When the plane was sighted, the crew was told to assemble on the main deck in plain view. Mihai observed that the plane was carrying "military men" (most likely private security forces), and guessed that a representative of the shipping company was also aboard. When, after two fly-bys, the plane's occupants were satisfied that all crew members were alive and accounted for, they released a parachuting bundle containing the ransom money. So strong were the monsoon winds, said Mihai, that the pirates had to chase the package in one of their supply boats after it landed dozens of metres away.

Once retrieved, the ransom was brought on deck and meticulously divided according to a pre-arranged formula. "The accountant had a laptop," said Mihai. "On it was an Excel table with the name of each pirate." Of the $1.8 million ransom, "The man who threatened to kill us received $150,000," Levenescu had told me earlier, almost certainly describing Mohamed Abdi, the head attacker. "The cook got $20,000."

After five or six hours, twenty-two pirates had received and counted their money and departed for the shore, leaving ten on board to oversee the lengthy preparations to ready the main engine after its long period of disuse. Twenty-four hours later, at exactly quarter past five on the morning of July 18—the time was etched in Mihai's memory—the last pirate left the deck of the *Victoria*.

* * *

For the Chief, the worst part of the experience was unquestionably the night on the bridge when he came closest to death. But he soon grew accustomed to living under the Damoclean sword of such threats. "At one point they sent the Germans an email," he said. "It read: 'If you don't send us the money we'll start randomly executing the crew, starting with the Captain.'"

I asked if he thought that the pirates would ever have carried out their threat.

"No," he replied. "It was just a tactic to push the owners into paying."

I pressed, "What makes you so sure?"

"Because if they had killed us, they wouldn't have gotten any money," came the matter-of-fact response.

Besides mass executions, the pirates also threatened to transport the crew onto land and scuttle the *Victoria*, a threat that Mihai did not view as credible. "I don't believe they would have done it," he said. "But who knows? They were unpredictable."

And if the shipping company had refused to pay?

"They wouldn't have let the ship go," he said. "But they might have released us, maybe after five or six months. Maybe."

As with Levenescu, Somalia was now on the Chief's personal travel ban list, as I discovered when I asked if he would ever accept a berth on another vessel transiting through Somali waters.

"No!" he exclaimed, shaking his head and chuckling. "Maybe I'd run into the pirates again—they'd say, 'Chief! You're back! You must like it so much here!'" Once again, my translator and I found ourselves laughing aloud at his infectious levity. Going into these interviews, I had been nervous that I would encounter mute and traumatized wrecks; never would I have expected the Chief's carefree attitude towards his experience.

The half-hour Mihai had originally promised us soon stretched into an hour and a half, leaving him over an hour late to pick up his wife. When his phone rang with her latest reminder, the Chief concluded that he had pushed his luck to the limit. Still chuckling, we got up and made our way out of the restaurant.

14

The Freakonomics of Piracy

MODERN SCIENCE MIGHT TAKE A SCEPTICAL VIEW OF COMPUTER'S psychic talents, but it is hard to argue with success, and his clairvoyant directions could not have been more effective in leading his pack to a helpless victim. Despite travelling in the Internationally Recommended Transit Corridor (IRTC) and being within 80 to 160 kilometres of a Turkish warship when she was attacked, the *Victoria* was captured with relative ease. What made her such an easy mark? It turns out that the vessel possessed several attributes that rendered her particularly vulnerable, listed in Table 2.

Table 2: Target Profile of the *Victoria*	
Characteristic	Comment
Maximum speed: 13 knots	Moderately slow (commercial vessels travel at speeds ranging from 5 to 23 knots)
Freeboard (at lowest point): Approx. 2 metres	Very low
Crew size: 11	Moderately small (large commercial tankers can have upwards of 30 crew members)
Passive security ("hardening"): High-powered water hoses (not used during attack), plates welded to windows, blocked stairwells	No barbed wire, electric fences, or safe zones
Active security: None	No armed guards, escort boats, or long-range acoustic devices

Weather conditions: Calm seas, sunny	No navigational difficulties for the attackers
Time of attack (as of sighting): 15:04	Daylight allowed for advance warning of pirate attack
Cargo: 10,000 tonnes of rice	Non-valuable cargo

In short, the *Victoria* was slow, low, and undermanned. The disadvantage conferred by her lack of speed is evident: with a thirteen-to-twenty-knot edge, Mohamed Abdi's team overtook the *Victoria* less than forty minutes after they were sighted. Once they reached her in advance of the Turkish attack helicopter, the difficult part was over. The pirates must have been delighted to find a freeboard of only two metres, close to the lowest possible for a ship that size. Finally, the *Victoria*'s small crew not only meant fewer variables to interfere with a smooth boarding (such as crew members blasting the attackers with high-powered hoses), but also fewer sets of eyes on deck watching for pirates.

The only element favouring the *Victoria*'s crew was the timing of the hijacking. Pirate attacks most often occur at dawn and dusk—to take advantage of reduced visibility—and the fact that the pirates chose to attack in the middle of the afternoon meant that the crew was afforded an unobstructed view of the oncoming attack craft.

* * *

Hussein Hersi's insider account in Chapter 12 provides a detailed sketch of the *Victoria* gang, both from an operational and a financial standpoint. But can we trust his information? "Pirate math" frequently does not add up, so I will subject it to an external audit.

The first step is to establish the full size of the gang. Former hostages Traian Mihai and Matei Levenescu both stated that there were usually twenty pirates on board the *Victoria* on a given day, but provided two different figures for the number who congregated on the days leading up to the ransom delivery: thirty-two, according to Mihai, and thirty-eight, according to Levenescu. If, as Hersi said, each member of the operation was required to be on board the ship in order to receive his share (and it is hard to imagine any gang member would *not* want to be present for the big day), then thirty-two to thirty-eight individuals represented the total membership of the gang; I have averaged the two estimates to reach a figure of thirty-five. Of these, Hersi's and Levenescu's testimonies account for fifteen: Computer, Loyan the interpreter, Mustuku the accountant, the "commander of the khat," nine attackers,[1] and two cooks. Presumably, the remaining twenty men were the "holders" who guarded the ship and crew, in rotating shifts, once it had been brought to Eyl.

* * *

Hersi supplied some detailed—though incomplete—payroll figures, including the salaries of Computer ($1.5 million), the nine attackers ($140,000 each), the twenty holders ($20,000 each), and the two cooks ($15,000 each). However, Hersi's estimates assumed a $3 million ransom, while the actual amount turned out to be only $1.8 million. To reflect the reduced total, I have scaled down each of Hersi's numbers by 40 per cent: Computer would have received $900,000, each attacker $84,000, each holder $12,000, and each cook $9,000. Regrettably, Hersi did not provide the incomes for the interpreter, the accountant, or the commander of the khat.

Unfortunately, these numbers sum to significantly more than $1.8 million even before including Loyan, Mustuku, and the commander of the khat, all of whom presumably collected respectable salaries. Where are Hersi's mistakes? Computer's 50 per cent share is probably accurate—it is well in line with the "industry standard" for the sole investor in a gang. The salaries paid to both the holders and the cooks are also probably roughly accurate; much less would not attract young men to a job that demanded almost two months of their time, and, while not as dangerous as that of the attackers, still carried substantial risks. The only remaining explanation is that

Hersi overestimated the amount received by the attackers, to the extent of about $40,000 per man.

Matei Levenescu, it is important to note, dissented from Hersi's account in two important ways. In his eyewitness description of the air delivery and subsequent partitioning of the ransom, Levenescu recalled that one member of the attacking team received a $150,000 share.[2] It is almost certain this was Mohamed Abdi, the first attacker to board the vessel. Abdi's higher share of the spoils was not the only indicator of his elevated status within the gang—he also served as the pirates' media spokesman, providing details of the ransom amount to journalists and confirming the ship's release. Levenescu also differed from Hersi in reporting that the pirates' cook—only one, he said (plus an assistant)—received a $20,000 share. I have accepted Levenescu's first-hand version of events over Hersi's, most of which was second-hand.

Using the combined testimony of Hersi, Levenescu, and Mihai, I was able to piece together a rough estimate of the *Victoria* gang's payroll (see Table 3). These figures debunk the myth that piracy turns the average Somali teenager into an overnight millionaire. Those at the very bottom of the pyramid, the holders and the cooks, barely made what is considered a living wage in the Western world: to maintain a pirate crew of twenty, each holder would have spent roughly two-thirds of his time, or 1,150 hours, on board the *Victoria* during her seventy-two days at Eyl, thus earning an hourly wage of $10.43. The head cook and assistant by all accounts never left the ship, and therefore would have earned wages of $11.57 and $5.21 per hour, respectively (a high-end restaurant meal in Somalia, for comparison, goes for about $10 to $15).

Even the higher payout earned by the attackers seems much less appealing when one considers the risks involved. The moment he steps into a pirate skiff, an attacker accepts about a 1–2 per cent chance of being killed, a 0.5–1 per cent chance of being wounded, and a 5–6 per cent chance of being arrested and prosecuted.[3] By comparison, America's deadliest civilian occupation, king crab fisherman, has an on-the-job fatality rate of about 0.4 per cent.[4] Granted, the $41,000 that an attacker earns buys a lot more in Somalia than it does in the United States. But given that most blue-collar pirates have a virtual army of destitute friends and relatives they are expected to share with, they do not typically experience a sustained rise in their standard of living.

Table 3: Payroll of the *Victoria* Gang		
	Hersi's estimate of salaries	My estimate of salaries
Officers		
Computer, commander-in-chief, investor	$900,000	$900,000
Loyan, interpreter	Not Given	$60,000*
Mustuku, accountant	Not Given	$60,000*
Commander of the khat, supply and logistics officer	Not given	$30,000*
Attackers (shock troops)		
Mohamed Abdi, first to board the ship	$84,000 (plus Land Cruiser bonus)	$150,000 (plus Land Cruiser bonus)
Eight others	$84,000 each	$41,000 each
Cooks		
Head cook	$9,000	$20,000
Cook's assistant	$9,000	$9,000
Holders		
Twenty men	$12,000 each	$12,000 each
*These figures are my own guesswork, based on the value of their skills relative to the other members of the operation.		

As in any pyramid scheme, the clear winner is the man at the top. Computer may or may not be all-knowing, as his reputation claims, but he certainly seems a lot savvier than the men working for him.

* * *

So much for income, but what about the gang's expenses? Hersi claimed that the gang spent $500,000 on supplies—purchased on credit—while awaiting the ransom. On the surface, this seems like

an exorbitant sum. Where could it all have gone? The gang's operating expenses fell into four categories, in order of decreasing cost:
khat, transportation and fuel, weapons, and food and beverage.
Since everything was paid for with credit granted on the basis of the
forthcoming ransom, the "pirate price" for these various goods and
services was approximately double the norm.

Khat was by far the biggest drain on the group's balance sheet.
The crew did not habitually chew khat with their captors, but each
of the twenty pirates on board would have easily consumed one kilogram per day, given not much else to do with his time. The Chief
noted (to his astonishment) that the pirates paid $38 per kilogram
for the drug—or $76, at credit prices.

The group's transportation and fuel expenses included three
items. Hersi related that the gang had two Land Cruisers on permanent retainer, primarily to transport members between Garowe
and Eyl. In Puntland, a Land Cruiser rents for $200–$300 per day;
assuming the pirates paid twice that, the cost of their premium shuttle service would have been close to $60,000.

The second item was the diesel used to power the *Victoria*'s emergency generator. During the first stage of her captivity, the crew used
this generator to provide the electricity for everyday conveniences:
lights, the mess, air conditioning, and so on. But by June, the *Victoria*'s
supply of diesel fuel had been depleted. The crew then resorted to the
extremely inefficient process of generating electricity using the ship's
main engine, until, shortly after I left Eyl, the supply of bunker fuel
reached critically low levels and the engine had to be shut down. At
this point, the pirates began to ferry drums of diesel from the shore to
power the emergency generator, which, according to Levenescu, they
only turned on at night. Marine emergency generators typically have
a power output of around a hundred kilowatts, and consume twenty-
five to thirty litres of diesel per hour at full load. Given the expense,
scarcity (due to the remoteness of Eyl), and logistical difficulties in
moving large amounts of fuel from the skiff to the deck of the ship, it is
likely that the pirates did not operate the generator above half its full

capacity. If they ran the generator between 7 p.m. and 5 a.m., at a cost of about $1.50 per litre of diesel (double the norm), they would have spent $225 on fuel during each of the *Victoria*'s final twenty-five days in captivity. Added to this bill was $6,800 for the four tonnes of diesel the pirates brought on board to power the ship's fuel heating system, in preparation for the *Victoria*'s release.

The gang's third transportation expense consisted of fuel for the supply skiffs, which two to three times daily ferried people and provisions to and from the *Victoria*. During my trip to Eyl I was lucky enough to witness the loading of an early morning transport (including the unfortunate goat), which was powered by a twenty-five-horsepower outboard motor. Assuming that each round trip took about fifteen minutes, the daily gasoline consumption for such a motor would have been about eight litres. With local gasoline prices at roughly $2.50 per litre, the boat would have consumed $20 of fuel per day.

As the *Victoria*'s captivity wore on, the gang became increasingly paranoid of outside attack. To defend themselves, Hersi related that they purchased two PKMs—standard-issue Soviet machine guns—and three thousand rounds of ammunition. Such weaponry is surprisingly expensive, even in Somalia; assuming that they paid twice the regular price, the total cost of these arms would have been around $30,000.

Food and drink were the least of the gang's expenses. Hersi said that the gang purchased and slaughtered two goats daily: one for the guards on the ship, and the other for the crew. Breakfast might have consisted of goat liver, or *beer*, perhaps served with *injera* bread in an onion and potato broth, and lunch and dinner would probably have been fried or minced goat meat served on pasta or rice (supplied free from the *Victoria*'s overflowing hold) with bell peppers, potatoes, tomatoes, lettuce, bananas, and limes. Accompanying the meals (and each khat session) would be sweet tea, 7-Up, goat's and camel's milk (to sop the rice), and bottled water. In Garowe, a goat costs roughly $25; using credit in the remoteness of Eyl, the pirates paid the inflated price of $100–$150 per goat. The cost of all other ingredients would have added up to no more than $100 per day.

The *Victoria* was held captive from May 5 until July 18—a total of seventy-five days—of which seventy-two were spent anchored at Eyl. Assuming an average of twenty pirates on board at a given time (the "company" was not responsible for the expenditures of those on leave), the expense sheet for Computer's operation might have totalled $230,000, as in Table 4. Even allowing for additional discretionary expenses of $50,000 on top of this already liberal estimate, we still fall almost halfway short of Hersi's $500,000 figure. One explanation is that Hersi's estimate was simply a baseless guess. But his frequent repetition of the figure suggests otherwise; perhaps $500,000 was the "official figure" bandied about in casual conversation by members of the gang.

Table 4: Expenses of the *Victoria* Gang		
	Cost per day	Cost for 72 days
Khat		
1 kg for each of 20 pirates on board @ $76/kg	$1,520	$109,440
Transportation/fuel		
Two Land Cruiser rentals @ $400/day	$800	$57,600
Diesel for emergency generator @ $1.50/L (10 hrs/night @ 15 Lph)	$225	$5,625 (25 days)
Four metric tons (4,559 L) diesel for heating system	n/a	$6,839
Gasoline for supply skiffs (8 L/day @ $2.50/L)	$20	$1,440
Weapons		
2 PKM machine guns @ $12,000 ea.	n/a	$24,000
Ammunition (3,000 rounds @ $2/round)	n/a	$6,000
Food		
Two goats* @ $125 ea.	$250	$12,500*
Vegetables, fruit, pasta	$60	$4,320
Beverages	$40	$2,880
Total	$230,644	

*According to Mihai, the pirates began to provide goats for the crew only three to four weeks before the *Victoria*'s release, and this figure has been adjusted accordingly.

Recalling that operating expenses were subtracted directly from Computer's 50 per cent share of the ransom, is it possible that the boss was exaggerating his contribution in order to justify his lion's share? Only Computer and the group's accountant are likely to have had an accurate knowledge of its financial structure. In light of the average pirate's lack of mathematical skills, a budget inflation of 100 per cent would hardly be too big an accounting glitch to put over on the group's lower-ranked members.

* * *

Computer had good reason to conceal the lucrative nature of his own payout. The necessary start-up capital—which went towards the purchase of a ten-to-twelve-metre boat, two outboard motors, weapons, food, and fuel—could not have exceeded $50,000 (see Table 5).

Of course, it is entirely possible that Computer already owned the boat and outboard motors, in which case his start-up costs would have been considerably discounted. But even if Computer's initial contribution was in fact as high as $48,500 and his operating expenses were $230,000, he would have netted $621,500—a return on initial investment of an enviable 1,300 per cent. Sadly, Computer rebuffed my repeated attempts to interview him, and even instructed his underlings to avoid me altogether. Some months later, I again tried to reach him through my local journalist contacts, but received the following curt riposte: "Impossible. He is a Puntland government fugitive—will be shot or arrested on sight."

I'll wager that Computer will see the soldiers coming from miles away.

* * *

In many ways a typical Gulf of Aden hijacking, the *Victoria* was an ideal subject for a profile of a pirate gang. As I delved deeper into the operations of the *Victoria* gang, I gradually became aware of the similarities to a like-minded study conducted by then-University of Chicago grad student Sudhir Venkatesh and popularized by authors Steven Levitt and Stephen J. Dubner in their bestselling book *Freakonomics*. In *Freakonomics*, Levitt and Dubner explore the detailed financial statements of an inner-city Chicago crack gang, revealing that the most junior members of the gang, the street dealers—or, as Levitt and Dubner call them, the foot soldiers—earn a paltry $3.30 per hour. The point they make is simple: despite the glamorized wealth of the drug trade, very few people make a decent wage out of dealing crack.

Table 5: Computer's Start-up Costs			
Description	Unit cost	Total cost	Notes
10–12 m boat:	$20,000	$20,000	A rough guess. Of course, Computer could have owned the boat and engines before the mission began
2x 350 HP outboard motors	$10,000	$20,000	Computer probably purchased the motors second-hand from Dubai
2x RPG launchers	$1,000	$2,000	Rough estimate, based on prices in Mogadishu's Bakaara market
4x grenades	$100	$400	See above
2,100 L gasoline	$1.25/L	$2,625	Traian Mihai observed that the pirates had 500 litres of fuel on their attack craft when they boarded the *Victoria*. With their gas-guzzling engines, Computer's gang would have used at least 1,600 litres to reach the Internationally Recognized Transit Corridor from their launch point. Thus, if Mihai's report was accurate, the pirates did not have nearly enough fuel to get back to Somalia
Week's stay in Bossaso	$40/man/day	$2,520	Food and khat for the nine-man attack team as they prepared for the mission
Food	$100/man	$900	Food for the nine-man attack team for an estimated ten days at sea
Total	$48,445		

A similar point can be made about Somali piracy. Media attention has focused on the multimillion-dollar ransoms paid to the pirates, but most of the members in a pirate gang earn barely more than a crack foot soldier. Once the ransom money is divided up, the middling amount received by the average gang member is quickly either spent or bled away by family and friends.

Even in the most high-profile hijacking cases, the ransom amounts can be deceiving. When Garaad complained (in Chapter 5) that everyone involved in the MV *Faina* hijacking "only got a few thousand," he probably had a legitimate grievance. By the time the five-month-long negotiation for the *Faina* ended, four or five distinct pirate organizations were involved, and over a hundred pirates were stationed on board the vessel itself. Even though the $3.2 million ransom paid to release the ship was the largest at the time, if the *Victoria* is any guide, virtually the entire amount could have been swallowed by the costs incurred during the *Faina*'s captivity.

The parallels between crack and piracy go beyond finances. Like drug dealing for inner-city youth, piracy provides one of the few avenues for a young Somali to gain status and respect. As Levitt and Dubner point out, crack foot soldiers are willing—in the short term—to accept a job paying far less than minimum wage because they view it as one of their best chances for long-term socioeconomic advancement. In Somalia, where the prospects for career development are undeniably worse than in even the most destitute of American ghettos, it is hardly surprising that piracy is the profession of choice for many ambitious young men.

15

The Road's End

ON MY FINAL DAY IN EYL, WE LEFT THE FAROLE COMPOUND IN Badey and passed through Dawad for the last time, stopping for a cup of morning *shah* in a cramped bodega. As we were sipping our teas, a maroon-and-chrome Land Cruiser pulled up to the shop. A few kids turned to me excitedly and pointed: "Burcad, burcad!"—pirates, pirates! The Land Cruiser revved its engine and sped away.

Dhanane, which lay on a promontory visible to the south of Eyl, should have been a half-hour drive down the coast. But as no such road existed, we were forced to strike inland for an hour and a half before turning onto a path running roughly parallel to the shoreline. As we headed back towards the ocean, our 4x4s began the arduous climb back up the ridge, their insides rocking and jarring like flight simulators. The "path" we were on barely deserved the name; it was fighting a losing battle with the mountain, asserting itself only in brief stretches between jutting slabs of rock. Stunted myrrh trees dug into the sandy soil, their roots tenaciously gripping the sloping rock face.

Upon reaching the top of the plateau I was again shocked by the stark change in landscape; it was completely desolate, reminiscent of the surface of Mars. The continual harsh winds had swept the plain clear down to the rock, leaving it denuded of vegetation save for scraggly patches of shrubs barely more substantial than lichens.

Against this empty landscape, reddish termite mounds assumed monolithic proportions, rising out of the ground like a string of sand fortresses guarding the passage. The bluish haze of the Indian Ocean was visible in the distance, barely distinguishable at the horizon from the brown of a seaside bluff. Slightly further to the south, nestled in front of a chalk-streaked cliff jutting into the sea, lay the town of Dhanane. We bounced along for another fifteen minutes, but the headland hardly seemed to get any closer; with no reference points, it remained an unchanging mass in the distance.

As we approached the town, a pair of 4x4s rumbled up the path towards us, likely a pirate supply convoy returning to Garowe after making a delivery in Dhanane. On the trail of Somali pirates, there was no sign more encouraging than near-new Toyota Surfs, the closest thing the pirates had to a company car. As the Surfs pulled alongside us, a driver-side window rolled halfway down and a few hands extended cautious greetings, which were reciprocated by our driver, Mahamoud.

"If you weren't here, we would capture or shoot them," Colonel Omar declared. I could not tell if he was joking.

If Eyl was the Wild West, then Dhanane was the wilderness—a hamlet of huts beginning about fifty metres back from the cliff-side, many with green-tinged thatched roofs the colour of a corroded penny. Rising ten metres above the ground, the spire of a lone radio tower dominated the town; a nearby mosque was the only stone building in sight. It was as if humanity had attempted to scratch proof of its existence into the bare rock, a testament that would be washed off the cliff by the first torrential rain. Of course, such a rain would never come in Somalia, but it seemed a miracle that the flimsy huts could withstand the vicious winds of the *hagaa*.

A few faded NGO signs marked the entrance to the village, probably planted during a brief detour by the tsunami relief expedition sent to Eyl in 2004. We drove slowly through the centre of town, past dwellings spilling rough-and-tumble towards the sea. The village was completely deserted, its inhabitants not yet awakened to our presence. We stopped the vehicles short of the cliff and strolled down to its edge.

The bluff on which Dhanane was situated wrapped around to cradle a large inlet at its base. Walking to the edge of the cliff, I gazed onto a white sand beach fifty metres directly below; the drop was precipitous, but a near-vertical path allowed access to it. Waves of rolling blue turned gently to green as they broke against the shallow incline of the beachhead. Subtract the wind, install a few shark nets, bring an end to the civil war, and Dhanane would have made a fine spot for a seaside resort. On the sand stood a solitary building resembling a beach house, surrounded by overturned fishing skiffs. There were no fishermen in sight, and it was easy to understand why; the winds in Dhanane were even stronger than those in Eyl, and in the horseshoe-shaped bay below they must have been close to tropical storm force. A pirate skiff would have been hard-pressed to make it past the first salvo of waves breaking against the shore.

My bodyguard Said grabbed my arm and pointed eagerly leftward on the horizon. There, almost obscured by the edge of the bluff, was the object of my trip to this obscure little town. It was the Dutch-owned cargo ship *Marathon*, hijacked on May 7, twenty-eight days previously, while transporting coke fuel through the Gulf of Aden safety corridor. There were eight Ukrainian crew members on board.

As I snapped away at these various sights, digital SLR in one hand, camcorder in the other, a number of young men detached themselves from the huts above and made their way to the cliffside to observe. They soon wandered over to Omar and began to question him.

"Why did you bring this spy?" one of them said. "Tell him that it's a Yemeni fishing ship," pointing to the *Marathon*, clearly hoping that I would go looking somewhere else for Europeans. He was hardly to blame for this cynical attitude, given the international media's failure to spare any ink for the scores of unreported attacks on Yemeni fishermen.

The curious youth soon tired of their windy watch-keeping and receded back into the town, glancing back at me over their shoulders.

We began to wind our way back up through the village, the orange tarpaulins of the hut walls snapping violently as we passed like sails luffing in the wind. We came to a small enclosure ringed by piles of stacked brushwood, where a few townspeople had gathered beside a small outdoor kiosk. Omar motioned to a thatched lean-to nearby, and I pushed through the canvas entrance and into the dark, cool interior. There were a few plastic chairs scattered in a circle around the wooden strut holding up the hut, and Omar and I sat down.

Two members of the local pirate chapter lounged on the woven mats lining the dirt floor of the lean-to. One, whom I later learned was the group's accountant, had recently arrived from Garowe in anticipation of the impending delivery of the ransom money; he lay curled in a semi-foetal position, his cellphone clutched in his left hand. Another member of the gang, sporting an oversized UNICEF T-shirt, joked that he had renounced piracy and was now working for the United Nations. Discarded khat leaves lay in two messy piles at his feet, flanked by several packs of British Tobacco cigarettes. Ombaali reclined next to him with his 7-Up in hand, and they chatted like old comrades.

I had no idea whose hut this was or who had invited us in, but soon a man dressed in brown khaki pants and vest entered and greeted us. His name was Dar Muse Gaben, and he soon revealed himself to be a high-ranking member of the local group, the man in charge of organizing and delivering supplies to his colleagues aboard the *Marathon*. Gaben took his work into his off-hours, it seemed, because he soon returned with a round of *shah* and several warm 7-Ups for Omar and me. After some prodding, Gaben cautiously agreed to answer a few of my questions.

"Illegal fishing, that's the only reason we're doing this," he said. Then, in an effort to sound convincing, "Last night, there were two illegal fishing ships right here. We tried to fight them, but they had anti-aircraft guns."

Though there was certainly no dearth of foreign fishing trawlers to attack, Gaben was set on an early retirement. "This is going to be my last ship," he assured me, almost apologetically, referring to the *Marathon*.

"We treat the hostages very well," he continued. "We bring them all the food and drink they want. They've become fat." He smiled broadly. "Let me tell you," he said, "they like it better on that ship than in the Ukraine."

Could I go on board and ask them myself? Gaben shook his head perturbedly, rose, and stormed out of the hut. I later discovered from media accounts of the *Marathon*'s release that the ship's welder, Serhiy Vartenkov, was already dead, shot and killed as the pirates boarded the vessel. The ship's cook, Georgi Gussakov, had also been shot and was in critical condition by the time the *Marathon* was released.

After a few more sips of 7-Up I wandered out after Gaben, but he had disappeared. Nearby, I spotted a group of local bushmen reclining against a wall, grinning openly at me through rows of straight white teeth. Two of the men enthusiastically agreed to my request to film them. The first looked to be in his early sixties, short and dark-skinned, cotton-white hair receding in a horseshoe pattern around a bulbous scalp; like many Somali elders, he dyed his beard with orange henna. He cradled a herder's staff between the loose folds of his *ma'awis*.

"We used to be fishermen, but we went back to the bush after it became too dangerous," he said. "We didn't become pirates. We don't even know who these guys are," he said, referring to my erstwhile tea companions. "We think they're from very far away."

"There are no soldiers here, and they know that," the second herdsman added. "And we hardly have any weapons. So they keep coming. They even used to steal our goats, though that doesn't happen as much anymore. There used to be more pirates here, but now there is only one ship left. This will be the last one, *inshallah*."

As I chatted with the bushmen, Gaben returned, accompanied by the young men who had earlier been studying me by the cliff. Each was carrying his gun slung over his shoulder. The atmosphere had become perceptibly tenser, and the townspeople began to slink away into the maze of huts until the area around the kiosk was deserted. The pirates moved to their row of parked 4x4s and milled around them anxiously, as if leaving open either option of a fight or flight response.

"You really freaked them out by asking to see the ship," Omar nervously explained. It was the same reaction I had provoked in Eyl, the only difference being that instead of moving their ship, the pirates were asking us to move. "There's nothing more to be gained by staying here," Omar advised.

The Colonel, meanwhile, broke into a wide grin and ordered me to follow his movements with my video camera. Out of habit I obeyed, tracking him in the viewfinder as he weaved his way through the crowd of posturing pirates. He returned after completing his round, winking and grinning at me.

"Eh, Levish? You said you wanted pictures of pirates," he said. Stunned, I thanked him for his help.

Not being inclined to wait around to find out how pirates dealt with spies in their midst, I agreed to Omar's request to leave. We quickly filed into our vehicles, and within a few minutes our mini-motorcade was out of Dhanane and back on the rocky trail.

It was time to go home.

* * *

The pirate board meeting onto which we stumbled had not been convened in vain. A few days later, on June 23, the *Marathon* was released for a reported ransom of $1.3 million.[1] As previously mentioned, the ship's welder had been killed by a stray bullet during the boarding operation; though initially denying that a death had occurred aboard a Dutch-flagged vessel, the government of the Netherlands soon issued a strongly worded promise to right the injustice. "I am shocked by the cowardly murder of a member of the crew," Dutch foreign minister Mamime Verhagen announced in a statement. "The Netherlands will do everything to end these practices, by putting Dutch navy ships into operations against piracy and supporting the creation of a regional tribunal so that the criminals do not escape punishment."[2]

The *Marathon* was one of the rare instances where casualties had been incurred among the crew of a hijacked ship. Up to this point, it had been possible for me to view pirates as a sympathetic breed of criminal like the bank robbers audiences cheer in movie theatres—the sort who never shoot the guards on the way in. For a pirate, killing hostages is not an economically rational decision, yet I had had the distinct impression that the Dhanane gang would have been as perfectly at ease with slaughtering their captives as ransoming them. Later, when reading news of the casualties the crew had suffered, I was struck by the chilling realization that I had shared tea with murderers.

It is often argued that movements based on violence or criminality become, by their very nature, increasingly radicalized as time passes, as the moderates are slowly squeezed out by the extremists. The gangs I encountered in Eyl and Dhanane were examples of what I term the "third wave" of piracy. Unlike the first wave of fishermen vigilantes in the mid-1990s, or the second wave of the mid-2000s, when the same men developed their operations into large-scale businesses, the third wave has consisted largely of opportunists without fishing backgrounds—often disaffected youth from the large inland nomad population. They mouth the worn-out mantra of the just crusade against illegal fishing like sanctimonious popes, with sly eyes and cynical smiles. But absent is the simple earnestness of Boyah and Momman, their brooding introspection regarding the morality of their actions, their sincere desire to lead a higher life.

The bosses in Dhanane exuded a cold ruthlessness that permitted a man to joke that his hostages were fat and sated, while one of them had been shot dead and another lay bleeding on the deck. These men had inherited Boyah's legacy.

Epilogue

The Problems of Puntland

I LAST SAW BOYAH A FEW DAYS BEFORE I LEFT PUNTLAND FOR THE final time. His Blue Jays T-shirt was absent, but as we parted he surprised me by seizing my hand and pulling me in for a pound hug, enveloping me in his massive frame. We had evidently come a long way from the menacing stares he had levelled at me during our first meeting six months previous.

Since that first meeting, Boyah has attained international fame as the self-appointed media spokesman of the Somali pirates, his name growing with every interview he has granted. Foreign journalists from the BBC, Al Jazeera, and the *New York Times,* among others, flocked to hear what Boyah had to tell them, in part because he guaranteed a good interview: he was frank, disarming, and always reliable for a great quote. His motivation was a simple wish to let the world know about the struggles that he and his brethren had faced growing up as poor fishermen. Unlike many of his successors, he was no petty thug or cheap sadist, and willingly subjected his past choices to a self-probing moral reflection. The remorse he expressed, I believe, was genuine.

In the end, Boyah paid a heavy price for his love of the spotlight. When his frankness during interviews extended to taking public credit for hijacking more than twenty-five ships, it was inevitable that he would catch the eye of the US government. After enduring continual criticism over his lax treatment of pirate leaders, President Farole finally caved under the weight of US and international pressure. On Tuesday, May 18, 2010, Boyah and ten other men were arrested as they were preparing to flee Garowe in three Toyota Surfs; in their possession were two pistols and, for all Boyah's earlier claims of being penniless, $29,500 in cash. As of February 2011, Boyah was still sitting in a cell, awaiting sentencing.

"Of course he'll go to jail," a Puntland government insider told me. "Life in prison."

From what I heard, Boyah had become disillusioned with the government's refusal to commission him and his men as coast guards, and decided to return to the sea on his own initiative. Following the arrest, the governor of Nugaal region claimed that Boyah, despite his highly publicized redemption movement, had never stopped covertly financing pirate activities.[1] The Puntland security forces had been tailing him for months.

It was a positive sign from the Puntland government, an indication that President Farole was willing to get tough with his own sub-clan in order to earn the trust of the international community. Such commitment from the Farole administration—free of the nepotistic proclivities bred by Somali clanism—will be critical if Puntland is to become a valid partner in the anti-piracy struggle.

* * *

Five years ago, the Somali pirates were little more than fishermen who had traded in their nets for assault rifles and rocket-propelled grenades. Since then, they have blossomed into maritime trade professionals, with an expanding capital base and a logistical and navigational sophistication that has allowed them to strike deep in the Indian Ocean, hundreds of kilometres beyond the reach of the international naval forces.

Though the naval presence continues to burgeon, pirate hijackings are on the rise, and as of February 2011 more vessels are being held hostage along the Somali coast than ever before. The international naval forces have yet to grasp that violence is best used as a scalpel, not a club, and that their efforts to bludgeon the Somali pirates out of existence through sheer military force alone are no more likely to succeed in the future than in the past.

How might Somali piracy look in another five years?

First, the business will probably be a lot more lucrative. The current trend of ransom inflation is almost certain to continue unabated; hijacked vessels and their cargos are often worth hundreds of millions of dollars (over and above the value of the crews' lives), and pirate negotiators have only just begun to realize how much shipowners are willing to pay. Each time a company agrees to a record-setting ransom, it sets a precedent that fuels the upward pressure on future payments.

Second, pirate gangs are likely to be much more organized. As the payoffs continue to rise, rival organizations, clan militias, and even Somali Islamist groups will be increasingly tempted to rip off successful pirate groups. This threat, in turn, may provoke the pirates to coalesce into more permanent criminal syndicates and establish standing armies of their own. Piracy might well develop into a mafia-style business, complete with infighting, turf wars, and mob hits.

Third, encounters at sea are likely to get a whole lot bloodier. Already, the use of firearms on all sides is on the rise; private security is becoming increasingly common on commercial vessels, the French government has stationed marines on the decks of its Indian Ocean fishing fleet, and Spain has followed suit by subsidizing the cost of armed guards on its own tuna boats. And the pirates are responding; whereas in the past, pirate attack groups used their weapons primarily as noisemakers—with the aim of frightening ships' crews into surrendering—it has recently become standard practice to fire directly at the attacked vessel and her crew.

The brutality has already begun to escalate. In February 2011 the Associated Press reported that the pirates had begun "systematically torturing" hostages, subjecting them to beatings, locking them in freezers, and ligating their genitals with plastic ties.[2] On February 18, there occurred a tragedy unprecedented in the brief history of Somali piracy. In circumstances not yet entirely clear, American retirees Sean and Jean Adam, along with crewmates Phyllis Macay and Bob Riggle, were murdered by pirates after their yacht, the S/V *Quest*, had been hijacked four hundred kilometres off the coast of Oman. Shadowed by four US warships, navy helicopters whirring overhead, the pirates reportedly panicked and began to fight amongst themselves over which course of action to take. Responding to the sounds of gunfire aboard the *Quest* (some accounts say that the pirates also hit a warship with a rocket-propelled grenade), US forces were speedily dispatched to the yacht, prompting the pirates to execute all four hostages. The hijacking brought a cruel end to the Adams' proselytizing voyage around the world, their vessel ballasted with thousands of Bibles to hand out along the way.

With the cost of future attacks increasingly likely to be measured in blood in lieu of dollars, bringing a swift end to the scourge of piracy has never been more imperative.

* * *

What might be done to solve the piracy problem?

Since the mid-1990s, Somali nation-building has been divided between those advocating for the "building block" approach—supporting stable, autonomous regions from the bottom up—and the top-down approach, as represented by the Transitional Federal Government (TFG). This latter strategy, which has held sway since 2000 (when the first in a series of transitional national governments was proclaimed), has been a disaster from the start. The TFG is a government in name only: its members have no constituents and its ministers no portfolios, and its continued existence rests only on the blind willingness of its international backers to believe that a fantasy is real. Yet the international community has remained steadfast in its patronage. At an April 2009 donor conference held in Brussels, for instance, Western nations pledged $250 million to support the TFG and fund the African Union's AMISOM peacekeeping mission, the only force preventing Shabaab from driving the few MPs remaining in Mogadishu into the sea. No money, conversely, was set aside either for Puntland or Somaliland.

Piracy in Puntland, I believe, is a direct symptom of the international community's failed strategy of nation-building in Somalia. The decline of Puntland's political and economic stability from 2005 to 2008 laid the groundwork for the subsequent piracy outbreak—a crisis that may have been averted had the international community diverted a fraction of its attention to stabilizing Puntland (by helping the administration meet its payrolls, for example). As Puntland came apart at the seams, the United States and other donors continued to put money towards the mortars and machine guns that would buy another stay of execution for the besieged members of Somalia's official national government.

* * *

If there is one thing on which every commentator on Somali piracy agrees, it is that the problem must be solved on land, not merely at sea. Startlingly few, however, explain what an on-the-ground solution might entail, other than the swift return of a functioning government to Somalia—as if the state collapse of the last two decades were the result of a lack of effort. Other analysts counsel military force, citing the United States' successful nineteenth-century war against the Barbary pirates—during which US marines ultimately invaded North Africa—as an educational precedent.[3] But although the UN Security Council has authorized land-based measures, the current security climate makes deploying ground forces on Somali soil a madman's proposition, and no country has volunteered (or will) its troops for such an errand.

Non-payment of ransoms is another policy option that has been discussed very seriously at the highest levels—both the UK government and the Baltic and International Maritime Council (the world's biggest shipping association), for example, have counselled against giving in to pirate demands. Concerns that the pirates may be linked to Al-Shabaab have also led to calls to treat pirate pay-offs like ransoms to terrorist groups—explicitly prohibited under any circumstances. Perhaps if shipping companies had taken a firm anti-ransom stance five years ago, Somali piracy would never have developed into the current epidemic. But the time for such brinksmanship is over; after over a decade of steadily increasing ransoms, the threat of withholding payments is no longer credible.

Notwithstanding the savage murders of the four American yachters, the pirates rarely kill, and it is possible—as Boyah and his colleagues have suggested to me—that the threat is largely a bluff. Unfortunately, even if shipping owners wished to gamble on this dubious assertion, the pirates still possess a viable option between the two extremes of murdering the crew or releasing the ship without a ransom: the threat to transfer the crew ashore and abandon or scuttle the hijacked vessel. Indeed, this manoeuvre has already been carried out on multiple occasions; in the case of the *Rockall* hijacking (see Chapter 4), a German couple was held in the mountains near Bossaso for months, and a similar fate befell Paul and Rachel Chandler, elderly British yachters who were held near Harardheere for over a year under intolerable conditions.

The problem with "getting tough" with the pirates is that just one misstep could occasion a monumental financial or even ecological disaster, to say nothing of the potential loss of life. As we saw in the case of the *Victoria*, pirate gangs often incur considerable operating expenses in expectation of a certain ransom payment, and potentially owe hundreds of thousands of dollars to dangerous creditors on land. In short, coming home empty-handed might prove as lethal to them as facing a team of Navy SEALs. They are scared, desperate, and unpredictable, and only one jittery finger on a grenade launcher would be needed to detonate an oil tanker and send a few hundred million dollars—more than the total of all ransoms paid to date—straight to the bottom of the ocean, leaving deadly toxic chemicals washing ashore on Somalia's beaches.

In essence, the risks of employing hardball tactics—either by refusing to pay ransoms or through direct military assaults—far outweigh the few million dollars such a strategy might save. The fact is, with only a fraction of 1 per cent of all ships passing through "pirate waters" being successfully hijacked, paying ransoms is economically sustainable for the long term (although this might change if ransom amounts continue to rise). Bowing to extortion may be humiliating, and the months of lost labour and capital inconvenient, but at least usually no one dies. The long-term cost of "giving in," on the other hand, is measured by the increasing ransoms paid to the pirates, and, with the higher stakes, the ever-growing chance of incurring loss of life.

One thing, at least, is clear: when the situation on the ground produces men desperate enough to set out into the Indian Ocean in four-metre skiffs without enough food and fuel to return—their only hope of survival either to capture a vessel or themselves be captured—military force alone will not be a sufficient deterrent. Short of convincing Somalia's warring factions to lay down their Kalashnikovs and come together to form a functioning national government overnight (which many analysts seem to treat as a realistic solution), Somali piracy is unlikely to be completely eradicated in the foreseeable future. Any feasible solution must therefore aim at the pragmatic mitigation, not the elimination, of piracy.

With that in mind, what can the international community do against piracy?

1. FINANCE AN EFFECTIVE AND WELL-PAID PUNTLAND POLICE TASK FORCE.

A coast guard is a legitimate last line of defence against piracy in a mature state, but in Puntland a much more cost-effective strategy would be to invest in a police task force capable of stopping the pirates before they reach the sea. Train and equip police officers, perhaps through an expansion of the police training program already operated by the UN Development Programme. Fund small permanent garrisons in Eyl, Garacad, and other coastal towns, and provide all-terrain vehicles that will allow for a rapid response to pirate threats. Salaries should be high enough—in the region of President Farole's suggestion of $300 per month—to deter corruption and reduce the allure that piracy has presented to members of the security forces in the past. In the longer term, provide funding for roads, radar stations equipped with high frequency radios, and other basic infrastructure in the coastal regions that will further improve response time.

2. FUND AN EXPANSION OF THE PUNTLAND PRISON SYSTEM.

The Puntland government is going to need somewhere to put suspects apprehended by its revamped police force, ideally without resorting to the mass pardons I witnessed at Bossaso prison. Accordingly, finance the construction of new prisons on Puntland soil, with the aim of increasing the region's prison capacity to roughly 1,500–2,000 inmates.

Instead of resorting to legal hocus-pocus to assign arbitrary jurisdiction over suspected pirates to Kenyan courts, establish qualified multinational tribunals to try them. Once the Puntland authorities have proved that they can be trusted to make prisoners actually serve their sentences—regardless of their clan or family connections—start to hand over convicted pirates to local prisons.

3. FOSTER INTELLIGENCE COORDINATION BETWEEN PUNTLAND AND INTERNATIONAL NAVAL FORCES.

The best source of intelligence on pirate activities is not EUNAVFOR or the CIA, but the local people on the ground. In order to tap this resource, create intelligence-gathering centres within Puntland. Set up pirate tip hotlines, publicize the relevant contact numbers, and offer modest rewards for information leading to the arrest of suspected pirates. Many local residents of Puntland's coastal areas are sufficiently fed up with the pirates to turn informer, and sufficiently poor that a moderate financial incentive would be enough to sway equivocators.

Finally, establish channels for coordinating ground-based intelligence with the international naval forces, ensuring regular communication between Puntland authorities and the NATO, EUNAVFOR, and CTF-151 command and control centres.

4. CLAMP DOWN ON ILLEGAL FISHING.

Although Somali piracy began as a backlash by disaffected fishermen, the hijacking of commercial vessels is now a self-sustaining business that has far outgrown its original impetus. Nonetheless, the continuing role of illegal fishing as a powerful founding myth, psychological justification, and effective PR tool should not be underestimated.

Somalis often point out to me the hypocrisy of foreign warships arresting pirates as long-liners fish unmolested within sight. Indeed, it hardly seems fair for international forces to apply one standard of justice to pirates and another to thieves. Given the political will, the EU has the legal authority to rein in the Spanish, Italian, and French fishing interests that continue to violate Somalia's exclusive economic zone. The Taiwanese, Thai, Chinese, and South Asian vessels that constitute the majority of the remaining violators would have to be stopped through other means. To that end, the international naval fleets patrolling Somali waters should expand their mandates to include interdicting foreign fishing vessels, or, at the very least, collecting photographic evidence of fishing violations to pass on to a regulatory body empowered to sanction offenders. Eliminating illegal fishing will not remove the financial incentive for piracy, but publicized prosecutions of vessels caught fishing illegally will help to undercut the pirates' claims of legitimacy.

Stymieing illegal fishing will also bring many benefits to those on land. Heavily armed trawlers, along with the more recent danger of foreign warships mistaking legitimate fishermen for pirates, currently make fishing far too dangerous an occupation for the average life-loving Somali. Cleansing Somali waters of thuggish foreign fishermen will aid in revitalizing Somalia's fishing industry, providing a vital source of income for destitute coastal dwellers and reducing the pool of potential pirate recruits. Action at sea should be matched on the ground by investments in fishing boats and gear, as well as processing plants and refrigerated transports.

5. ENCOURAGE OR REQUIRE PASSIVE SECURITY MEASURES ABOARD COMMERCIAL VESSELS.

Simple security measures—such as extra watches, barbed wire, travelling in convoys, and lockdown areas in which the crew can barricade themselves (my "turtle defence")—are extremely effective at deterring pirate attacks. Ideally, the International Maritime Organization should adopt binding regulations to force owners of vessels transiting through Somali waters to implement a bare minimum standard of such practices.

* * *

Implementing the above recommendations would not require additional foreign aid to Somalia, but rather the reinvestment of the hundreds of millions of dollars already being spent on the bloated—and largely ineffectual—international marine flotillas. If the (mostly Western) countries contributing to the naval effort—the United States, France, and the United Kingdom principal among them—coordinated with one another to cut the annual budgets of the NATO, EU, and US-led coalition task forces by as little as 10 per cent (approximately \$100–\$110 million per year), sufficient funds would be freed to finance my suggested course of action.

The method of delivering financial and technical assistance, however, is as critical as the assistance itself. After years of foreign meddling in their affairs, Somalis have become wary of outside intervention, and Puntland's cooperation with Westerners, particularly the United States, could provoke and attract support to an Islamist insurgency. The simultaneous Al-Shabaab suicide bombings in Bossaso and Hargeysa (Somaliland) in October 2008 demonstrated that the Islamists have both the capacity and the will to strike at their northern neighbours when they perceive them to be cozying up to the United States.[4] In mid-2010, moreover, an Al-Shabaab-linked insurgency sprang up in northern Puntland, led by the Warsangali warlord Mohamed Said Atom from his mountain base in Galgala, thirty kilometres outside Bossaso. Consequently, the visible foreign presence on the ground would have to be kept to a minimum; even unarmed military or police advisors on Somali soil would risk a very high chance of eliciting, or exacerbating, an extremist response.

Is the Puntland government up to the task? Many would argue that the current administration is too kleptocratic, institutionally weak, and clan-oriented to be a trustworthy partner. Some—such as the UN Monitoring Group on Somalia—have come close to calling Puntland a criminal state, and might easily argue that funding the Puntland government is merely one step removed from buying off the pirates themselves.[5] Moreover, with the deaths of American yachters in February 2011, it is increasingly tempting to equate giving aid to Somali political institutions with helping the people responsible for the brutal murder of US citizens.

To these detractors, I have two responses. First, Puntland is all we've got. If an on-the-ground solution is required, then perpetuating the farce that the TFG is in control of the entire country is an unproductive delusion. Second, even if one assumes the worst excesses of corruption from Puntland government officials, muscling in on the international donor scene would be, for them, a far more profitable racket than piracy. In order to be assured of continued international assistance, the Puntland government would have to deliver concrete results, and if the price were scuttling its alleged pirate associates, their choice would be easy. My point here is not to suggest another way to line the pockets of corrupt officials; rather, it is a cynical assessment of how we might incentivize such officials into working for our advantage.

I have one last caveat. Enhancing the Puntland government's capacity to enforce law and order will not end piracy completely, because pirate bases south of Puntland—most notably Harardheere and Hobyo—have become the new centres of the trade. However, success in Puntland would provide a model for similar action in the far weaker semi-autonomous region of Galmudug, where these two towns are situated (though the Galmudug administration is yet to bring them under its control). The lynchpin of my approach is that valid local partners—wherever they may be found—are vital to any serious attempt to curtail Somali piracy. The same dogmatic inflexibility that has permitted the TFG-focused nation-building approach to consistently triumph against all reason must not be allowed to infect our counter-piracy thinking. Like an earthquake that exposes the faults in a foundation, piracy has revealed the flaws underpinning the world's strategy in dealing with Somalia. Perhaps it is time to tear down the house and begin anew.

* * *

At a chaotic guardhouse at Bossaso airstrip, scurrying travellers clamoured for boarding passes from a few overburdened officials. Upon handing over my passport I learned that, on my way into Somalia, the customs agent had scribbled the incorrect exit date on my visa stamp. Now, an official informed me that I had been in the country illegally for the past ten days and would be required to pay a fine of $200. I had spent the last of my US dollars on the wages of my bodyguards, Said and Abdirashid, and had no money for my exit ransom. Colonel Omar was stuck with the bill; he fixed me with one of his menacing glances, as if deciding whether he should arrest me, let me go, or shoot me. Beyond the chain-link fence separating the parking lot from the sand-covered airstrip, a mob was pressing around the gangway; the plane was starting to board. I left the Colonel grumbling at me and shouting at the official, and made my way onto the runway, past a solitary guard who made no motion to check my passport.

The Ilyushin Il-18 turboprop was Soviet-made, the seat fabric torn and seatbelts broken, but it was larger and seemingly sturdier than the rattletrap Antonov that had brought me into Somalia. I left Puntland decidedly less apprehensive than I had first arrived.

For me, Somalia will always be a land of adventure, my memories of it forged in a mixture of adrenaline and wonder. In the span of a few weeks, I had gone from writing marketing reports to tracking down pirates in one of the world's most dangerous countries, under the protection of a man I had never before met. The romanticism of the journey was intoxicating.

Like their seventeenth-century forebears, the Somali pirates were outnumbered and outgunned, yet dared to challenge the might of the world's navies, casting themselves as heroic defenders of their seas against the forces of foreign exploitation. It was hard not to feel some slight admiration for their reckless courage, regardless of the iniquity of its ends. In reality, the pirates more resembled self-interested, amoral, and often barbaric gangsters than principled crusaders, as any hostage seafarer could attest to. "It is when the pirates count their booty," author William Bolitho once wrote, "that they become mere thieves."[6]

As the plane gained altitude, Bossaso shrank to a pale yellow smudge in the side window. A pair of Australian cameramen chatted loudly in the seats in front of me. Far below, the Gulf of Aden stretched to the horizon, blue and unbroken.

Appendix 1

Simplified Somali Clan Tree

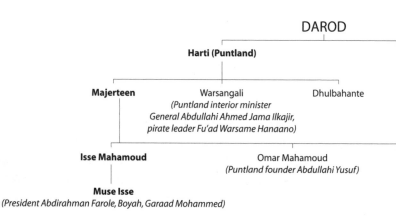

DAROD

Harti (Puntland)

Majerteen Warsangali Dhulbahante
(Puntland interior minister
General Abdullahi Ahmed Jama Ilkajir,
pirate leader Fu'ad Warsame Hanaano)

Isse Mahamoud Omar Mahamoud
(Puntland founder Abdullahi Yusuf)

Muse Isse
(President Abdirahman Farole, Boyah, Garaad Mohammed)

HAWIYE (Central/Southern Somalia)

Abgal Habir Gedir
(Warlord Mohamed Farah Aidid)

Sa'ad **Suleiman**
(Afweyne, other Harardheere pirates)

DIR

Gadabursi
Biinaal
Isse

Marehan
(former Somali dictator Mohamed Siad Barre) Ogaden

Osman Mahamoud
*(former Puntland president
Mohamud Muse Hersi)*

ISAAQ* (Somaliland)

Habir Awal
Habir Geelo
Garhajis
Habir Jaalo

Ayr   Sarur

RAHANWEYN

Digil
Mirifle

*Considered by some to be a sub-group of the Dir.

Appendix 2

The *Victoria* Gang

IN CHAPTER 14, WE LOOKED AT THE FEATURES OF THE *VICTORIA* that made her a tempting target. But what of her captors? How did Computer's organization measure up to a typical pirate gang? Stig Jarle Hansen's extensive research into the organization and operational methods of pirate groups allows us to establish a comparative framework with which to place the *Victoria* gang in perspective.[1] I will examine seven criteria in turn:

1. Size
2. Investment structure
3. Cost structure
4. Attack strategy
5. Technology
6. Role of the diaspora
7. Other

1. SIZE

According to Hansen, "an average group tends to consist of around 12 to 35 individuals." At 35 members, Computer's organization was large, though still smaller than the top-tier operations, such as the hundreds-strong consortium of gangs involved in the *Faina* hijacking.

2. INVESTMENT STRUCTURE

Venture Capital

Hansen describes three methods of capital financing for pirate operations, which I label the "single investor," "co-operative," and "private equity" investment models. Under the single investor model, one man—often a local businessman—funds the entire operation, from the boats to the guns and the communication equipment. The co-operative, on the other hand, involves a number of equal shareholders joining together, each bringing his own guns and food (though the boat is owned by a specific member of the group). Finally, the private equity model consists of an individual who first raises capital from a number of willing investors, then proceeds to organize and direct the mission (like Afweyne, in the early days).

The *Victoria* gang operated under the single investor model, with Computer supplying the entire start-up capital and hence claiming a large slice of the company's revenues. "In Puntland," Hansen writes, "local researchers have identified 51 investors, mid-level businessmen mostly from the clans of the respective pirate group." Computer's name is probably on that list—particularly if, as suggested in Chapter 14, he is a known Puntland government fugitive.

Payroll

The majority of pirate gangs work on straight commission, a system Hansen playfully labels "no prey, no pay." Their paycheques, in other words, are contingent on the successful capture and ransoming of a suitable vessel. This commission structure was clearly employed by Computer's group; without the *Victoria*, the gang members' remuneration would have consisted of nothing more than a one-way pleasure cruise in the Gulf of Aden.

3. COST STRUCTURE
Start-up Costs
According to Hansen, the cost of financing a pirate operation ranges from $300 to as high as $30,000. At almost $50,000, Computer's initial capital outlay was off Hansen's scale. To blame for his extravagant bill were the dual heavy-duty outboard motors he outfitted to the back of his unusually large attack boat; at 350 horsepower, they were among the most powerful and expensive available.

Operating Expenses
Operating expenses for a typical pirate group, Hansen writes, might run "as low as $100 per day." At an estimated $3,000 per day, Computer's gang spent money at a rate several orders of magnitude higher. In their love of deficit spending, however, Computer's gang was typical. Hansen writes that a hijacked ship is often maintained on credit, and there is no doubt that this was the case with Computer's operation.

4. ATTACK STRATEGY
Number of Attack Craft
The most common pirate attack strategy, Hansen argues, involves two skiffs (each typically holding five or six pirates), with one covering the other as its occupants attempt to scale the target vessel. Deploying one turbo-charged attack craft carrying nine hijackers, Computer's modus operandi was atypical. Putting all your pirates in one boat has its perils; if, for instance, the *Victoria* crew had put up any resistance—such as blasting the would-be boarders with deck hoses—the absence of cover fire might have proved problematic. However, such a strategy also had several advantages: a more comfortable standard of living, additional room to store food and fuel, and more convincing fisherman camouflage.

Solitary Boarder

According to Hansen, standard operating procedure for a pirate boarding dictates that one lone man scale the sides of the target vessel before all others; in the words of Bossaso-based pirate "Red Beard": "One man goes first and that man gives information back to us and we all board the ship then." In this respect, the *Victoria* gang followed the industry norm; their trailblazer, of course, was Mohamed Abdi.

"Attack" and "Hold" Teams

"The groups are often, but not always, divided into an attack team and hold team," writes Hansen. This attacker/holder dichotomy was certainly an organizational feature of Computer's group. The attackers, like an entitled officer corps, enjoyed a higher status than the holders, and greater flexibility when it came to taking shore leave. Furthermore, the "three leaders" identified by hostage Traian Mihai all came from the attacker caste, and each attacker received a significantly higher payout than the holders.

5. TECHNOLOGY

Though Computer's psychic directions undoubtedly gave the *Victoria* hijackers a unique advantage over other pirate groups, a sceptic might wonder if they had any additional help from modern technology. Hansen notes that pirates often possess such gadgets as night vision goggles, satellite telecommunications systems, and occasionally automatic identification systems that allow them to read the transponders of passing vessels. Added to this list should be basic marine navigation devices, such as GPS and radar systems.

There is no evidence to suggest that the *Victoria* hijackers possessed any of these accoutrements. The *Victoria* was carrying a cargo of rice, and was not the kind of glamorous prize about which a pirate would brag to his friends at the local khat *suq*. (Romanian media sources went so far as to report that the pirates may have mistaken the *Victoria* for an oil transport.[2]) Regardless, Computer's group would probably not have targeted the *Victoria* if they had been able to read transponders or had detailed intelligence on vessel itineraries. Indeed, given the pirates' utter lack of understanding of the *Victoria*'s radar display (as humorously recounted by Mihai), their attack craft almost certainly did not possess a marine radar system.

The more likely scenario is that the *Victoria* found *them*. With limited range and navigational technologies, the pirates were content to float in the IRTC and await a target of opportunity, like patient fishermen waiting for a nibble. In some respects, Levenescu may have been correct when he scornfully claimed that the IRTC had made the pirates' job easier: though they faced a higher risk of death or capture, the transit corridor saved them the trouble of deciding where to hunt.

Another hypothetical indicator of a sophisticated pirate gang is the practice of gathering intelligence (cargo, itineraries, insurance details) on potential targets, either through "spotters"—informants located in major ports—or through membership in an online maritime tracking service, such as Lloyd's Marine Intelligence Unit. For the same rationale as discussed above, there is little reason to think the *Victoria* hijackers made use of either of these resources.

In all probability, their most sophisticated technology was their own eyes, which would have proved quite capable of detecting the *Victoria*—and her telltale deck cranes—at a distance of ten kilometres.

6. ROLE OF THE DIASPORA

There has been much discussion in the media regarding the supposed transnational criminal networks controlling Somali pirate gangs from behind the scenes. As with many such myths, the drive for a good story often overwhelms the facts.

Though the existence of a transnational criminal conspiracy is highly overstated, the true level of the Somali diaspora's involvement in piracy is less certain, and Hansen's research does not help resolve the ambiguity. One of his pirate interviewees claimed that Somali expats from Kenya, Ethiopia, and the Gulf states sometimes provide technology such as goggles and telecommunications systems, as well as their translation services, but only rarely contribute money.

Like the clan networks within the country, the Somali diaspora is extremely integrated and close-knit, with Somali expats constantly moving in and out of Somalia even as they carry on normal lives in their adoptive homelands. The support provided by the diaspora—remittances, access to markets, business connections, and professional advice—is absolutely essential to making life inside Somalia liveable. "Pirate entrepreneurs" will seek to access these resources in the same way as legitimate local businessmen, but this is no more transnational crime than the foreign brother of a US citizen helping him to cheat on his income taxes.

The only known affiliation the *Victoria* gang had to the diaspora was through Loyan, their interpreter (Mihai told us that Loyan had studied in India for at least five years, which meant he must have held foreign citizenship, as it is virtually impossible to travel on a Somali passport). Men such as Loyan—English-speaking opportunists taking extended vacations in their homeland—are the real face of the so-called transnational criminal empire of Somali piracy.

7. OTHER
The Yemen Connection

Pirate attacks on Yemeni fishing ships, which are then converted for use as pirate motherships, have been well documented, and there are some indications that the *Victoria* gang may have been guilty of a double hijacking, the first involving a Yemeni vessel.

According to Hussein Hersi, his cousins left Somalia in two small attack skiffs, but both Matei Levenescu and Traian Mihai reported being attacked by one boat between ten and twelve metres in length. Is it possible that the *Victoria* hijackers departed Somalia in smaller skiffs, and then proceeded to hijack a Yemeni dhow somewhere in the Gulf of Aden, abandoning the vessel's previous occupants in their skiffs?

"The Somali side of the Gulf is too well patrolled by foreign warships," Hersi told me, "and the commercial ships stay two or three hundred miles away from the Yemeni coast. So the pirates go over to the Yemeni side; they pretend to be Yemeni fishermen, but at night they attack the actual Yemenis and capture their fishing dhows. "They're always changing tactics, you know. The warships go this way, the pirates go the other," he said, motioning in two directions with his hand.

It was not clear if Hersi was referring to his cousins' gang in particular, or to the practices of Gulf of Aden pirates in general. But the dimensions of the attack ship described by Levenescu and Mihai fit the proportions of a small Yemeni dhow; and the fact that the *Victoria* was captured only 120 kilometres south of the Yemeni coast confirms that the pirates had been operating from the Yemeni side of the Gulf of Aden, and had quite possibly hidden from coalition forces by pretending to be Yemeni fishermen.

On the other hand, Computer's psychic timeline, as reported by Hersi, allowed only eight hours between launching the mission and encountering the *Victoria*. If so, the pirates would have barely had enough time to reach Yemeni waters and hijack the dhow before meeting the *Victoria* (at a top speed of twenty knots, the hijackers would have needed almost seven hours just to reach the position where they encountered the *Victoria*).

Relationship with the Puntland Authorities

No blanket statement can define the "typical relationship" between pirate gangs and the Puntland government forces, which has ranged from direct armed confrontation to allegations of complicity and outright involvement. As evidence of possible corruption, Hansen cites Boyah's statement that 30 per cent of ransom money goes to bribes (in my view an absurd claim, which Boyah has since retracted on multiple occasions). But another of Hansen's interviews suggests a more evasive strategy: "We usually hide ourselves and put the ship we capture in (*sic*) far from the shore and move from place to place when we see [the Puntland police] around," said a pirate named Sultan.

Their actions show that the *Victoria* gang came closer to adopting the latter approach, as illustrated from their flight from Eyl upon my arrival with government forces. Though Levenescu suggested that the purpose of their departure was to harvest drinking water, the timing of the trip may have been influenced by the sudden appearance of uniformed government soldiers in Eyl, several of them closely related to President Farole himself.

Finally, by electing to spend its money on soldiers' uniforms rather than on bribes, the gang coped with the Puntland authorities through subterfuge rather than confrontation or negotiation. One must wonder if even this minimalist effort was necessary; when I was in Eyl I saw no local authorities worth bribing, and no military presence other than my own escort.

Appendix 3

Piracy Timeline

1991: The Somali state collapses as rebel factions descend on the capital, Mogadishu. President Mohamed Siad Barre flees the country.

JANUARY 12, 1991: In the first recorded piracy incident in modern Somalia, the cargo ship MV *Naviluck* is boarded by bandits off Puntland's coast. Part of the crew is taken ashore and executed, while the boat is ransacked and subsequently set ablaze.

OCTOBER 1993: US efforts to arrest warlord Mohamed Farah Aidid lead to the infamous "Black Hawk Down" incident, in which eighteen US Army Rangers are killed by Somali militants.

MARCH 1995: The last UN peacekeeping forces withdraw from Somalia, leaving the country in a state of protracted civil conflict.

MAY 5, 1998: A pan-clan conference held in Garowe proclaims the creation of Puntland State of Somalia. Garowe is chosen as the region's capital.

NOVEMBER 1999: Hart Security, a British private security firm, signs a contract to provide coast guard services in Puntland. The company operates there until 2002, when it is replaced by the Somali-Canadian Coast Guard (SomCan).

APRIL–MAY 2000: The Transitional National Government (TNG) is formed at the Somali National Peace Conference, held in Djibouti.

NOVEMBER 2001: The election of Jama Ali Jama to the Puntland presidency sparks a brief civil conflict when Abdullahi Yusuf Ahmed refuses to step down. Six months later, Yusuf emerges victorious.

MAY 2002: The Somali-Canadian Coast Guard (SomCan), owned by a group of Toronto-based Somali businessmen, assumes coast guard duties in Puntland. The government dismisses the company in March 2005 after SomCan marines hijack a Thai fishing boat.

OCTOBER 10, 2004: The TNG is reconstituted as the Transitional Federal Government (TFG), and Abdullahi Yusuf is elected president. Shortly thereafter, General Mohamud Muse Hersi takes over the Puntland presidency.

DECEMBER 26, 2004: The Indian Ocean tsunami, one of the worst natural disasters in recorded history, strikes the eastern coast of Somalia, causing devastation in Eyl and other waterside towns. Dozens of submerged toxic waste canisters wash ashore, revealing the extent of illegal dumping in Somali waters.

JUNE 27, 2005: The World Food Programme transport MV *Semlow* is hijacked by pirates under the command of Mohamed Abdi Hassan "Afweyne." Attacks on food aid transports continue until the French navy begins escorting shipments two years later.

JUNE 2006: The Islamic Courts Union (ICU), a grassroots religious movement, seizes power in Mogadishu and much of southern Somalia. The ICU takes control of Harardheere and Hobyo, and briefly manages to suppress piracy.

DECEMBER 2006: US-backed Ethiopian forces invade Somalia, overthrowing the ICU and forcing its moderates to flee to Eritrea and Djibouti. Hardline ICU militias split off to form Al-Shabaab, or "The Youth," and undertake a violent insurgency against the occupying forces.

OCTOBER 28, 2007: A pirate attack group led by Abdullahi Abshir Boyah hijacks the MV *Golden Nori*, a Japanese chemical tanker, fifteen kilometres off the Somali coast.

APRIL 2008: President Hersi ceases to pay his Puntland security forces. Following the end of the summer monsoon season in August, piracy explodes.

JULY 2008: A rejuvenated SomCan enters into a one-year contract with the administration of President Hersi to resume its coast guard duties. The following year, President Farole declines to extend its contract.

SEPTEMBER 25, 2008: Eyl- and Harardheere-based pirates jointly capture the MV *Faina*, a Ukrainian vessel transporting tanks intended for the government of South Sudan. After a four-month standoff, the pirates receive a then-unprecedented ransom of $3.2 million.

OCTOBER 2008: NATO announces plans for a seven-warship counter-piracy task force in Somali waters. In the following months, the European Union and the United States deploy their own fleets, EU Naval Force Somalia (NAVFOR) and Combined Task Force 151 (CTF-151).

NOVEMBER 15, 2008: Somali pirates associated with Afweyne hijack the MV *Sirius Star*, a Saudi supertanker carrying $100 million in crude oil. The attack occurs almost eight hundred kilometres south of Somalia, the farthest Somali pirates have ventured to date.

DECEMBER 2008: Kenya signs a memorandum of understanding with the United Kingdom to prosecute suspected pirates captured on the high seas. Similar deals follow with the EU and the United States.

JANUARY 2009: Ethiopian troops withdraw from Somalia, and Al-Shabaab quickly assumes control over much of the south of the country. The TFG merges with the exiled ICU leadership to form a 550-member parliament. Sheikh Sharif Ahmed, former ICU head, is chosen president of the new body.

JANUARY 8, 2009: Former Puntland finance minister Abdirahman Farole is elected president of Puntland. A former academic, Farole becomes only the third Somali civilian leader since 1969.

APRIL 8, 2009: Members of Garaad Mohammed's pirate organization briefly seize the MV *Maersk Alabama*, the first US merchant ship to be commandeered in two hundred years. Four attackers flee the ship in the Alabama's lifeboat, taking Captain Richard Phillips with them. After a tense four-day standoff, US Navy SEALs kill three of the pirates and take the fourth into custody.

MAY 5, 2009: The MV *Victoria*, a German-owned container ship, is hijacked by a gang of Eyl-based pirates operating under the instructions of Abdulkhadar "Computer," a reported psychic. The ship is released after seventy-five days, garnering a ransom of $1.8 million.

NOVEMBER 6, 2010: Pirates release the South Korean oil tanker *Samho Dream* for a record-setting ransom of $9.5 million.

JANUARY 21, 2011: South Korean commandos storm the hijacked chemical tanker MV *Samho Jewelry*, freeing the crew and killing eight pirates. The rescue marked the first military assault on a commercial vessel whose crew had not barricaded themselves within a "safe room."

FEBRUARY 18, 2011: Pirates hijack the yacht S/V *Quest* four hundred kilometres off the coast of Oman. Surrounded by US warships, the pirates execute their four American hostages.

Acknowledgements

A VERY SPECIAL THANKS TO MY HOST AND PARTNER, RADIO Garowe and Garowe Online (www.garoweonline.com) founder Mohamad Abdirahman Farole, his brothers Omar and Mahad, and his cousins, Abdirizak Ahmed and the redoubtable Colonel Omar Abdullahi Farole. I would also like to extend my deepest gratitude to my invaluable consultant, Somali-American journalist Yusuf Hassan. Finally, my thanks to my trusty bodyguards, Said and Abdirashid, who got me back alive—twice—and to Boyah, who welcomed me into his world.

To my parents, Maria and Kailash, unwavering in their support as this project developed from cockeyed suicide mission to unimagined success, and to Laura, for her love, understanding, and flawless application of *Marry Me* doctrine.

I am extraordinarily grateful to my unofficial editors, the friends who gave countless hours of their valuable time to help me become a better writer: Lauren Amundsen (who mercilessly beat the flowery metaphor out of me), as well as Kevin Weitzman, Geoff Burt, and Ross Gray.

I wish to thank all those who helped me along the way, from Toronto to Garowe, London, Nairobi, and beyond: Teddy Florea, Katharine Houreld, Kevin Mwachiro, Jamal Abdi, Rene Dalgaard, Hussein Hersi, Abdiwahid Mahamed Hersi Joaar, Said Orey, Ion

Tita-Calin, Stig Jarle Hansen, Ryan Bigge, Avril Benoit, Reva Seth, Shin Imai, Bill Burt, Daniel Sekulich, Thymaya Payne, Mohamed Dahir Hassan, and the Kenyan prison service, especially Wanini Kireri, David Macharia, and Patrick Mwenda.

I would like to express my sincerest appreciation to Daniel Crewe and Lisa Owens at Profile, Vicky Wilson at Knopf, Noelle Zitzer at HarperCollins, Sarah Wight (my superbly-talented copyeditor), and in particular to my editor Jim Gifford, who saw beyond the CV.

Finally, my inestimable thanks to my agent, Rick Broadhead, for his tireless patience and hard work as I trod my first steps along a very unfamiliar path.

To those whom I have neglected to mention: please accept the omission as one of memory, and not of gratitude.

Endnotes

PROLOGUE: WHERE THE WHITE MAN RUNS AWAY

1. All figures are in US dollars.

CHAPTER 1: BOYAH

1. Name has been changed.

2. The United Nations Development Programme (UNDP) corroborates part of Boyah's claim: a 2005 report states that "[illegal] fishing is increasing day by day and destroying coral reefs, fish nursery areas, capturing endangered species and depleting fish stocks rapidly." Also according to the report, illegal, unregulated, and unreported fishing vessels "often take the fishing gear from the local fishermen, and sometimes even kill people in the process." Illegal fishing ships, it continues, come as close as a kilometre to the coast, causing extensive damage to the local marine ecosystem. Mohamed Mohamud Mohamed and Mahamud Hirad Herzi, *Poverty Reduction and Economic Recovery: Feasibility Report on the Fisheries Sector in Puntland* (Bossaso: Ocean Training and Promotion/UNDP Somalia, April 2005), http://mirror.undp.org/somalia/publications.htm, 16, xiii, xiv.

CHAPTER 2: A SHORT HISTORY OF PIRACY

I am indebted to Stig Jarle Hansen for his excellent work on the history and origins of piracy in Somalia, much of which is reproduced in this chapter.

1. Aidan Hartley, *The Zanzibar Chest* (London: Harper Perennial, 2004), 184.

2. United Nations Human Settlements Programme (UN-Habitat), *Garowe: First Steps Towards Strategic Urban Planning* (Nairobi: UN-Habitat, 2008), http://www.unhabitat.org/pmss, 4.

3. Although cousins on the Somali clan tree, the Majerteen, Dhulbahante, and Warsangali have never been the best of friends. Dating back to before the Majerteen sultanates of the eighteenth and nineteenth centuries, the Majerteen have traditionally dominated their Harti kinsmen, a pattern that continues to the present day. There were allegations that, before and during the Garowe conference, Abdullahi Yusuf strong-armed Warsangali and Dhulbahante leaders into supporting the creation of Puntland, which was certain to be controlled primarily by the Majerteen. In any case, the Dhulbahante- and Warsangali-inhabited regions of Puntland have never been much more than nominally under the control of the region's central government; in 2005, Warsangali leaders in Sanaag region established their own short-lived breakaway mini-state, Makhir, and in 2007 many Dhulbahante clan leaders switched their allegiance to Somaliland, resulting in the secession of the town of Las Anod.

4. Quoted in Jeffrey Gettleman, "For Somali Pirates, Worst Enemy May Be on Shore," *New York Times*, May 8, 2009, http://www.nytimes.com.

5. Stig Jarle Hansen, *Piracy in the Greater Gulf of Aden: Myths, Misconceptions and Remedies*, NIBR Report 2009:29 (Oslo: Norwegian Institute for Urban and Regional Research, 2009), http://en.nibr.no, 20.

6. Ibid., 20.

7. Ibid., 22.

8. Anonymous interviewee quoted ibid., 23–24.

9. Quoted ibid., 24.

10. UN Monitoring Group on Somalia, *Report of the Monitoring Group on Somalia pursuant to Security Council resolution 1630 (2005)*, S/2006/229, May 4, 2006, http://www.un.org/sc/committees/751/mongroup.shtml, 27.

11. Kismaayo, though far south of Puntland, contains a substantial population of Isse Mahamoud, which is Garaad's clan.

12. "Hijackers of Food-Laden Ship Make New Demands," IRIN, August 15, 2005, http://www.irinnews.org.

13. The *Faina* was originally hijacked by Afweyne's militias, who brought it to Harardheere. But when the ransom negotiations dragged on for months and operating expenses continued to mount, the gang was forced to turn to the Eyl pirate group to share the costs.

14. Hansen, *Piracy*, 23.

15. United Nations Office for the Coordination of Humanitarian Affairs, *Annual Report 2005 Activities and Use of Extrabudgetary Funds* (New York, 2005), http://ochaonline.un.org, 170.

16. In Eyl, 40 boats were destroyed and 70 damaged, out of a total of 145. Hermann M. Fritz and Jose C. Borrero, "Field Survey after the December 2004 Indian Ocean Tsunami," *Earthquake Spectra* 22, no. S3 (June 2006): S219; United Nations Development Programme, *Tsunami Inter-Agency Assessment Mission: Hafun to Gara'ad, Northeast Somali Coastline, 28 Jan–8 Feb 2005*, March 30, 2005, http://www.undp.org/cpr/disred/tsunami/news/march05.htm, 4.

17. Interestingly, however, poverty levels within Somalia do not appear to be directly correlated to the prevalence of piracy. Hansen, *Piracy*, 15.

18. "Exchange Rate Drops in Puntland Markets," Garowe Online, March 7, 2009, http://www.garoweonline.com.

19. Ibid.

20. The salary of a Darawish soldier remained fixed at one million shillings per month.

21. Hansen, *Piracy*, 33.

22. International Crisis Group, *Somalia: The Trouble with Puntland,* Africa Briefing no. 64 (Nairobi/Brussels: August 12, 2009), http://www.crisisgroup.org, 3.

23. Hansen, *Piracy*, 33.

CHAPTER 3: PIRATE LORE

1. I have used International Maritime Bureau statistics here (rather than ECO-TERRA's, which I employ elsewhere in the book), since the IMB figures more accurately represent the number of *commercial* ships hijacked while transiting through

the Gulf of Aden. IMB Piracy Reporting Centre, http://www.icc-ccs.org/home/piracy-reporting-centre.

2. "Somali Adulterer Stoned to Death," BBC News, November 6, 2009, http://www.bbc.co.uk/news.

3. Quoted in Martin Plaut, "Pirates 'Working with Islamists,'" BBC News, November 19, 2008, http://www.bbc.co.uk/news.

4. Jeffrey Gettleman, "In Somali Civil War, Both Sides Embrace Pirates," *New York Times*, September 1, 2010, http://www.nytimes.com.

5. Ibid.

6. Quoted in Martin Abbugao, "Somali Pirates Controlled by Syndicates: Interpol," Agence France-Presse, October 14, 2009.

7. Mike Pflanz, "Somali Pirates 'Helped by Intelligence Gathered in London,'" *Telegraph* (London), May 11, 2009, http://www.telegraph.co.uk.

8. See, for example, Tom Odula, "Pirate Ransom Money May Explain Kenya Property Boom," *Huffington Post*, January 1, 2010, http://www.huffingtonpost.com.

CHAPTER 4: OF PIRATES, COAST GUARDS, AND FISHERMEN

1. UN Monitoring Group on Somalia, *Report of the Monitoring Group on Somalia submitted in accordance with resolution 1853 (2008)*, S/2010/91, March 10, 2010, http://www.un.org/sc/committees/751/mongroup.shtml, 40.

2. Ombaali's math does not add up. If, as he claims, $1.8 million and $1.6 million were paid to release the two vessels, a 20 per cent share of both ransoms, divided equally amongst the thirty-five holders, would have earned Ombaali just over $19,000 (this, as we will see in Chapter 14, is much more in line with a pirate foot soldier's average wage).

3. Stig Jarle Hansen, *Piracy in the Greater Gulf of Aden: Myths, Misconceptions and Remedies*, NIBR Report 2009:29 (Oslo: Norwegian Institute for Urban and Regional Research, 2009), http://en.nibr.no, 35.

4. Marine experts have estimated that Somalia could support sustainable marine production of between 300,000 and 500,000 tonnes per year; yet prior to the

civil war, official output stood at 20,000 tonnes, a mere 4 per cent of this potential (Andrew Mwangura, "Militia vs. Trawlers: Who Is the Villain?" East Africa Magazine, July 9, 2001). In Puntland, development of the fisheries sectors—as with all industries—has lagged even behind the south of the country. Local fishermen have no access to export markets other than through the Somali middlemen who peddle their rock lobsters to fish importers in the Gulf states; there is also a single industrial-scale tuna canning plant, located in the northern coastal town of Las Qoray. Road and refrigeration infrastructures are so bad that the coastal communities cannot find customers in their domestic market—little fish from Eyl is transported even as far as Garowe, two hundred kilometres distant.

5. Quoted in International Crisis Group, *Somalia: The Trouble with Puntland*, Africa Briefing no. 64, Nairobi/Brussels: August 12, 2009, http://www.crisisgroup.org, 11.

6. Quoted in Jonathon Gatehouse, "This Cabbie Hunts Pirates," *Macleans*, January 12, 2009.

7. Stig Jarle Hansen, "Private Security and Local Politics in Somalia," *Review of African Political Economy* 118 (2008): 588.

8. Choong also claimed that Sirichai falsely labels its tuna products "Product of Thailand" and markets them in Kenya. Muhammad Shamsaddin Megalommatis, "The MV Faina Piracy Crisis Chronicle-VII," http://www.california-chronicle.com, December 7, 2008.

9. A patrol run from SomCan's base in Bossaso to Garacad, spanning almost the entire Puntland coast, requires approximately sixty drums of diesel, or twelve thousand litres. At $150 per drum, the fuel for a one-way trip costs $9,000.

10. A short time after this violent encounter, the SomCan ship responded to an American naval communiqué requesting the Puntland government's help in transporting a shipload of stranded Somali fishermen to shore. SomCan found the marooned sailors adrift in an inoperative speedboat off the coastal town of Bargaal. The fishermen had been forced, at gunpoint, to exchange vessels with a gang of pirates who were experiencing technical problems with their attack craft's engine. The fishermen had been adrift for two days in the pirates' discarded boat before being spotted by a US warship. For all the pirates' talk about their solemn duty to cleanse Somali waters of illegal fishing ships, their own countrymen were apparently not immune to being targeted when the greater good demanded it.

11. Roger Middleton, *Piracy in Somalia: Threatening Global Trade, Feeding Local Wars* (London: Chatham House, October 2008), http://www.chathamhouse.org.uk, 7.

12. Katharine Houreld, "Blackwater Founder Trains Somalis," Associated Press, January 20, 2011; "Puntland Signed an Agreement with Saracen Company to train its Marine Forces," Garowe Online, November 18, 2010, http://www.garoweonline.com.

13. Mark Mazzetti and Eric Schmitt, "Blackwater Founder Said to Back Mercenaries," *New York Times*, January 20, 2011, http://www.nytimes.com.

14. Katharine Houreld, "1,000-Man Militia Being Trained in North Somalia," Associated Press, December 1, 2010.

CHAPTER 5: GARAAD

1. Richard Phillips, *A Captain's Duty* (New York: Hyperion, 2010), 247–48. Phillips, apparently, did not consider it within the ambit of a captain's duty to heed maritime safety bulletins concerning pirate activity. Following the *Alabama* incident, several of his crewmates, including the ship's navigator and chief engineer, publicly attacked Phillips for his negligence in ignoring warnings to stay at least 950 kilometres from the Somali coast. A map of the attack location shows that Phillips had put the *Alabama* at unacceptable risk; she was only about 550 kilometres east of Harardheere when she was hijacked—right at the pirates' doorstep. See John Curran, "Crew Blames Capt. for Pirate Attack," Associated Press, December 2, 2009.

2. "French Warship Detains Pirates, US Call for Action," Agence France-Presse, April 15, 2009.

CHAPTER 6: FLOWER OF PARADISE

1. Despite its historical use in Koranic study, khat was declared un-Islamic and banned after the Islamic Courts Union assumed control over southern Somalis in 2006, provoking widespread street protests.

2. David Anderson, Susan Beckerleg, Dagol Hailu, and Axel Klein, *The Khat Controversy: Stimulating the Debate on Drugs* (Oxford: Berg, 2007), 1.

3. Anderson et al., *Khat Controversy*, 61.

4. This may be an optimistic assessment; during my trip to Bossaso in President Farole's entourage, we stopped for a night in the city of Qardho, where the president's good offices were sought to mediate a dispute over two young men who had been killed by Puntland police while attempting to rob a khat truck. The boys' clan elders were demanding that the police officers be executed in retribution for their actions.

5. For an interesting discussion of khat use amongst Somali militants, see Michael Odenwald, Harald Hinkel, Elisabeth Schauer, Frank Neuner, Maggie Schauer, Thomas R. Elbert, and Brigitte Rockstroh, "The Consumption of Khat and Other Drugs in Somali Combatants: A Cross-Sectional Study," *PLoS Medicine* 4, no. 12 (2007), http://www.plosmedicine.org.

6. United Nations World Food Programme, Puntland: Food Security and Vulnerability Assessment (Nairobi: WFP Somalia, April 2007), http://documents.wfp.org; Danish Refugee Council, CDRD M&E Specialist Field Trip to Puntland, 2009, http://www.somcdrd.org.

7. Puntland Ministry of Planning and Statistics, Puntland Facts and Figures 2003 (Garowe: 2003), http://siteresources.worldbank.org.

8. Of the population, 43 per cent is aged fifteen or over. If the population distribution for men and women is identical, which cannot be the case, then 21.5 per cent of the men are at least fifteen. As a rough estimate it is adequate.

9. I have not used these three women's real names. From the way she described it, Maryan's union with Garaad was a form of Islamic pleasure marriage, an institution designed to provide a veneer of religious propriety to a casual sexual relationship (see Chapter 12). When I asked Maryan where her "husband" was, she nonchalantly replied, "I have no idea."

10. A 2004 paper estimated that 57 per cent of Somalia's foreign exchange had made its way to Kenya through the khat trade in the few years prior. Cited in Anderson et al., *Khat Controversy*, 61.

11. Tim Marshall, "Yemen: Legal High Is 'Fueling' Extremism,'" Sky News, January 15, 2010, http://news.sky.com.

12. "Somali Gunmen 'Renounce Piracy,'" BBC News, May 25, 2009, http://www.bbc.co.uk/news.

CHAPTER 7: THE LAND OF PUNT

1. Quoted in Jalal al-Sharaabi, Khaled Mahmoud, and Courtney C. Radsch, "Somali Leaders Accuse Islamists of Piracy," Al Arabiya News Channel, December 2, 2008, http://www.alarabiya.net.

2. Abdirahman Farole, speech before the US House of Representatives Subcommittee on Africa and Global Health, June 25, 2009, author's copy.

3. "Anti-Piracy Campaign Begins Today in Puntland," Garowe Online, April 24, 2009, http://www.garoweonline.com.

4. Ibid.

5. Puntland also employs an extensive system of religious, or sharia, law courts, which deal mostly with matters of family law.

6. Quoted in "Puntland Has Sacrificed for Its Peace, Says Pres. Farole," Garowe Online, November 17, 2010, http://www.garoweonline.com/.

7. UN Monitoring Group on Somalia, *Report of the Monitoring Group on Somalia pursuant to Security Council resolution 1853* (2008), S/2010/91, March 10, 2010, http://www.un.org/sc/committees/751/mongroup.shtml, 39.

8. According to the terms of the arrangement, Range Resources was granted exploration rights for $25 million to be paid in monthly instalments of $200,000.

9. "Puntland Govt Arrests Official with Alleged Links to Pirates," Garowe Online, February 24, 2008, http://www.garoweonline.com.

10. UN Monitoring Group on Somalia, Report, March 10, 2010, 41.

11. "Puntland Leader Sacks Deputy Police Chief," Garowe Online, October 13, 2008, http://www.garoweonline.com.

12. Not only did Farole fail to win an ally in Congress, House committee chair Donald Payne issued a report highly critical of the Puntland administration, accusing it of a litany of human rights abuses. Alisha Ryu, "US Congressman Criticizes Puntland for Abusive Behavior," Voice of America, November 23, 2009, http://www.voanews.com.

13. "Puntland's Leader Says UN Report Is 'Politically Motivated,'" Garowe Online, March 22, 2010, http://www.garoweonline.com.

CHAPTER 8: MOMMAN

1. UN High Commission for Refugees, Mixed Migration Task Force, Mixed Migration Task Force Update No. 8, August 2009, http://ochaonline.un.org.

CHAPTER 9: THE POLICEMEN OF THE SEA

1. These figures have been taken from the Nairobi-based NGO ECOTERRA, and include attacks that may not have been reported to more conventionally cited sources, such as the International Maritime Bureau.

2. These success rates are probably somewhat exaggerated, due to the number of failed pirate attacks that go unreported to any authority.

3. Stig Jarle Hansen, *Piracy in the Greater Gulf of Aden: Myths, Misconceptions and Remedies*, NIBR Report 2009:29 (Oslo: Norwegian Institute for Urban and Regional Research, 2009), http://en.nibr.no, 36.

4. Only two deaths have been attributed to NAVFOR, however. The majority of the fatalities (thirty-eight) were caused by individual navies (figures are from the Belgian defence news website Bruxelles 2, http://bruxelles2.over-blog.com). The journalist tracking these statistics stopped in May 2010 because he found it too difficult to obtain accurate information.

5. ECOTERRA, Somali Marine & Coastal Monitor 291, November 19, 2009.

6. Quoted in Kathryn Westcott, "'Pirate' death puts spotlight on 'guns for hire,'" BBC News, March 24, 2010, http://www.bbc.co.uk/news.

7. US Department of Transportation, *Economic Impact of Piracy in the Gulf of Aden on Global Trade*, September 2010, http://www.marad.dot.gov.

8. See David Osler, "Sonic Solution May Not Be a Sound Investment," *Lloyd's List*, December 2, 2008.

9. "Chinese Ship Uses Molotov Cocktails to Fight Off Somali Pirates," *Telegraph* (London), December 19, 2008, http://www.telegraph.co.uk.

10. After first announcing its intention to prosecute the ten captured pirates in Moscow, the Russian government reversed its position and decided to release the men in an inflatable boat without any navigational equipment. Afterwards, the Russian defence ministry reported that the pirates had "probably died" at sea. The summary

execution scenario is far more likely, and supported by a comment by President Dmitry Medvedev on the day the *Moscow University* was stormed: "We'll have to do what our forefathers did when they met the pirates." Mansur Mirovalev, "Pirates 'Have All Died,' Russia Says, after Decrying 'Imperfections' in International Law," Associated Press, May 11, 2010.

11. Based on International Maritime Bureau statistics, IMB Piracy Reporting Centre, http://www.icc-ccs.org/home/piracy-reporting-centre.

12. This estimate is based on the cost to the shipping companies; once financial, legal, and private security fees are tacked on, the total cost of delivering a ransom roughly doubles.

CHAPTER 10: THE LAW OF THE SEA

1. Marie Woolf, "Pirates Can Claim UK Asylum," *Times* (London), April 13, 2008, http://www.thetimes.co.uk.

2. Preceding the UNCLOS treaty of 1982, Somalia was one of a handful of states to claim a territorial sea of two hundred nautical miles, through its Law No. 37 of 1972. One of the primary motivators behind UNCLOS was the need to standardize the width of territorial seas, which the convention achieved by limiting its signatories to a territorial sea of twelve nautical miles. Though Somalia was amongst the first countries to ratify UNCLOS, Law No. 37 was never subsequently repealed, leaving an ambiguity surrounding the status of Somalia's territorial seas. "From the behaviour of states patrolling the waters off the coast of Somalia it would seem clear that they assume that the external limit of the Somali territorial sea is 12 miles," writes Tullio Treves, a judge at the International Tribunal for the Law of the Sea in Hamburg. "Whether this is also the assumption of the TFG [Somali Transitional Federal Government] is uncertain." Treves, "Piracy, Law of the Sea, and Use of Force: Developments of the Coast of Somalia," *European Journal of International Law* 20, no. 4 (Apr. 2009): 408.

3. The Security Council extended this patchwork legal arrangement for another twelve months in December 2008 (Resolution 1846), and again in November 2009 (Resolution 1897).

4. Resolution 1816 and its successors were issued under Chapter VII of the UN Charter, which authorizes the use of military force to counter threats to "international peace and security." Given that Chapter VII permits the violation of national sovereignty, Resolution 1816's emphasis on obtaining the authorization of the So-

mali government seems redundant. According to Tullio Treves, the requirement served three objectives: "The first is to pay homage to state sovereignty . . . The second is to strengthen the TFG, which, while maintaining the Somali presence at the United Nations, does not exercise effective power in Somalia, and in particular lacks the capacity to fight pirate activities off its coasts. The third, through the designation by the TFG of the states whose vessels are authorized to act in its territorial sea, would seem to consist in limiting the foreign fleets' presence in Somali waters to those of the states most involved, and to states ready to cooperate with each other." Treves, "Piracy, Law of the Sea, and Use of Force," 407.

5. After the far-reaching expansion of piracy into the Indian Ocean, the Seychelles also entered into an agreement with the EU to detain suspected pirates, though its capacity to try them is extremely limited.

6. David Morgan, "U.S. Delivers Seven Somali Pirate Suspects to Kenya," Reuters, March 5, 2009.

7. James Gathii, "Jurisdiction to Prosecute Non-National Pirates Captured by Third States under Kenyan and International Law," *Loyola of Los Angeles International and Comparative Law Review* 31 (Summer 2009): 25–26.

8. Quoted in Christopher Thompson, "Suspected Somali Pirates in the Dock," *Financial Times*, January 8, 2010, http://www.ft.com.

9. Quoted in Gathii, "Jurisdiction to Prosecute Non-National Pirates," 19.

10. The legal argument used to reject the appeal rested on two principles: first, that piracy on the high seas was a crime under the Kenyan penal code; second, that piracy was a crime under international customary law, or *jus gentium*, and thus the Kenyan High Court was justified in extending its jurisdiction beyond the nation's borders. Ibid., 4, 8–9.

11. "Jail Sentence for Somali pirates," BBC News, November 1, 2006, http://www.bbc.co.uk/news.

12. Quoted in Gathii, "Jurisdiction to Prosecute Non-National Pirates," 11–12. Article 101 of the UN Convention on the Law of the Sea defines piracy as follows:

(a) any illegal acts of violence or detention, or any act of depredation, committed for private ends by the crew or the passengers of a private ship or a private aircraft, and directed:

(i) on the high seas, against another ship or aircraft, or against persons or property on board such ship or aircraft;

(ii) against a ship, aircraft, persons or property in a place outside the jurisdiction of any State;

(b) any act of voluntary participation in the operation of a ship or of an aircraft with knowledge of facts making it a pirate ship or aircraft;

(c) any act of inciting or of intentionally facilitating an act described in subparagraph (a) or (b).

13. Gathii, "Jurisdiction to Prosecute Non-National Pirates," 19.

14. Quoted ibid., 26.

15. Ibid., 24.

16. In response to a Russian-led Security Council initiative in April 2010, UN secretary-general Ban Ki-moon proposed seven options for prosecuting suspected Somali pirates, including the creation of an international tribunal. To date, the Security Council has rejected this option due to its prohibitive cost, as well as the difficulty of finding a nation to host the proceedings. In January 2011, the UN's special advisor on piracy, Jack Lang, issued a report urging the creation of regional piracy tribunals in Puntland, Somaliland, and Tanzania. The proposal, estimated to cost $25 million over three years, also called for the construction of additional prisons in Somalia.

CHAPTER 11: INTO THE PIRATES' LAIR

1. Jonathan Clayton, "Somalia's Secret Dumps of Toxic Waste Washed Ashore by Tsunami," *Times* (London), March 4, 2005, http://www.thetimes.co.uk. The claims of the local people and the initial UN Environmental Programme assessment mission were challenged by a subsequent UN fact-finding mission to Puntland's coastal areas, which failed to find evidence of widespread radiation sickness. "UN Mission to Puntland on Toxic Waste in the Coastal Areas of Somalia," *Somaliland Times*, October 7, 2005, http://www.somalilandtimes.net.

CHAPTER 12: PIRATE INSIDER

1. Though tempting to believe (and completely consistent with other accounts of

pirate behaviour), Hersi's claims contradict the statements of both former *Victoria* hostages I interviewed, Matei Levenescu and Traian Mihai, who asserted that the pirates on the ship never consumed alcohol and never progressed beyond fist fights. The incidents Hersi discussed may have taken place on land.

2. In the case of the *Victoria*, intra-group tensions may have been due to the lack of familial homogeneity within the gang. According to former hostage Traian Mihai, the gang was composed of multiple families from various towns in Puntland; however, they were almost certainly all members of the Isse Mahamoud sub-clan.

3. This is almost certainly an exaggeration, though if one considers the money the gang spent on khat (see Chapter 14), potentially not a very gross one.

CHAPTER 13: THE CADET AND THE CHIEF

1. German defence ministry spokesman Thomas Raabe reported that a Turkish frigate had been within eighty to one hundred nautical miles at the time of the attack. Katharine Houreld, "Somali Pirates Seize German Ship, 11 Crew," Associated Press, May 6, 2009.

2. Informed as it is by his own unfortunate experience, Levenescu's condemnation of the transit corridor—not to mention the international naval forces—is hardly fair. The IRTC, in conjunction with scheduled convoys and greater naval coordination, greatly reduced the number of successful attacks in the Gulf of Aden.

3. So hazardous were the winds that in one instance a supply boat being hoisted by one of the *Victoria*'s deck cranes was blown onto the deck, damaging its hull.

4. The other hostage I interviewed, Traian Mihai, noted that one of the three leaders, a "foreigner" to Eyl, spent only two days on shore during the entire length of the *Victoria*'s captivity.

5. Not surprisingly, Somalis have a predisposition for diabetes. The primary cause is supposedly genetic, though the Somali cultural proclivity for using tea and other drinks as mediums for consuming sugar probably has something to do with it.

6. This start-up sequence is necessary to heat the ship's highly viscous bunker fuel to a temperature of seventy degrees Celsius, the point at which it is properly combustible. All large cargo ships possess a diesel-powered heating unit specifically for this purpose.

7. Mihai was able to fill in a few details of Loyan's biography. Contrary to Hersi's description, Loyan spoke English fluently, having studied for five years at an Indian university. This fact suggests that, like Hersi, he is a relatively well-off member of the Somali diaspora.

8. There could hardly be better evidence of the hijackers' fear of the Puntland security forces. This behaviour is inconsistent with claims by various commentators that the Puntland government is complicit—or even actively involved—in piracy. It is also evidence that the Puntland security forces are disorganized to the point that an easily obtainable set of clothing is all the identification required to prove membership.

CHAPTER 14: THE FREAKONOMICS OF PIRACY

1. There are three differing accounts of the number of men who assaulted the *Victoria*: Hersi claims there were ten men in two boats; Matei Levenescu says there were nine in one boat; and the media reports of the incident state that there were eight attackers. Given that he was an eyewitness, Levenescu's figure is almost certainly the accurate one, and it is the number I will use in this analysis.

2. The $150,000 paid to one attacker (Mohamed Abdi) might explain why Hersi was under the impression that each member of the attacking team would receive a commensurate share ($140,000 of a $3 million ransom, according to him).

3. These estimates are based on a tally of the total number of pirates killed (60), injured (24), and taken into custody (454) by the combined international naval forces since August 2008, as of May 2010. These figures are taken from the news blog Bruxelles2 (http://bruxelles2.over-blog.com), which compiles data from EU-NAVFOR, NATO, the US Navy, the US Department of Justice, and the Royal Navy. Given the large number of assumptions and unknown variables (such as the number of pirates dying from causes other than naval intervention, such as starvation or dehydration), my estimates are only a very rough account of the perils of piracy.

4. Les Christie, "America's Most Dangerous Jobs," CNNMoney.com, October 13, 2003.

CHAPTER 15: THE ROAD'S END

1. When I spoke to them in Dhanane, the pirates told me that they were expecting a ransom of $2.5 million.

2. Quoted in Sapa-AFP, "Dead Crew Member Identified," Independent Online, June 24, 2009, http://www.iol.co.za.

EPILOGUE: THE PROBLEMS OF PUNTLAND

1. Malkhadir Muhumed, "Pirate on US Wanted List Arrested in Somalia," Associated Press, May 20, 2010.

2. Katharine Houreld, "Somali Pirates Torturing Hostages," Associated Press, February 1, 2011.

3. For example, in April 2009 former US ambassador to the UN John Bolton told Fox News that a ground invasion of Somalia was the only way "to end [the piracy] problem once and for all." Slightly more reasonable voices have recommended targeted bombings, a strategy that would claim the lives of far more civilians than pirates and serve only to inflame anti-Western sentiments.

4. Al-Shabaab's targets were thoughtfully chosen to deliver that message. In Hargeysa, the organization bombed the presidential palace, the Ethiopian embassy, and UN Development Programme headquarters, perhaps in response to Somaliland president Dahir Riyale Kahin's plans to pass a (largely toothless) anti-terror law. In Bossaso, the target was the Puntland Intelligence Service, a CIA proxy funded by the American government. The two bombings claimed the lives of at least thirty people.

5. UN Monitoring Group on Somalia, *Report of the Monitoring Group on Somalia pursuant to Security Council resolution 1853* (2008), S/2010/91, March 10, 2010, http://www.un.org/sc/committees/751/mongroup.shtml, 39.

6. William Bolitho, *Twelve Against the Gods* (New York: Simon and Schuster, 1929), 8.

APPENDIX 2: THE *VICTORIA* GANG

1. The material in the following analysis draws heavily from Stig Jarle Hansen's comprehensive report, *Piracy in the Greater Gulf of Aden: Myths, Misconceptions and Remedies*, NIBR Report 2009:29 (Oslo: Norwegian Institute for Urban and Regional Research, 2009), http://en.nibr.no. All subsequent quotations are from this report.

2. Ion Tita-Calin, "*Dezvăluirile foştilor prizonieri ai piraţilor somalezi*" [Revelations from former Somali pirate prisoners], *Cuget Liber*, July 28, 2009, http://www.cugetliber.ro.

Picture Credits

Thanks to Mohamad Farole for permission to use a number of his photographs: 5, 6, 7, 8, 9, 10, 11, 12, 13, 14, 15, 17, 19; also to AP Photo, 24. All other photographs belong to Jay Bahadur.

Index